CURRICULUM

From Theory to Practice

WESLEY NULL

ROWMAN & LITTLEFIELD PUBLISHERS, INC.
Lanham • Boulder • New York • Toronto • Plymouth, UK

Published by Rowman & Littlefield Publishers, Inc.
A wholly owned subsidary of The Rowman & Littlefield Publishing Group, Inc.
4501 Forbes Boulevard, Suite 200, Lanham, Maryland 20706
http://www.rowmanlittlefield.com

Estover Road, Plymouth PL6 7PY, United Kingdom

British Library Cataloguing in Publication Information Available

Library of Congress Cataloging-in-Publication Data

Null, Wesley, 1973–
    Curriculum : from theory to practice / Wesley Null.
        p. cm.
    Includes bibliographical references and index.
    ISBN 978-1-4422-0914-5 (cloth : alk. paper) — ISBN 978-1-4422-0915-2 (pbk. : alk. paper) —
    ISBN 978-1-4422-0916-9
    1. Curriculum planning. 2. Critical pedagogy. I. Title.
    LB2806.15.N85 2011
    375—dc22   2010051614

∞™ The paper used in this publication meets the minimum requirements of American National Standard for Information Sciences—Permanence of Paper for Printed Library Materials, ANSI/NISO Z39.48-1992.

Printed in the United States of America

FOR MY PARENTS

Master teachers and curriculum makers

We wish all men to be educated in all the virtues.

—JOHN AMOS COMENIUS, *The Great Didactic*

Contents

Figures and Textboxes

Figures

Textboxes

Foreword

The Future of Our Making: Recapturing the Identity of Curriculum

DAVID M. CALLEJO-PÉREZ

Carl A. Gerstacker Endowed Chair in Education,
Saginaw Valley State University

GROWING UP playing baseball in Miami, I always understood two things about the Cuban style of baseball: hitting is an art and baseball is a reckless discipline. Coaches, fellow players, and parents yelled to attack the ball, whether hitting or fielding, and to imagine and harness forces of action when throwing, catching, swinging, tagging up, or running. In short, we had to play baseball like we lived our lives—it was one and the same. In much the same way, curriculum is an art and a reckless discipline. William Schubert writes, "What is fundamentally curricular and what is fundamentally human are of the same fabric."[1] Curriculum also exists in a state of angst, between science and art; practice and theory; justice and oppression; and democracy and totalitarianism.[2]

In *Curriculum: From Theory to Practice*, Wesley Null provides readers with a guided journey through curriculum—discussions of its history and etymology—especially its context and role within the American mind. Whether John Franklin Bobbitt, Ralph Tyler, Joseph Schwab, John Dewey, Paulo Freire, Michael Apple, Frantz Fanon, Maxine Greene, Elliot Eisner, William Pinar, or Pierre Bourdieu, the question driving their study of what and how we teach and learn in schools always centered on the deeper idea that there needed to be an ethical and philosophical force driving the curriculum.

Curriculum, Null explains, is at the center of the most permanent and ephemeral issues in education. Controversial as they may seem, the answers may only be found if we evolve the profundity of the questions about curriculum. Ultimately, Wesley Null, like Paulo Freire, begins and ends his work with the proposal that curriculum needs to be a liberating path that leads to humanization.[3] Thus, in his work, Null provides readers with traditions and thinkers who have and continue to shape the field. This historical analysis guides us to Null's method of deliberative curriculum that seeks to address the identity crisis facing curriculum today. This philosophical and liberating approach emerging from Joseph Schwab and William Reid's scholarship provides readers with a thoughtful direction for change in universities, schools, and classrooms. Building on tradition, the author's historical analysis provides possibilities to discuss and address practical problems facing curriculum today with an eye toward providing a narrative for problem solving through deliberative curriculum.

I want readers to see that this book has the potential to change how we discuss curriculum much like Michael Lewis's *Moneyball* did for baseball.[4] In *Moneyball*, Lewis writes, "A baseball team, of all things, was at the center of a story about the possibilities—and the limits—of reason in human affairs. Baseball—of all things—was an example of how an unscientific culture responds, or fails to respond, to the scientific method."[5] In his book, Lewis describes the stark difference between the field of play, where freedom is cherished, and the uneasiness of the space just beyond where "executives and scouts make their living" (287). The situation is the same for curriculum, the flow of where it occurs and uneasiness of the place where it is created and learned is explored deftly in this work by Null. In *Moneyball*, Lewis is able to take us through a journey that examines and deconstructs the standard operating procedures of Major League Baseball while asking why we continue to practice the way we do in spite of reason and to imagine why we continue to do what we do in light of the failures we see. Likewise, Null's journey seeks to shed light (reason) on curricular practices. He walks readers through the maze of curriculum development, implementation, practice, and evaluation in order to explain why we do what we do and how reason can inform our practice and, beyond that, change society.

Null offers the foundation for a reconciliation of the curriculum field based on his historical and comparative analyses of curriculum thought and practice. I can say that a comprehensive and public conversation in the curriculum field about curriculum theory has not taken center stage since the AERA Professors of Curriculum meeting in Montreal in 1999, which followed the written debate in the January 1999 issue of *Educational Researcher*. Although the recent article William Schubert published in *Curriculum Inquiry*, entitled "Journeys of Expansion and Synopsis: Tensions in Books That Shaped Curriculum Inquiry, 1968–Present," attempts to summarize and reconcile curricular arguments and positions, we have yet to bridge the great divide among curriculum thought, teacher education, and schooling.[6] Null's book is not just an intellectual exercise that analyzes curriculum; it is more than a critique. He offers examples of practice and hope for change through the building of a bridge sorely needed in our field. Null addresses the difficult questions of curriculum theory and practice and empowers readers to ask and respond to why they should care about curriculum. The historical and philosophical investigation presented here examines the different ways curriculum has been theorized and practiced. The author is able to build on current questions and reopen debates that many of us in curriculum and teacher education need to address.

Curriculum and its place in schools has a history, although one may wish to disown certain ideas and practices while defending others, revising or forgetting them; but slight as they may be in the literature, they remain cited in footnotes, quoted in chapters and articles, altered perhaps but still there to serve as a foundation for oncoming generations—gerontophagy for future curriculists. Criticism is the lifeblood of curriculum studies, and I hope that the historical analysis put forth by Null enlivens us to seek to explain (rather than defend) our beliefs and practices. Thus, it is my hope that we can use this work to reconstruct and set forth a new context for the conception of the ideas that have dominated our field. I also hope we listen to the author's critiques and suggestions—that we are willing to liberate curriculum, in thought and practice, and to act on that liberation.

Robert Dahl writes that in the "long history of democracy, few events, if any, have been more dramatic and important than the collapse of many authoritarian regimes in the 1980s and the ensuing efforts to construct democratic systems in their place."[7] Two such efforts in the curriculum field are 1986's *Curriculum: Perspective, Paradigm, and Possibility* by William Schubert and 1995's *Understanding Curriculum: An Introduction to the Study of Historical and Contemporary Curriculum Discourses* by William Pinar, William Reynolds, Patrick Slattery, and Peter Taubman.[8] It has been a long time in our field since we have had—to borrow Bill Pinar's words—a "synoptic text" that offers both a place for our traditions and a challenge to our future. Maybe it is our banality that such works occur once every decade or more; but as Null writes, these texts provide sources for conversation and debate among professors, teachers, and school officials. I would also add the importance of a text for those who, as Eisner describes in the *Educational Imagination*, consume and make decisions about curriculum.[9]

Knowing the author for more than ten years, I find the vulnerability with which he writes for us refreshing. In this book, he emerges from a journey in which he discussed the curriculum field, examined its history, and suggested changes to impact teacher education, colleges of education, and K–12 schools.[10] As the iconic historian Eric Hobsbawn wrote, "The test of the historian's life is whether he or she can ask and answer questions, especially 'what if' questions, about the matters of passionate significance to themselves and the world, as though they were journalists reporting things long past—and yet, not as a stranger but as one deeply involved. These are not questions about real history, which is not about what we might like, but about what happened, and could perhaps have happened otherwise but did not."[11]

This past year I have thought about similar issues related to the role of the field of curriculum studies in higher education, and I believe that it would be in our best interest if we examined curriculum theory and its place within teacher education programs.[12] After careful thought, I realized that our work exists within a state of impermanence because so much of what we believe and practice emerges from institutions and traditions—a common ground within higher education—that no longer make sense given the way our students think and practice. Ironically, educational programs continue to trudge along not noting that their evolution has no direction that allows concrete predictions about the social, cultural, and political consequences of their actions. This impermanence is noteworthy because what separated curriculum studies in education from most other programs was a sense of a common core that typically included curriculum theory, educational foundations, curriculum history, and evaluation or policy. Whether all of these courses or a combination of them were part of a program, they provided a common basis of coursework that was unique within teacher education.

What important things can curriculists teach and learn that will endure? This question is one rarely asked. When it is asked and answered, the answers almost always relate to testing, standards, esoteric research, and funded projects. With apologies to Charles Dickens, it is the best of times and it is the worst of times in education. It is an age of unprecedented spending for program growth; it is an age of record budget deficits and cutbacks. In countless states across the United States, new programs (e.g., charter schools) have risen to replace traditional ones and accommodate a growing number of students who need assistance (see KIPP and Teach for America). Yet a faltering economy has put the squeeze on operating budgets and has made constituents less likely to support ambitious proposals (e.g., new schools or hiring more teachers). As a result, as money is given at a record pace to support education, schools and their graduates are falling behind because they come to learn each day in programs that are inadequate and poorly supported. The push for improving the quality in curriculum, then, is more than just a question of aesthetics. Freire viewed students as the means to enrich the educative process, as the place where the curricular conversation (dialogical education) feasts on one's experience.[13] Teaching has changed radically in the last decade, and parents, schools, and children have begun to search for schools that are different. Schools are also giving more of their work to others including community organizations, nongovernmental organizations (NGOs), and private firms in search for programs that can help them deal with the "at-risk" populations they see each day.

■ A Call to Action: Angst, Art, and Reckless Discipline

In the last twenty years, curriculists explored issues of memory in the creation of the imagined community of curriculum studies. In this work, Wesley Null extends that argument beyond its origins, promoting levels of connections toward the idea of what it means to be a curriculum worker from the point of a generalist who can lead the growing changes in colleges of education, the education of teachers, and educational policy. Null's work emerges from the moral tradition that sees curriculum as occurring in two planes, one believed to be a painting of the past and yet dynamic in its own development, and the other perceived as different from the past yet influenced by its own attempt to reinterpret history. Our job, as Null writes, is to liberate curriculum from the burden of expertise and thereby enter into a curricular exchange with the students who inform, make, and change meanings that drive the curriculum and its language. In creating curriculum through language, I agree with Michael Kreyling when he suggests that we should "keep the conversation going, and keep it balanced between the artefactual and non-artefactual realities."[14] Understanding curriculum without understanding the "projects that have created, indicted, refurbished, or rebirthed it; is impossible."[15] In curriculum, reflection and action feed one another; collectively, they make curriculum a process, and as curriculists we are in it, body and mind.

Lessons from *Curriculum: From Theory to Practice* include that tomorrow's educational leaders need to be equipped not only with a historical perspective, but also a visionary one. How do we develop this vision? Through understanding the roots of curriculum theory with the accompanying political and social influences, tomorrow's leaders can begin to form ideas for future change and direction. In an era of standardization and accountability, institutions of higher education, and specifically colleges of education within these institutions, have both an opportunity and an obligation to nurture and prepare effective leaders for all levels of schooling. Their preparation should be grounded in a set of moral principles that foster achievement of high outcomes for teaching and learning at multiple levels. The program should include an interdisciplinary perspective that is threaded across the program, emphasizing inquiry, reflection, and collaboration embedded within a context for beginning teachers to meet the needs of diverse learners. Educational leaders who can respond not only to the directives of the educational enterprise that address accountability, quality, and efficiency within the system but also to issues pertaining to the individual, community, and social justice require programs that weave throughout their curriculum opportunities for students to think critically while examining their values and beliefs about schooling, teaching, learning, and educational policy. Critical reflection of this sort has the potential to cause individuals to change their sometimes-entrenched normative beliefs about education and related issues. It also serves as a catalyst to promote a change in behavior. Teacher education is becoming a method of advancing reform efforts with an ever increasing emphasis on instructional methodology without an opportunity for students to examine the ideas behind social theory, politics, and a substantive view of curriculum. Students enrolled in teacher education programs are inundated with basic information that is necessary to advance the status quo of educational practices without a thought as to the nature of the curricular decisions handed down or the implications of their implementation. True reflection in education needs to become part of teaching practices in order to advance the professionalism of teaching.

Preface

DOZENS OF books on curriculum are published every year. Only time will tell if *Curriculum* will stand out in a crowd, but my hope is that it provides a unique contribution to the field not only because of the way it depicts five curricular traditions, but also because of the way it addresses curriculum problems. I hope the book will introduce students to the exciting field of curriculum while at the same time showing experienced scholars some new ways to approach an old subject.

My journey with curriculum began in the summer of 1995 when I took a graduate course entitled "Curriculum: Theory into Practice" from Dr. Alan W. Garrett at Eastern New Mexico University. Alan combined stories and structure in a way that I found fascinating. The concept of curriculum at first seemed a bit impersonal, but during that course I came to realize that curriculum is as much a personal quest as it is an institution. When I began graduate school, I thought I was primarily interested in the foundations of education (i.e., the history and philosophy of education), but I have since learned that curriculum has a way of integrating thought and action that foundations of education will never have. As someone who is part educational historian, I remain deeply involved in the foundations of education field, but, at least professionally, I know that I am most satisfied when teaching "Curriculum Theory and Practice," my version of Alan's course that I teach at Baylor.

My goal with *Curriculum* has been to offer an approach to curriculum theory and practice that hits the mean between several extremes that, when put into practice, harm the effort to create good curriculum and teaching. The nature of these extremes will become apparent throughout the text, but they revolve around the questions of theory and practice, the personal and the institutional aspects of curriculum, and the proper balance between experience and knowledge when creating curriculum. Good curriculum makers, and indeed good teachers, know they must constantly search for ways to balance—in theory and practice—all of these complex dimensions of curriculum and teaching. This task is sometimes easier said than done, but I do know that curriculum is the path to finding the mean between so many extremes. I am hopeful that the cases presented in part II and the curriculum dilemmas in the appendix will provide readers with the opportunity to find this mean in both discussion and practice.

My interest in writing this book began as I was working with William A. Reid on the second edition to his *The Pursuit of Curriculum: Schooling and the Public Interest.* After working on that book with Bill, I decided that the tradition he has worked to uphold for many years has the potential to remake not only curriculum but entire communities as well. The four years I have worked to produce this book have been full of countless ups and downs, both personal and professional. During this time, my personal curriculum has brought into my life new babies, a positive tenure decision, colleagues leaving and arriving, soccer coaching when I knew nothing about the sport, piano recitals, gymnastics, a first fishing trip with my son, and a cancer scare for my wife. Some of these experiences have been liberating and others not, but I must say that, because of friends and family, the final push to finish this book has been nothing short of liberating. I hope reading it will do the same for those who spend time with what I have written.

Wesley Null
Waco, Texas
August 2010

■ Supplementary Materials

Supplementary teaching and learning tools have been developed to accompany this text. Please contact Rowman & Littlefield at textbooks@rowman.com for more information. Available materials include

- **PowerPoint Presentations**. Instructional approaches for each chapter, answers to activities and text questions, and downloadable slides of text figures and tables.
- **Test Bank**. Available only through the book's password-protected website.
- **Teacher's Manual**. Test bank answer key and supplemental readings.

Acknowledgments

NO AUTHOR has ever written a book without the support of friends and family. I must begin by thanking my wife, Dana, and our two beautiful children, Corbin and Raegan, for their endless support, encouragement, and inspiration. I also want to thank my many colleagues at Baylor University who serve as a constant source of advice and engaging discussion. I especially want to acknowledge the friendship and professional guidance of David A. Smith, Perry Glanzer, Jon Engelhardt, Andy Wisely, Dwight Allman, Tom Hibbs, David Lyle Jeffrey, Elizabeth Corey, Susan Colon, Elizabeth Davis, Barry Harvey, Scott Moore, Sarah-Jane Murray, Anna Shaw, Don Schmeltekopf, Jim Marcum, Al Beck, Jules Sweet, Diane Haun, Tom Riley, Gretchen Schwarz, Tony Talbert, Larry Browning, Trena Wilkerson, Sandi Cooper, Rachelle Meyer, and Elden Barrett. In addition, I was fortunate to have the terrific support of four Baylor graduate students during the time I worked on this project. I want to acknowledge the excellent research and editing skills of Melissa Merritt, Michelle Horan, Connee Duran, and Claudiu Cimpean. I am deeply grateful for their diligence while copying articles, searching for books, and verifying references.

I should acknowledge my Fall 2009 Curriculum Theory and Practice course at Baylor. They were the first to read and discuss a draft of this manuscript, leading to conversations that improved the text in countless ways. Thanks to all of you for your insightful contributions.

Beyond Baylor, I should mention the inspiration I have received from Diane Ravitch, E. D. Hirsch, Jr., Lucien

Ellington, Jacob Needleman, Wilfred M. McClay, Ian Westbury, Jared Stallones, Gerry Gutek, Bob Yinger, John Beineke, Chara Haeussler Bohan, Peter Hlebowitsh, Bill Wraga, Blanche Brick, Doug Simpson, Craig Kridel, Lynn Burlbaw, Don Warren, Richard Glotzer, Mark Groen, Greg Barrett, Joseph Watras, Jennifer Jolly, Shelley Chapman, Sam Katz, Corey Locke, Todd Ream, Todd Kettler, and Mindy Spearman.

Perhaps my greatest satisfaction from publishing books comes when I hear from K–12 teachers who have run across my work and chosen to send me a message. These are the people who do the challenging but tremendously rewarding work of educating children every day. They are nothing short of heroes in our culture. I want to thank Richard Munro for his passion and dedication to the teaching profession, Diana Senechal for her support and insightful reading of my work, Anna Spitzer Quandt for her enthusiasm and commitment to the teachers college tradition, and Mary Duty for her love of history and her commitment to civic virtue. I also want to thank Annie Gosar for reading what I write and responding with remarkable kindness and insight.

Patti Belcher has been a dedicated and thoughtful editor who has improved the readability of this text in a variety of ways. I want to thank Patti for seeing the value in this project and for the time she has dedicated to improving my writing.

I want to thank the reviewers of the manuscript, who offered comments and suggestions that were both helpful and generous: Dr. Andrew J. Milson, University of Texas, Arlington; Dr. C. Matt Seimears, Emporia State University, Kansas; and Dr. David M. Callejo-Pérez, Saginaw Valley State University, who ultimately wrote the foreword.

Last but not least, I want to thank the three teachers of curriculum whose work has impacted me the most: Alan W. Garrett, O. L. Davis, Jr., and William A. Reid. Alan inspired my fascination with curriculum, O. L. challenged me to write better than I ever thought I could, and Bill has tutored me patiently with his wisdom and perceptive touch. This book would not exist without their teaching.

Despite all of this support, I know this text remains imperfect. No work of curriculum is ever done. Whatever inaccuracies or omissions remain in the final result are of course my responsibility and mine alone.

A Note to the Reader

Theory to Practice

THIS BOOK features special sidebars throughout, identified by an apple icon. We call them "Theory to Practice." Understanding the theories of education is one thing, but knowing how to apply them in real-life situations is invaluable. We help you make that initial connection through the "Theory to Practice" examples, and we have made them easy to find with the apple icon. Use these examples as the first step to applying this knowledge in your own way and in your particular circumstances. Refer to them when observing teachers and discuss them in your courses. By doing so, your knowledge of education and teaching will grow, and your success as a teacher will follow as well.

Pay special attention! The apple will alert you to methods that can be implemented in a classroom situation based on theories being discussed in the text.

Introduction

What Is Curriculum and Why Does It Matter?

EVERYONE WHO discusses teachers, schools, or education uses the term *curriculum*. The word is unavoidable. Few people, however, stop to think about what curriculum means or what it takes to create a good curriculum. Even fewer people ask questions about what curriculum is *for*, what should serve as the proper foundation for curriculum making, and how we should go about making curriculum decisions. These decisions should tie knowledge together, build community, and serve the common good. This book is about these questions and these goals. The best place to start is by making a distinction between curriculum and education.

■ Curriculum versus Education

Curriculum is the heart of education. The reason is twofold. First, curriculum is about what should be taught. Second, it combines thought, action, and purpose. "Education" is an abstract, nebulous concept that takes place through families, churches, the media, and many other cultural influences that surround children.[1] Curriculum, however, is a specific, tangible subject that is always tied to decision making within institutions, whether they are schools, churches, nonprofit agencies, or governmental programs. Unlike education, curriculum requires those who discuss it to address what subject matter should be taught. Education is frequently discussed without regard to subject matter, but every discussion of curriculum must address subject matter in one way or another. At the same time, subject matter is only one source of content for curriculum making. Social scientific studies in education often focus so exclusively on process that they seriously neglect, if not downright ignore, curriculum. This tendency to discuss "education" without addressing curriculum is a significant barrier that curriculum specialists, teachers, and indeed the general public must overcome if we expect to create good schools.

In addition to subject matter, curriculum raises numerous questions about sources of content for curriculum making. For example, any curriculum must address *why* subject matter should be taught. Because of its history and etymology, curriculum is inevitably a teleological term. This *why* aspect of curriculum must take into account questions of purpose and ultimate goals. Unlike much "education" debate today, curriculum cannot be discussed—let alone created—without addressing this question of purpose. Subject matter is of course one of the sources of knowledge that must be included in a curriculum. At the same time, however, subject matter—think of history, literature, or science—is primarily a tool that teachers and curriculum makers use to achieve the larger goals embedded in any curriculum. The topic of curriculum raises these questions not only because of its history, but also because the term is tied to institutions, which must communicate their reasons for existence if they expect to flourish.[2]

Education is almost always discussed as if it were a modern social science disconnected from ultimate ends. Our modern, empirically driven culture deinstitutionalizes "education," stripping it of its teleological roots. It is much more difficult, however, to do this with curriculum. Curriculum has retained its institutional identity in the face of our modern world. Concentrating on curriculum can help us to rediscover the deeper ideals that were once foundational to education.

Recognizing this distinction between curriculum and education also helps us to become more effective teachers, more thoughtful curriculum makers, and more astute consumers of educational rhetoric. Focusing on curriculum enables us to become better citizens because of the renewed sense of purpose that deliberations about curriculum can provide, whether they take place in schools, homes, churches, legislatures, or anywhere else. Distinguishing between education and curriculum can help us to realize that much of what passes for talk about "education" today is shallow and devoid of meaning, if not deceptive.

Curriculum is distinct from education in other ways as well. Curriculum forces us to think about ethics, whereas education is frequently discussed as if it can be divorced from questions of right and wrong. Curriculum is about the substance of what should be taught (an ethical matter), whereas "education" is often presented as if it can or should be a social science disconnected from the moral question of curriculum. "Education" is analyzed in this way whether the conversation takes place in elementary schools, high schools, community colleges, universities, think tanks, the legislature, or the media. We often find people with backgrounds in economics, psychology, and political science making pronouncements about "what must be done" in education. Rarely, however, do these "experts" address the moral question of curriculum. The basis for their claims about "education" almost always derives from their standing as specialized researchers who explain social phenomena, not as citizens who contribute to curriculum deliberation.[3]

Explanations about social phenomena have real value. By themselves, however, they do not provide us with what we need to make good curriculum decisions. The source can be economics, psychology, sociology, history, or any other intellectual specialty, but the result is the same. Explanations can be *useful* in making curricular decisions, but they are not sufficient in and of themselves for making curriculum. The attempt to separate education as a social science from curriculum as a moral practice is not only impossible, but dangerous. Trying to create a science of education divorced from curriculum is equal to training someone how to fire a weapon but failing to teach them when and why to do it.

Now is a momentous time, however, in intellectual history. Recent changes in social science and moral philosophy indicate that the twenty-first century will be a time of reintegrating the social sciences and moral philosophy.[4] Specialists in curriculum (or curriculists as this text refers to them) and others who make curriculum decisions need to pay attention to what is happening in other fields that integrate theory and practice. One example is medicine.[5] There was a time when discussions of medicine attempted to be "objective" and value-free, but no longer. Recent debates about healthcare reform illustrate this point powerfully. Like medicine, education and curriculum cannot be "objective" or value-free. The language that surrounds so-called scientific debates about education does not do a good job integrating theory and practice, nor does it succeed at combining social science and moral philosophy. This book will make the case that the language of curriculum deliberation has a much better chance of succeeding at this task.

A major goal of *Curriculum* is to help anyone interested in educational improvement to recognize when rhetoric about education is masking the underlying *curricular* issues that are the essence of education. Many people—in the media and elsewhere—make pronouncements using the word *education*, when in reality they are making assertions about curriculum without even realizing it. Often these assertions about "what must be done" in the name of education are incomplete, hollow, and doctrinaire. This book addresses this problem by providing an introduction to five curricular traditions and then offering a deeper vision for what curriculum is, can, and should be. The goal is for readers to reenvision what can and should be done in the name of education by infusing our approach to education with a richer conception of curriculum. A significant first step is to think and speak more clearly about curriculum at all levels.

One of the main reasons schools struggle is because states have spent a great deal of time and money on the creation of efficient systems of education but have ignored the most significant ingredient in any school: its curriculum. Spending money to create large systems of schooling while ignoring curriculum would be like dedicating billions of dollars to create a new space shuttle but allocating little time or money to the path the ship will take, the purpose of the space program, or the characteristics of the people who will pilot the ship.

Perhaps we have ceased to engage in meaningful deliberations about curriculum because we have stopped asking deeper questions about the purpose of schooling. If that is the case, curriculum can help us to raise these questions again. We cannot, must not, and should not continue to evade discussions of curriculum by allowing social science researchers to make assertions about what must be done in education while at the same time dismissing the term, topic, and moral practice of curriculum making. That is one of the central arguments of this book. Educators at all levels—and especially curriculum specialists—need to learn how and why to ask challenging *curricular* questions, which are inevitably moral, social, and political in nature. Asking curricular questions in the face of rhetoric from empirical specialists can be difficult, but asking them is essential if we are to provide a liberating curriculum to all young people. Not only curriculum specialists, but also members of the general public need to learn to ask curriculum questions.

■ Curriculum Questions

What should be taught, to whom, under what circumstances, how, and with what end in mind? Put more concretely, what should be taught to these students, in this school, at this time, how, and to what end? What process should we use to decide what our curriculum ought to be within a particular school, college, or university context? These are *curriculum* questions. They are *not* questions that can be answered only with economics, psychology, political science, history, biology, mathematics, or any other intellectual specialty. They also cannot be answered only by looking at the skills that employers want their workers to possess. Curriculum questions can only be answered through thoughtful inquiry into *curriculum*. This point seems so obvious, but it is often forgotten in heated debates about schooling.

Curriculum is at the center of every controversial issue within teaching and schooling today. Debates rage on with regard to moral education, sex education, religious education, state-mandated testing, intelligent design, whole language versus phonics in the teaching of reading, prayer in schools, and other hot-button topics. What is the common theme that unites these debates? At their foundation, they are curricular in nature. Partisan advocates for one view or another may discuss these issues as if they are about education, but in reality they are about curriculum and education *at the same time*. They are curricular because they are ethical and teleological, leading us inevitably to the subject of purpose.

What is curriculum? What is it *for*? *Who* is it for? Who should make curriculum decisions? How should these decisions be made? How should we structure the decision-making process? What should we do to make a good curriculum, and what should people who specialize in curriculum development (or curriculum deliberation) do in order to make curriculum better? What characteristics, or virtues, should these people possess? Dealing with these questions is essential if an educational institution expects to be effective—and indeed successful—in any long-term, substantive way.

Theoretic debates routinely take place in state legislatures or in the U.S. Senate, but at some point any abstract political battle must come into contact with real-world practical decision making in classrooms and schools. This book is about this transition that always takes place between theoretic visions for what curriculum "must do" or "should do" and the practical, decision-making world of classrooms and schools. Good curriculum making takes into account both of these extremes as well as all points in between.

What should be the nature of this transition between vision and classroom decision making? How should we take theoretic plans for what curriculum must or should do and turn these plans into an enacted curriculum within a particular classroom, school, or school district? What should be the internal and external characteristics of the curriculists who have worked to understand this transition and, as a result, can help it to take place more smoothly?

In addressing these questions, the purpose of this book is twofold. It begins by describing five curriculum traditions that have been powerful for hundreds of years. I have attempted to discuss these five traditions in a manner that presents their strengths and weaknesses as fairly as possible. Nevertheless, readers should recognize that the deliberative tradition, discussed in chapter 6, is the one that I believe provides the best foundation for high-quality curriculum and teaching. Whether they are reading this book for a course or on their own, I hope readers will find a way to challenge my view that a deliberative tradition provides the best way forward. Secondly, this book uses specific cases, drawn from my background as a curriculum specialist and teacher, to show how the deliberative tradition operates in practice. The case studies provide students of curriculum with the opportunity to discuss and deliberate about the unique, contextual problems that always surround curriculum decisions.

■ Why Curriculum Matters

Another hope I have for this book is that readers will discover that curriculum turns out to be a quite exciting subject, despite the reputation it may have as a boring topic. Instead of merely a lesson plan or a list of boring topics, curriculum turns out to matter as a subject, a field of study, and a moral practice. In this respect, curriculum shares many characteristics with philosophy, specifically moral philosophy. People write books, take courses, share views, and engage in disagreements about what curriculum is and should be. For these reasons, curriculum is a subject that will never go away, especially in our modern society that relies on institutions, credentialing, and structure. Curriculum also parallels philosophy because both fields attempt to see knowledge, reality, and practice in their entirety. Both aim to see the relationships between the various fields by concentrating on the "big picture" while at the same time developing specialization in one area, for example, continental philosophy in the field of philosophy or science curriculum in the field of curriculum. In addition, curriculum and philosophy both rely upon reason and logic, but both also can be tied closely to matters of religion and faith.

Curriculum matters as a specialized field of study as well. Universities, national and state departments of education, local school districts, and individual schools rely upon curriculum specialists. If curriculum specialists are to be employed in these roles, they need specialized preparation that will help them and the institutions they serve. In our world of competing interest groups and conflicting views on a host of social and political topics, curriculum specialists must be creative, thoughtful, and socially astute people who understand the various levels of curriculum planning and execution. During their preparation in graduate school or as undergraduates, the best curriculum specialists have studied state curriculum guidelines, but they also know how to take these documents and shape them appropriately within specific institutional contexts. Making this transition between curriculum as an abstract document and curriculum as a living classroom force requires that curriculists be taught how and why curriculum is as much a moral practice as it is a body of knowledge.

Curriculum is about taking a subject, preparing it for classroom use, and following through so that it makes a lasting impact on students. This shift from curriculum as an abstract body of knowledge to curriculum as a social force requires those who make curriculum decisions to address questions of teleology, ethics, and local circumstances. Specialized knowledge of one area outside of curriculum—whether it be mathematics, history, or chemistry—is essential but not sufficient when the task is curriculum making. The sooner we liberate curriculum from the idea that it is nothing but subject matter sequentially organized in an abstract way, the sooner we will be on our way to realizing the ideal of a liberating curriculum for all.

◼ What Is a Liberating Curriculum?

What is a liberating curriculum? I ask this question because curriculum should liberate students from narrow ways of thinking. It should open them up to new possibilities, but within the boundaries of tradition. A liberating curriculum is a necessary component of a liberal education. A liberating curriculum transforms the inner constitution of a person's character so that he or she can lead a life of reason, reflection, and deliberation. Moreover, a liberating curriculum is a course of study that draws upon all of the talents and abilities of students to make them more humane and compassionate. A liberating curriculum connects students with the traditions that provide the foundational knowledge necessary for understanding social and political life, while at the same time preparing them to deliberate wisely about decisions that further these traditions.

Describing what a liberating curriculum is *not* is sometimes easier than describing what it is. Curriculum needs to be liberated from ways of thinking that have shackled its growth and quality for decades. These restrictive ways of thinking include the attempt to reduce curriculum to a mechanical script that all teachers are expected to parrot, without teachers thinking for themselves or taking into account the students they teach. Another is the tendency to reduce curriculum to nothing but a syllabus on the one hand or an efficiency problem on the other. Others reduce curriculum to an impersonal list of topics divorced from meaning, purpose, and humanity. Beyond that, there are Utopian dreamers who focus so much on what could be that they forget that curriculum must start with reality and all its imperfections. There are also makeshift practitioners who reject the need to connect curriculum to a broader vision for what schooling can or should achieve. Then there are revolutionaries who promote a curriculum that foments revolution but fails to discuss what should be done once the revolution has taken place. There are theorizers who emphasize personal experience to such an extent that they forget curriculum also must address community, citizenship, institutions, and concern for the common good. Certain intellectual specialists also sometimes seek to control curriculum. They wrongly assume that the structure of their academic specialty doubles as a legitimate curriculum. Finally, there are economically driven executives who see curriculum as nothing but a tool to train the next generation of compliant workers. All of these views limit the creation of a liberating curriculum.

Curriculum can address some of the problems raised by these limited ways of thinking, each of which has something to offer. However, when curriculum is captured by any one of these perspectives, it loses its life, vitality, and direction. By "a liberating curriculum," I mean a path, a way of life that enhances the social, moral, political, intellectual, and spiritual faculties of every student. I mean something similar to what philosopher Pierre Hadot means when he speaks of philosophy and wisdom. Hadot writes, "For real wisdom does not merely cause us to know: it makes us 'be' in a different way."[6] The best hope for offering this path, this way of life, is to build upon what I call, following others, a deliberative approach to curriculum practice.

■ Thesis and Structure of the Book

My thesis has three parts. The first is that curriculum is in chains and must be liberated if we expect to have better schooling. The second is that, in order to create a truly liberating curriculum, we must begin by liberating *the concept* of curriculum before we can address specific curriculum problems. Third, in order for curriculum to be truly liberating for real students in real schools and universities, we must move from liberating *the idea* of curriculum within our *minds* to *deliberating* about specific curriculum problems within contemporary institutions.

The structure of *Curriculum* consists of two parts. Part I, "Curriculum Traditions," addresses the first two parts of the thesis, having to do primarily with the *idea* of curriculum. Part II, "From Theory to Practice," shows the practice of curriculum deliberation at work within specific educational institutions. This structure is designed to (1) show what curriculum theory is, (2) describe how deliberative curriculum theory differs from four other curriculum traditions, and (3) provide specific examples of how deliberative curriculum theory operates in practice.

■ Brief Book Overview

Before expanding on what good curriculum deliberation is and ought to be, part I examines four other well-known traditions within the curriculum field. Drawing in part upon curriculum philosopher William A. Reid's *The Pursuit of Curriculum,* part I provides a description of five philosophies of curriculum that are prevalent today and have been influential for centuries.[7] I have incorporated Reid's language by using the terms *systematic, existentialist, radical, pragmatic,* and *deliberative.* In *The Pursuit of Curriculum,* Reid discusses four, not five, curriculum traditions. I have retained Reid's terms but have added a fifth tradition that I label pragmatic. Each tradition provides a vision for curriculum that has strengths and weaknesses, which are discussed toward the end of each chapter.

Chapter 1 describes how I came to organize the book in this way. I begin with background on the idea of liberal education before touching briefly on the impact of Joseph Schwab on the field of curriculum.[8] I also describe how I see this book building on the work of Schwab and Reid. Chapters 2 through 6 present major figures who have shaped—and continue to shape—each of the five traditions. Each chapter discusses why each tradition has been powerful at different times in American history. *Curriculum,* however, is not a work of history. It is a work of curriculum philosophy and practice.

The subject of chapter 6 is the deliberative tradition. I aim to show how the deliberative tradition is uniquely suited to addressing the problems that curriculum entails. The deliberative tradition does not reject the other four in their entirety, but rather it incorporates them by maximizing the strengths and weaknesses of each. To highlight the strengths and weaknesses of each tradition, I use the five "curriculum commonplaces" first presented by Joseph Schwab.[9] Chapter 1 discusses the notion of "commonplaces" to show how it is useful in making sense of the five traditions.

Chapters 7, 8, and 9 raise specific practical questions that curriculum workers face each day. These chapters describe representative examples of common curriculum problems within schools, colleges, and universities. They then show what a deliberative curriculum worker likely would do in order to resolve the problems that arise. These chapters take the form of a narrative in which the scene is presented. Each case includes discussion of the characters involved and the specifics surrounding each set of curriculum problems. Each chapter then discusses potential resolutions that address the problems under consideration. The scenarios should be useful to anyone interested in curriculum at all levels, but especially for college and university faculty who teach courses in curriculum development, theory, and practice. In order to broaden the scope of the audience for this book, part II includes case studies from public and private schools at the K–12 and the higher education levels.

Chapter 10, the concluding chapter, discusses the characteristics—or virtues—that must and should be upheld by curriculists who wish to extend the deliberative tradition. The final chapter also argues why the deliberative tradition provides the most realistic path to a liberating curriculum for all. Before moving on to part II and particular cases, however, a broader perspective on the relationship between liberal education and curriculum sets the stage for the five curriculum traditions.

■ Discussion Questions

1. What is the difference between curriculum and education?

2. What are some examples of curriculum questions? What makes them "curricular"?

3. How does the idea of "teleology" relate to curriculum?

4. What are some ways that curriculum is similar to philosophy?

5. What does the phrase "a liberating curriculum" mean?

6. What does it mean for curriculum to be a "moral practice"?

7. The thesis of this book has three parts. What are they?

CURRICULUM
TRADITIONS

CHAPTER 1

The March to Liberal Curriculum for All

LIBERAL EDUCATION is an ideal that has shaped curriculum and teaching for centuries. Forgotten to many people today, the term *liberal* in liberal education has nothing to do with contemporary politics or left-leaning views on hot-button issues. Liberal education, rather, refers to an interdisciplinary approach to curriculum and teaching that pursues the goal of liberating minds so that they can become more fully human, make rational judgments, and provide civic leadership. Liberal education is the opposite of indoctrination. Liberally educated citizens do not merely recite the views of others. They have shaped their character in such a way that they can consider issues from many perspectives. They have developed their personal viewpoints carefully and have learned to support them with well-reasoned arguments and persuasive reasoning.

The idea of liberal curriculum stretches across generational and geographical boundaries. Its roots reach back at least to the ancient Greek philosophies of Plato and Aristotle during the fifth and fourth centuries BCE. Both recognized that true education—meaning an education fit for human beings—must strengthen human nature and cultivate leaders who shape communities toward happiness and harmony. Central to liberal education is the concept of a liberal curriculum. Rarely discussed, the creation of a liberal curriculum is the only way that liberal education can be achieved. A liberating curriculum should turn students into free thinkers who can draw upon many fields of knowledge, pursue truth, and solve problems.

To be free-minded means to use our minds to think independently while at the same time basing our judgments on a well-conceived view of tradition and purpose. Liberally educated citizens have learned to base their judgments on reason and thereby avoid surrendering to their passions, following the dictates of others, or merely pursuing material wealth.

The gift of reason distinguishes human beings from other creatures. Nonrational beings merely react to stimuli. They never engage in genuine thought or deliberation. Human beings, especially if they have studied a liberal curriculum, have the ability to think, speak, and deliberate. Some people, however, remain in a state of reaction and rarely think, primarily because they have never experienced a curriculum that awakens their ability to reason and deliberate. Since all human beings possess the gift of reason, any curriculum for liberal education must focus on strengthening rational thought, as well as other human faculties like speech, persuasion, and discipline.

In a democratic state, a liberal curriculum should be offered to every citizen. The ideal of universal liberal education, however, has never been achieved. The reason is because we have not paid sufficient attention to the subject of curriculum that gives rise to the liberal arts ideal. To address this issue, part I of *Curriculum: From Theory to Practice* focuses on five traditions that have answered the question of curricular content in different ways. Part II then introduces readers to specific cases that revolve around common curricular problems. Before addressing the five traditions in part I, however, the first step is to gain perspective on the origins of a liberal curriculum. Attention to this history helps us to understand the ideal we are trying to achieve and also make sense of why this ideal has never been put into practice.

■ Origins of a Liberal Curriculum

Greeks like Plato and Aristotle and Christian educational philosophers like St. Augustine and John Amos Comenius recognized the significance of reason when creating a liberal curriculum. Plato made reason the most powerful force in his well-known work, *The Republic*. A liberal curriculum to Plato is one that teaches young people to control emotion and appetite—the lesser aspects of human nature—by strengthening reason and self-discipline. The process of studying such a curriculum makes reason the most powerful force in people's lives. A well-ordered soul, to Plato, is one that keeps reason and emotion in their proper relationship by using logic to direct thoughts, actions, and decisions.

Plato's best, most powerful curriculum, however, was not for everyone. He reserved a truly liberating curriculum for those who had demonstrated their power to reason when they were young, making them the most fit prospects for ruling in his ideal city. The only way a community could attain true happiness was if these reason-driven citizens came to hold power over the important decisions made in the city. These philosopher-kings, as Plato called them, were the only citizens who engaged in genuine deliberation. He holds them up as the only citizens who will pursue a curriculum that strengthens their ability to reason and deliberate. Sharing this most highly prized curriculum with others was viewed as unnecessary and even harmful to the city.

Aristotle, working in Plato's shadow, similarly identified reason as the unique human ability that separates good citizens from bad, leaders from followers, and liberated citizens from servants. In works such as the *Nicomachean Ethics* and

Plato's Cave

Plato's *Republic* is regarded as one of the most influential books ever published on curriculum and teaching. The highlight of the book is known as the Allegory of the Cave, which is found in Book VII. In that book, Plato describes the kind of education that he believes leaders of any city need to have. Plato compares uneducated people to prisoners who have been living in a cave for their entire lives. These prisoners have come to believe that the shadows they see on the wall of the cave are the truth. He then depicts teaching as the process of liberating prisoners by showing them that the shadows they have been staring at their entire lives are not real, but rather reflections of something else. Teachers then persuade students to turn toward the light, climb out of the cave, and eventually stare directly at the sun, which is the source of all truth, beauty, and goodness. Teachers and students climb together out of the cave, meaning that both are responsible for their respective parts of the teaching and learning process. Plato's cave metaphor is found repeatedly in literature, philosophy, religion, and many other fields throughout the history of the West. One such example is found in the movie *The Matrix*. The matrix represents the shadows on the wall of the cave, and the prisoners are the humans who provide electricity to run the matrix. The character of Morpheus, played by Laurence Fishburne, is the teacher who leads the prisoners, including Neo played by Keanu Reeves, out of the darkness and into the light.

Politics, Aristotle, like Plato, ties his views on a liberating curriculum to the concept of the soul. Although a bit more complex than Plato's, Aristotle's depiction of a well-ordered (meaning liberated) soul places reason in control of animalistic impulses like appetite and desire. Again, a curriculum fit for human beings, to Aristotle, is one that introduces students to subjects, conversations, and experiences that strengthen virtues like courage, friendliness, and practical wisdom—all of which are rooted in reason, including the proper relationship between reason and emotion. Aristotle stresses moral virtues like courage and magnanimity more than Plato, but a curriculum that cultivates the proper relationship between reason and emotion remains the foundation for a liberating curriculum to Aristotle. To him, a curriculum that ignores the subjects and practices that facilitate reason will never lead to liberation, nor will it make students sufficiently human.

Looking back upon ancient Greeks like Plato and Aristotle from the perspective of the early twenty-first century reveals that the beauty of their views also has its liabilities. If our goal is democratic education, then the works of Plato and Aristotle provide limited guidance. In his description of regime types in the *Republic,* for example, Plato ranks democracy as one of the worst regimes, only one step above tyranny.[1] Similarly, in Aristotle's *Politics,* Aristotle categorizes democracy as a "deviant" regime, one that only comes into existence when a polity becomes controlled by people who pursue their own interests as opposed to the interests of the community as a whole.[2] In Aristotle's view, democracy, tyranny, and oligarchy come into existence when self-interest and emotion take over a community, leading to these "deviant" regimes.

To counteract the problems inherent in democracy, Plato and Aristotle argue that communities must be ruled by elites who have the character to make society flourish. This aristocratic viewpoint runs counter to a democratic philosophy that rejects the division of citizens into rulers and followers. The views of Plato and Aristotle are rooted in a particular view of human nature. Its clearest description can be found in the *Republic,* where Plato divides citizens into three "soul types": gold, silver, and bronze.[3] In Plato's ideal community, each soul type is provided the type of curriculum that is best suited to his or her nature. Universal education is not the goal. The goal is to provide each student with what he or she needs to serve the ends of the state.

The roots of tracking can be found in Plato's argument for a different curriculum for each type of soul in the city.

With some minor revisions, Aristotle accepts Plato's division of citizens into rulers and followers. Aristotle similarly rejects the ideal of universal education. To Plato and Aristotle, only those citizens who possess the most desirable soul types can be truly educated in a liberated sense. Some citizens are destined to be servile and slave-like, while others are destined to rule. No amount of liberal education can change this reality. Some citizens are responsible for deliberating and making decisions on behalf of the community, while others are responsible for following the decisions made by the elites.

The views of Plato and Aristotle in this respect lead to a substantial gap between "theory" and "practice." This gap is closely tied to the distinction between aristocrats and lesser citizens in the community. The curriculum presented to future leaders is rooted in reflection, conversation, dialectic, and abstraction. The curriculum designed for future workers, on the other hand, is designed to train lesser citizens for their roles as laborers or soldiers who serve the city in a strictly physical sense. Curriculum, as a result, becomes liberating for some but not for others. Deliberation is confined to those who have received the necessary preparation for deliberative activity; others are excluded. The roots of the common distinction between today's college prep and "vocational" tracks within curriculum can be found in these classical works of Plato and Aristotle.[4]

The Christian Era and the Liberal Arts Ideal

Opportunities for expanding the notion of a liberal curriculum to a larger segment of the population changed somewhat with the birth of the Christian era. Christianity's message is that Christ died for everyone, not just for a specific segment of the population. To use Plato's metaphor, the Christian message was available to all regardless of "soul type," which makes a liberal curriculum available to all. At the same time, however, the Christian tradition also transformed the content of the curriculum. A truly liberating curriculum in a Christian sense requires that students embrace the faith that Christ presented. In addition to standard Greek virtues—wisdom, science, courage, and magnanimity—Christianity introduced new virtues. Faith, hope, and love became the new ends toward which a liberal arts curriculum ought to be pursued. Christian thinkers such as St. Augustine, St. Thomas Aquinas, and John Amos Comenius sought to balance reason with faith, while at the same time extending the Christian tradition.[5] Virtues like wisdom, science, and courage remain essential to a Christian liberal arts curriculum, but they become tools to pursuing the broader virtues of faith, hope, and love. A truly liberated person from a Christian perspective is one who is wise, but wise for the right reasons: to serve God, love our fellow man, and pattern ourselves after the life of Christ.

Deliberation also changes with the birth of the Christian era. Deliberators must draw upon the Christian virtues as they decide upon a course of action. Depending upon interpretations of scripture, the various Christian denominations allow different segments of the population to hold political power, thereby participating in the deliberative process. Faith traditions that retain sharp distinctions between clergy and laity reject the practice of extending the deliberative process to all members of a community. In this scenario, clergy interpret scripture, and members of the laity are expected to accept these interpretations on authority. On the other hand, some Protestant traditions, especially those that were closely tied to the rise of democracy, reject the distinction between clergy and laity, opening up the deliberative process to more members of the community. The goal of teaching all members of the community to deliberate is especially elevated in the work of John Amos Comenius, a seventeenth-century educational philosopher and curriculist.[6] Known as the father of universal education, Comenius had the ability to engage in philosophical dialogue with the leading thinkers of his time while at the same time communicating with everyday citizens about how and what to teach their children.

Deliberation in the United States and other Western societies has been heavily influenced by the Christian tradition that dominated curricular thought and practice throughout the Middle Ages. The goal of deliberations within a Christian context was different from those in Greek or modern democratic societies. The goal of deliberation during the Middle Ages was to extend the Christian tradition by introducing each successive generation to the story of redemption. Democracy can be a means to the goals inherent in Christian deliberation, but any regime type—whether it is democracy or aristocracy—cannot be an end in itself. As democracy gained prominence as an ideal end, however, it often conflicted with the dominant interpretations of faith that prevailed during the late nineteenth and early twentieth centuries. Further attention to democracy and its role in shaping curriculum brings us to the modern era and the most recent steps in the march toward a universal liberal curriculum.

The Rise of Democracy

With the rise of democracy as an ideal, new challenges arose for education and curriculum. Democratic education—defined as equal educational opportunity for all—became the new end toward which modern societies began to move. The idea of a liberal curriculum for some and a servile curriculum for others could no longer hold when equal educational opportunity became the goal. The "liberating" aspects of the curriculum—those designed to cultivate reason, thought, reflection, and refinement—somehow had to be integrated with the "vocational" dimensions of curriculum, which focus on application. When aristocratic views of politics dominated the culture, the "liberal" and "vocational" aspects of curriculum could remain separate because different people were trained for different roles in society. In the modern world of the nineteenth century, however, this distinction began to crumble.

The rise of nation-states altered education and curriculum considerably. Increasingly powerful nations in Europe and individual states in the United States created public education systems that began to educate an increasingly large percentage of children. Public education systems also began to dominate the content of curriculum. Universal education became a goal to be attained through state-funded institutions. The church, or individual tutors, no longer held sway over what students learned. The creation of common schools (later referred to as public schools) and normal schools (later referred to as teachers colleges) were institutions created to expand educational opportunity to populations that had not had access to education before.[7]

The most significant challenge that faced these new institutions was curriculum. Common schools, for example, had to decide if they would rely upon a more elite-oriented curriculum that emphasized reason, reflection, and foreign languages or teach something else. New questions immediately arose. Should the new schools pursue the ancient ideals of liberal arts curriculum or emphasize economy-driven subjects like manual training and cooking? Or, should they attempt to do something in between these two perspectives by creating a curriculum that combined reflection, foreign languages, and vocational training? If so, how could this

The terminology of "teachers colleges" is the more well-known phrase. When they were first created, however, institutions for teacher education in the United States were called "normal schools." By the early to mid 1920s, all of them had dropped the phrase "normal school" and adopted the name "teachers college."

balanced curriculum be implemented in practice? How could the curriculum be liberating and economically useful at the same time? Is such an integration possible?

These questions were front and center for those who had to develop curriculum for the newly created common schools. Similar questions arose for the new teachers colleges. These institutions had to create a curriculum that served the needs of future teachers and simultaneously prepared them to teach the common school curriculum. What curriculum would provide future teachers with an appropriate amount of liberal education while at the same time preparing them for the challenging task of running a common school? What, in practice, ought to be the appropriate relationship between the liberal and the vocational aspects of teacher education curriculum? How can programs be established that both liberate future teachers and prepare them to run schools effectively?

These questions do not have easy answers, but what tied the efforts of curriculists together as they faced them was the desire to expand equal educational opportunity to all. In their response to the above questions, reformers often defined curriculum differently in various parts of the country. Their desire, nevertheless, was the same: universal education. The different ways in which nineteenth- and twentieth-century reformers made sense of universal curriculum can be found in the five traditions presented in the following chapters.

These same reformers were intensely interested in moral education and preparation for citizenship, even if they did not stress deliberation. Citizenship required adherence to religious principles, fidelity to rules, and preparation for participation in the institutions that held America together (e.g., the family, church, school, and politics).[8] Moral education, however, has changed since the nineteenth century. Deliberation was once marginalized, but now it has resurfaced. Curriculum theorists and political philosophers have only in the last fifty years begun to emphasize deliberation and its connection to moral education.[9]

Universal Liberal Curriculum and Deliberation

A central assumption of this book is that this relatively recent shift toward deliberation should be linked more closely with curriculum. Curriculum is something that we seek to enact through decision making, not just something we want to understand. Understanding is of course an important part of curriculum, but it is not the goal of curriculum itself. The sooner we begin to see curriculum as a practical activity that requires deliberation, the sooner we will create better teachers, curriculum makers, and schools.

Because deliberation is at the heart of what this book argues, the story of how it relates to the rise of universal education is essential. Deliberation also deserves attention because of its connection to citizenship. No citizen is fully engaged in the life of her nation unless she is recognized as a deliberative participant. All citizens in a democracy, moreover, should encounter a curriculum that prepares them for their lives as civic participants. Before the rise of democracy as an ideal, the idea of educating all citizens for deliberative activity was hampered by the assumption that not all people have the capacity to deliberate, at least not to the extent that merits true citizenship. Moreover, universal deliberation was restricted by the assumption that curriculum should be differentiated so that some students are liberated for political activity and others are trained for labor.

Some historical reflection on deliberation is perhaps necessary at this point. Deliberation first became prominent in the work of Aristotle. Socrates is known for his love of conversation, but deliberation is different from conversation. The goal of conversation, both to Socrates and in the minds of many people today, is understanding, or perhaps enjoyment or communication. Because of his emphasis on deliberation as opposed to Socratic conversation, Aristotle is known as the father of political deliberation. The goal of deliberation is not just to understand, enjoy, or communicate, although all of these are important factors in deliberation. The goal, rather, is to make a *decision*. Decisions always take place within a specific context and are influenced by the individual circumstances that impinge upon that context. Deliberation is grounded, tactile, and specific, whereas conversation is abstract and general.

In his argument for political education for future aristocratic statesmen, Aristotle ties the ability to deliberate with the virtue of practical wisdom, which he maintains is essential to the maintenance of a healthy state.[10] Deliberation, briefly described as the ability to make wise decisions after having considered all possible options, is only open to students who have the innate capacity to do it well. They have pursued the kind of curriculum that Aristotle lays out in the *Ethics,* they have demonstrated their political abilities in challenging circumstances, and they can make judgments that benefit the

The concept of deliberation has grown increasingly influential during the past forty years. Deliberation has witnessed a revival of sorts, especially in the fields of political science and philosophy.

city as a whole. In keeping with the underlying support for aristocracy that pervades the *Ethics,* Aristotle presents a view of decision making that leaves deliberation to an elite class. This class of special citizens is charged with the task of making decisions for everyone else. The lesser, nondeliberating citizens are then required to implement the directives laid down by Aristotle's elite.

Aristotle does not address the question of curriculum in any significant detail, but a logical extension of his views on political education leads to the position that he would see deliberation as essential to good curriculum making. From an Aristotelian perspective, however, the scope of curriculum deliberation should remain limited to the people who hold political power over curriculum. Not all members of society have the character and background to participate in curriculum deliberations; therefore, the curriculum—and deliberations about it—should remain the purview of the elite. Curriculum should be written by elites who hand it over to others for implementation.

In a democracy, however, the number of stakeholders involved in curriculum deliberation must expand. This expansion should take place not only because curriculum is improved when deliberation takes place at all levels, but also because democracy requires that all citizens have input into what is taught. Universal deliberation must grow in tandem with universal education. In addition, universal education must be accompanied by a curriculum that provides all students with the tools they need to deliberate wisely. Without such a curriculum, a country asks its citizens to participate in a process for which they have not been prepared.

John Dewey and Democratic Education

The relationship between democracy and education has been a common topic that scholars have addressed for at least a century. Well-known discussions of this topic, however, have paid little attention to curriculum. Works on educational research and philosophy have addressed education in a broad, abstract sense, but not the specifics that come with curriculum. For example, John Dewey's *Democracy and Education,* which is universally recognized as the most influential book ever published on democracy and education, includes chapters that address subjects such as geography, history, and social studies. Nowhere in the book, however, does Dewey provide an in-depth discussion of curriculum and curriculum making. His book reads like an anthropology treatise and not a book on democracy and its relation to curriculum.

Dewey makes broad statements that are difficult to defend when the subject is curriculum decisions within specific schools. For example, Dewey writes, "We cannot establish a hierarchy of values among studies."[11] Dewey does not explain his position any further. If a school or school district wants to identify science, mathematics, Latin, Greek, or philosophy as subjects that are most important, why is this not possible? All a school district has to do is set curriculum policy that identifies certain courses that are required for all students. Of course, private schools are freer to adjust their curriculum than public schools, especially during the current age of state and national standards. Still, however, public school districts can (and frequently do) make decisions that identify certain core subjects as most important and then require these subjects for all students. Like much of his other writing, Dewey is ambiguous, especially when it comes to the subjects within the curriculum that he views as most significant. He is notoriously silent on this topic. Dewey expects readers to accept his assertions because of the science that he puts behind them. Abstract arguments, however, are not sufficient when the subject is curriculum.

Another example indicates how Dewey avoids curriculum. Chapter 15 of *Democracy and Education* is entitled "Play and Work in the Curriculum." With the exception of the title, Dewey does not use the term curriculum *even once*. With his title, Dewey claims to be writing on curriculum, but then avoids the term and the specifics that come with it.[12] Dewey also does not broach the question of what methods should be used to arrive at curricular content. To the extent that Dewey addresses curriculum questions, he answers them in a theoretic way that pays scant attention to the practical side of curriculum making.

Despite the fact that Dewey is known as one of the fathers of pragmatic philosophy, he does not provide sufficient guidance for how to address the daily decisions that practitioners face. Dewey deserves credit for successfully bringing democracy and education together in the way a political philosopher perhaps should do, but he did not take on the more difficult challenge of bringing democracy and *curriculum* together in a realistic way. Joseph Schwab, however, did confront that challenge in a provocative way.

■ Joseph Schwab's Challenge to Curriculum

During the 1960s and 1970s, Joseph Schwab changed the face of curriculum.[13] I explore Schwab's work in more detail in chapter 6, but a few specifics regarding his argument are useful in understanding the march toward universal liberal curriculum. In his "practical" papers, Schwab, a professor of education and natural sciences at the University of Chicago, makes critical distinctions that are foundational to the argument of this book. In "The Practical: A Language for Curriculum," for example, Schwab argues that curriculum is a moral practice and not a theoretic science.[14] This assertion runs counter to almost all twentieth-century writing on curriculum. It also connects the field of curriculum with a philosophical tradition that stretches back to Plato, Aristotle, and St. Augustine. To argue his case, Schwab makes a distinction between what he calls "theoretic inquiry" and "practical inquiry." He demonstrates how these two modes of inquiry differ in at least three significant ways: by outcome, subject matter, and method.

The outcome of theoretic inquiry is understanding. The outcome of practical inquiry, on the other hand, is to make a *decision* about what should be done within a particular social and political context. Understanding can and should be part of practical inquiry, but, within the world of practicality, understanding is always a means to the end of decision making.

In addition to outcome, Schwab shows how theoretic and practical inquiry differ because of the subject matter they address. In theoretic inquiry, the subject matter is a puzzle or a question that is interesting to the researchers who conduct the study. The outcome of a lab-based experiment, for example, is almost always more questions for researchers to ponder in their quest to understand a particular phenomenon. Lab-based researchers are not so much interested in questions like "Should we do this or that . . ." but rather questions like "What is the nature of this object?" or "How will these molecules react in this situation?" Questions of a "What should we do?" variety deal with states of affairs, not with states of mind.

A third way in which theoretic and practical inquiry differ is with regard to method. The method of theoretic inquiry is logic, either deductive or inductive. Knowledge is produced by making logical connections based on deductions from mathematical models or as a result of inductions that arise from observations of the phenomena under study. In practical inquiry, on the other hand, the method of inquiry is not pure logic, but rather deliberation. Decision makers seek out problems, discuss the nature of what they have found, collect data, consider alternatives, and arrive at a decision for action. If they wish to create a liberating curriculum, deliberators must take into account a variety of factors that always influence practical action. Of these factors, five stand out as most significant. They have arisen constantly in educational philosophy and curricular practice for centuries. In the third of his practical papers, "The Practical 3: Translation into Curriculum," Schwab refers to these five factors as commonplaces.[15] Following Schwab, this text argues that these five commonplaces are essential if any attempt at curriculum reform expects to succeed. A more in-depth consideration of the commonplaces is warranted not just because of their role in curriculum making, but also because the following five chapters use these commonplaces to compare and contrast the five traditions.

> The commonplaces connect curriculum with its humanistic roots, which have not been emphasized in the field for quite some time.

■ The Five Commonplaces of Curriculum

Why the Language of Commonplaces?

What is a commonplace and why did Schwab choose this somewhat uncommon term? In choosing *commonplaces*, Schwab connected curriculum to a tradition quite different from what dominated the field during his time. He was drawing upon the subject of rhetoric, whereas curriculum theory and curriculum development had almost invariably drawn upon the natural sciences and behavioral psychology for guidance. The term *commonplaces* translates into Latin as *locus communis. Communis* is similar to community, so the idea of a commonplace is a word, phrase, or idea that is commonly accepted as true, or "commonsensical," throughout a community. A commonplace is somewhat like the notion of "conventional wisdom" today. A commonplace is something that everyone accepts as "right" or "true," regardless of whether the idea turns out to be true upon deeper investigation. For example, the idea that "schools should meet the needs and interests of students" is both a slogan and a commonplace. Because this idea has been so powerful since the early 1900s, it has come to be understood as conventional wisdom, or as a commonplace. To rebut the argument that "schools should meet the needs and interests of students" requires an equally compelling—if not commonplace—argument, one that is widely accepted throughout a community as well. Commonplaces are difficult to refute because they operate at the level of assumptions that are widely accepted as infallible.

In the ancient sense of rhetoric found in the works of writers such as Aristotle and Augustine, a commonplace is also understood as a path that can be taken to persuade an audience. Writers and speakers who have been trained in the art of rhetoric can draw upon the commonplaces that surround their subject. Speakers can use their knowledge of these commonplaces to persuade citizens to support their views. By connecting the practice of curriculum making to the art of rhetoric, Schwab opened up many new possibilities for curriculists. He was challenging curriculists to become persuasive artists as opposed to efficient technicians. He used the language of commonplaces to connect curriculum not only to rhetoric but to other humanities fields as well.

Rather than seeking to discover a "one best method" that would produce uniform curricula, Schwab presented curriculum makers with five commonplaces that are found in any attempt to make curriculum. These commonplaces are powerful because each is accepted as a true part of any good curriculum. Their widespread acceptance is what makes each a commonplace. The five he identified are teachers, learners, subject matter, context, and curriculum making. He maintains that all five have something to offer anyone who makes curriculum. He also asserts that the failure to consider any one of these factors will lead to an incomplete, ineffective curriculum. The challenge for curriculum deliberators is to balance these commonplaces while at the same time avoiding the trap of thinking that any one of them is sufficient, by itself, to make a good curriculum. We must tend to all five as we consider alternatives, produce curriculum documents, and enact curriculum within individual schools and classrooms. Some attention to each of the commonplaces helps to set the stage for their use in the following chapters.

Commonplace #1: Teachers

The point that *teachers* are a central force in curriculum is self-evident. No curriculum can be taught without a teacher. Even in the process of reading a book outside of a school or another institutional context, there is always an author who serves as a teacher. Teachers are the agents who take an official (or unofficial) curriculum and present it to students within a specific classroom. Who are they? What is their background? How long have they been teaching at this school? What have they experienced? Are they resistant or open to change? All of these questions belong to the teacher commonplace.

Overemphasis is the most common mistake that arises when the teacher commonplace is the subject of discussion. Since everyone knows that teachers are an essential factor in any curriculum, the tendency to exaggerate and make teachers the only or even the primary force is always present. When teachers are presented as the sole or even the principal force in curriculum, then the other commonplaces—often learners—are diminished. When this happens, the power of curriculum—and the liberating force it can provide—is undermined. The point that teachers are one of the five essential curriculum commonplaces, however, is obvious.

Commonplace #2: Learners

The commonplace of learners is every bit as self-evident as the commonplace of teachers. Of course, teachers always teach something to *someone*. If those who make a curriculum ignore the needs, interests, and backgrounds of students, then the curriculum they offer will not make an impact. What interests do these students have? What are their backgrounds? What subjects do they prefer? How motivated are they to learn? What stage of development are they in? How will they likely react to new and different ideas? What kind of life outside of school do these students have? These are questions raised by the learner commonplace.

Similar to the commonplace of teachers, the learner commonplace is often subject to exaggeration. The problem with placing too much value on learners was particularly evident during the first half of the twentieth century, at least in the United States, when "child-centered learning," "learner-centered instruction," "developmentally appropriate instruction," and other similarly named movements were popular. The power of individualism in American culture also has led to a frequent exaggeration of the importance of the learner commonplace.

The use of "learners," however, also implies more than the students who are involved in the learning process. The commonplace of learners also refers to the idea of "learning" as the ultimate end for education. A common assumption is that "learning" is what the purpose of education ought to be. Rarely has this assumption been challenged, at least in the popular press and in policy discussions of curriculum. Schwab, however, challenges this "learning is the end of education" assumption by identifying learners as only one of five commonplaces and by making the distinction between theoretic and practical inquiry. If learning is the only end of education, then we would never be taught how to take what we have learned and apply it within practical situations. With the identification of learners and learning as one of five commonplaces, Schwab places learning within the larger context of moral and intellectual inquiry. From this perspective, learning should not be seen as an end in itself, but rather as a means to acting in the world.

Commonplace #3: Subject Matter

Like the other commonplaces, subject matter is essential to curriculum. Teachers teach learners *something*. The challenge, once again, is to view subject matter as part of a larger curricular whole. The most prevalent way in which subject matter is privileged over the other four commonplaces is when it is referred to as "content," thereby presuming that "content" is not found elsewhere in the family of commonplaces. The point of the five commonplaces is that curricular content is found in *all of them,* not just one. This is a point that modern readers find difficult to comprehend. Americans are accustomed to thinking in terms of sharp distinctions between "content" and "method," without regard to other factors within curriculum. If a deeper view of curriculum is to thrive, conversations must move beyond shallow terms that place "content" on one side of curriculum and "methods" on the other. Good curriculum always integrates both.

Modern science has played a significant role in the predominance of the subject matter commonplace. Science during the Enlightenment period had the tendency to make subject matter the preeminent if not the only factor present in curriculum discussions. For instance, many scholars and university professors view curriculum as nothing but an extension of their specialized field. The problem with this view is that privileging subject matter devalues the other commonplaces and emasculates good curriculum making. Similar to the case with the commonplaces of teachers and learners, the tendency on the part of scholars is to assume that subject matter deserves more attention than teachers, learners, context, and curriculum making. The consequence of this flawed assumption is that it results in an ineffective, unsuccessful, and ultimately nonliberating curriculum.

Commonplace #4: Context

Context refers to the setting in which a curriculum is taught. Teachers always teach something to someone *somewhere*. Curriculum documents can of course be created without regard to individual schools, but any curriculum document must at some point come into contact with the reality of a specific school and classroom context. Schwab used "milieu" instead of context to refer to this commonplace, but the point is the same. This text uses "context" because it is the more contemporary term for the point that Schwab was making.

Context shares similarities with the learner commonplace, but it also differs in significant ways. Whereas the learner commonplace focuses on the students who are being taught and their developmental readiness, context takes into account the larger community in which a specific school exists. For example, context raises questions about the history of *this* community, *this* neighborhood, and *this* school district. How long has this school been in existence? What are the expectations of the parents who send their children to this school? Do most of this school's graduates choose to remain in the community after graduation? If so, what roles will they be expected to perform? How do parents and other leaders within this community judge the effectiveness of the school? What is the nature of the curriculum that has been taught in the past and how does it relate to the community in which the school exists?

As with the other commonplaces, the context commonplace is prone to exaggeration. One consequence is that overemphasizing context leads to a curriculum that does not create new possibilities for students. Students become trained for what has been done in the community in the past, as opposed to being liberated so that they consider new paths. Overemphasis on context also can lead to the reproduction of the current barriers that exist within a community—whether they are based on race, class, or gender—without any attempt to break them down.

At the other extreme, ignoring the context commonplace can lead to a curriculum that is not supported by the community in which the school exists. If parents and community leaders begin to hold the view that a school teaches a curriculum that does not support (or further) the goals of that community, then the school will lose its social, political, and economic support. Like the other commonplaces, the factor of context must be kept in mind as deliberators decide what action to take.

Commonplace #5: Curriculum Making

The curriculum making commonplace is often the most difficult to comprehend. It is, however, the commonplace that holds the others together. It includes at least three essential dimensions: *practice, purpose,* and *integration.*

When it comes to *practice,* perhaps the best way to explain the curriculum making commonplace is to say that something must put the other commonplaces in motion before teaching can take place. In other words, the four commonplaces exist in an abstract way unless we place them in relationship to one another *in practice.* The term *making* is insightful in this respect. Curriculum *making* is the only commonplace that is referred to with an active term, in this case a gerund instead of a noun. The idea of curriculum *making* is active. It is about doing, not reflecting. What curriculum makers *do* is what matters most. Without the practice of curriculum making through the work of curriculum *makers*, discussion of the other four commonplaces remains academic and abstract. No education, certainly not a liberating one, can take place without high-quality, active curriculum making.

The curriculum making commonplace also takes into account the question of *purpose.* No school can liberate unless the teachers and school administrators within it have thought seriously about the purpose behind the curriculum they teach. Curriculum making not only puts the other four commonplaces in motion, it also puts them in motion toward an ideal end. One of the great aspects of the term *curriculum* is that it assumes a *telos,* or end. Nobody creates a curriculum just for the sake of thinking about it. A curriculum is created to *do something,* specifically to impact students in a certain direction. The commonplace of curriculum making acknowledges this purposive aspect of curriculum.

Integration is a third component of curriculum making. Integration takes place within the five commonplaces and with regard to the subject matters that are represented in the subject matter commonplace. As they search for problems, deliberate about possibilities, and engage in the overall practice of curriculum making, deliberators must learn to integrate subject matter and the other four commonplaces simultaneously. The best deliberators balance the five commonplaces in conversation and decision making. They also know how to make connections between the subject matters that make up the subject matter commonplace. Effective deliberators can move from commonplace to commonplace and, in a sense, "take the side" of whatever commonplace is not receiving appropriate attention.

■ A Map for Curriculum Makers

In addition to Schwab's five commonplaces, another device within curriculum literature that I have found most helpful is William A. Reid's map for curriculum makers. In *The Pursuit of Curriculum*, Reid provides curriculists with a way of thinking that is useful not only to people who create curriculum in an official sense, but also to anyone who is interested in educational reform.[16] Reid believes that curriculum is the purview of entire communities, not just experts. He argues that all citizens have a stake in what should be taught in schools.[17] Reid's map enables us to clarify what we believe about curriculum.

Reid compares curriculum to politics. Both are practical fields that operate in a world of uncertainty and not precision. Unlike chemistry or mathematics, politics and curriculum reach conclusions that are fuzzy in nature because of the circumstances in which decisions about them are made. In Reid's hands, curriculum philosophy looks a lot like political philosophy, at least political philosophy in an ancient or premodern sense of the term. Reid is following Schwab in his argument that curriculum researchers and practitioners should reconnect themselves to humanistic fields like rhetoric and moral philosophy, as opposed to technical fields like chemistry and behavioral psychology.

In *The Pursuit of Curriculum*, Reid chose not to publish an illustration of his curriculum map. Since my work builds upon Reid's, however, I have chosen to provide an illustration of the map, with my own revisions and additions (see figure 1.1). I have used slightly different terms as well as included

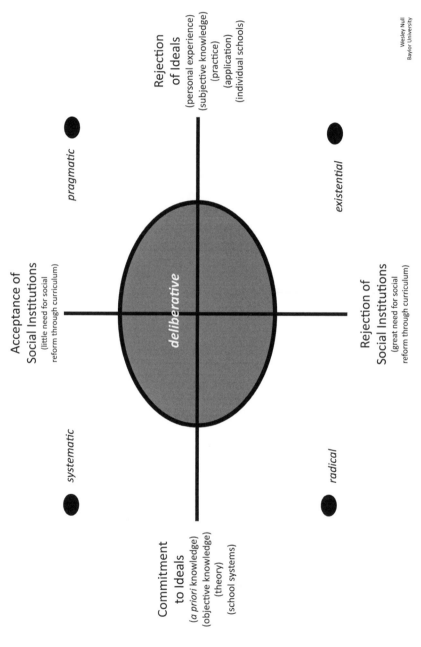

Rejection
of Ideals
(personal experience)
(subjective knowledge)
(practice)
(application)
(individual schools)

pragmatic

existential

Acceptance of
Social Institutions
(little need for social
reform through curriculum)

deliberative

Rejection of
Social Institutions
(great need for social
reform through curriculum)

systematic

radical

Commitment
to Ideals
(*a priori* knowledge)
(objective knowledge)
(theory)
(school systems)

Figure 1.1. Curriculum Map

Wesley Null
Baylor University

a fifth curricular tradition, the pragmatic (found in the top right quadrant of the map). The changes I have made, however, do not alter the essential structure of the map.

The Horizontal Axis

The two axes of the curriculum map represent the institutional and practical dimensions inherent in any curriculum. The vertical axis depicts the institutional aspect of curriculum, whereas the horizontal axis illustrates practice. The two ends of each axis indicate the extreme views held with regard to these two aspects of curriculum. In other words, an extreme view on the left of the horizontal axis indicates a theoretic, purely idealistic vision disconnected from specific, practical concerns within individual schools. This extreme makes commitment to ideals paramount and simultaneously diminishes practice, application, and the specific nature of curriculum problems. At the same time, an extreme view on the right of the horizontal axis represents just the opposite position: complete rejection of ideals and simultaneous emphasis on specific circumstances to the detriment of larger questions of theory, ideal ends, and objective knowledge.

Another way to look at the horizontal axis is to view those who hold the extreme ideal position as people who search for objective facts and thereby reject the idea of subjective knowledge. Similarly, an extreme view on the application side of this continuum rejects the notion of objective facts and replaces it with reliance upon personal experiences and nothing else. People who view curriculum in this way tend to argue for a curriculum that is "true to me" or "personally meaningful," not one that is factual or "scientific" in an empirical sense.

The Vertical Axis

The vertical axis depicts the institutional character of curriculum. Reid argues that the idea of curriculum cannot be separated from the idea of institution. In other words, without institutions, curriculum cannot exist. He then analyzes the way people think and write about curriculum as an institutional entity. His analysis has led him to identify two extremes. One, found at the top of the vertical line, accepts the current status of curriculum and thereby sees no need to make significant revisions to the institutional structure of curriculum. Those who hold this view do not believe that curriculum is a tool that should be used to foment social reform.

This extreme view assumes that, once it is institutionalized, a curriculum is good, positive in its effects, and neutral. The task that remains is to ensure that the institutionalized curriculum is delivered in an increasingly efficient way.

At the other extreme (found at the bottom of the vertical line), we find people who see nothing good in the current institutionalized curriculum. They want it to be overthrown in its entirety. This view argues that a good curriculum is one that challenges the institutional status quo and even incites revolution, instead of one that merely accepts the status quo.

The Curriculum Map and the Five Curricular Traditions

Introducing the curriculum map in chapter 1 is useful because it helps readers to understand the five curriculum traditions that are used throughout the remainder of the book, especially in chapters 2 through 6. The black dots on the map identify where four of the traditions are found. A deliberative view, of course, is found in the center. Chapters 2 through 6 refer to the curriculum map on occasion to help readers understand the similarities and differences between each perspective. Because of its influence throughout history and its ubiquitous presence today, the best place to begin is with an approach to curriculum that emphasizes system and efficiency—not deliberation. It is to the systematic tradition within curriculum that we now turn.

■ Discussion Questions

1. What is the primary goal of a liberal curriculum to Plato and Aristotle?

2. On what basis did Plato make the case that not all young people should receive the same curriculum?

3. How does the liberal arts ideal change with the birth of the Christian era?

4. What is the connection between citizenship and deliberation?

5. How are deliberation and practical wisdom related?

6. How does the relationship between liberal and vocational curriculum change with the birth of democratic education as an ideal?

7. According to Joseph Schwab, what is the difference between theoretic and practical inquiry and how does this distinction relate to curriculum?

8. Briefly describe the five curriculum commonplaces.

9. Briefly explain the two axes on the curriculum map.

CHAPTER 2

Systematic Curriculum

SOME PEOPLE argue that education is a business. They see schools as factories that produce students (or student learning), teachers as workers who mold students into a finished product, and school principals as managers whose job is to increase efficiency by eliminating waste. This way of thinking is particularly evident, for example, in a statement found on the cover of *Chief Executive* magazine in April 2005, which read: "American schools are broken. Here's what CEOs are doing to fix them."[1] The magazine praises CEOs for their "committed effort" to "champion school reform."[2] It then urges CEOs to transfer their business knowledge to the world of education and curriculum in order to fix the "broken schools" that are in need of the expertise that CEOs can provide.[3] The editorial for this issue also argues for increased competition, more efforts to break the "intellectual monopoly" that dominates school policy, and the implementation of "sweeping solutions" that will produce an efficient system of curriculum and teaching. *Chief Executive* magazine implores CEOs to get involved in educational reform, speaking directly to their readers by saying, "CEOs are used to thinking about entire industries or sectors, so you should apply your systematic thinking to K–12 education."[4]

Numerous terms could be used to refer to this way of thinking, but *system* is the most accurate and appropriate. It encapsulates the views of these thinkers without dismissing or denigrating them. Business leaders, and those who think similarly, can accept the label systematic because it captures the way they present themselves to the public. Businessmen see themselves as system builders, and the idea of system captures the strengths and the liabilities of this approach.

The strengths and liabilities of this approach, systematic curriculum, will become apparent by the end of this four-part chapter. First, however, we begin with an introduction to the systematic tradition by demonstrating how this view is found in No Child Left Behind and in the relatively new curriculum standards movement. The next section introduces historical figures John Franklin Bobbitt and Werrett Wallace Charters in order to explain the roots of a systematic view and how it has gained power at different times in American history. Section three makes a distinction between "free-market system" and "bureaucratic system" with the goal of describing how a systematic view has evolved during the past two decades into something quite different from what Bobbitt and Charters had in mind. The chapter concludes by connecting the systematic tradition to the curriculum commonplaces before addressing the strengths and weaknesses of this view.

■ No Child Left Behind and Systematic Curriculum

An obvious example of systems thinking applied to curriculum can be found in No Child Left Behind (NCLB), signed into law by President George W. Bush in January 2002. The influence of NCLB has been profound. The views on curriculum embedded within it fit squarely into the systematic tradition. The law's dominant goal is to prepare students to compete economically in the global marketplace. To achieve this goal, the authors argue for what they refer to as "scientifically based research." They believe that randomized, control-group studies provide the only route to creating the kind of public school system they desire. They define "scientifically based research" (SBR) as "research that involves the application of rigorous, systematic and objective procedures to obtain reliable and valid knowledge relevant to education activities and programs."[5]

There are multiple assumptions related to curriculum theory and practice embedded within this statement. Unpacking NCLB as a whole and what this definition of SBR means can help us to understand the systematic tradition and how it influences curriculum today. The above definition includes rhetoric that is virtually impossible to oppose. Who would want research that is not rigorous and systematic? What is the alternative? Research that is flabby and random? The difficulty with scholarship on education and curriculum is not producing studies that are rigorous and systematic, but rather with coming to consensus on what people mean when they use terms like *rigorous*, *systematic*, and *objective*.

To the writers of NCLB, research into curriculum can and must be truly objective in the same way that research on the effects of drugs can be objective. Supporters of NCLB frequently compare educational research with medicine, typically in a way that bemoans the fact that educational research is not truly "scientific" in the way they believe medicine is. For example, the *Parents Guide* to NCLB produced by the U.S. Department of Education praises NCLB because it

> moves the testing of educational practices toward the medical model used by scientists to assess the effectiveness of medications, therapies and the like. Studies that test random samples of the population and that involve a control group are scientifically controlled. To gain scientifically based research about a particular educational program or practice, it must be the subject of such a study.[6]

Although the term *curriculum* is not used in this quotation, curriculum is what the statement refers to when it uses the phrase a "particular educational program." Curriculum, to these writers, is similar to a drug like an antibiotic or a vaccine. Curriculum research must (and presumably should) measure the effects produced on students by curriculum A compared with curriculum B. Curriculum research of this type also must use randomized trials in highly controlled settings. For a study to be considered scientific, everything in the school other than the curriculum must be controlled—including teachers, the school context, the backgrounds and interests of the students, the influence of school administrators, and any other outside factors that impinge on the school's culture. Studies of this type seek to prove objectively which curriculum is most effective and therefore should be universalized to all schools.

For purposes of curriculum, a closer look at the relationship between research and practice within the systematic approach is necessary and insightful. The link between theoretic knowledge produced by SBR and the practices of classroom teachers is straightforward and logical. Teachers are responsible for following the prescriptions produced by the latest studies. They must change their curriculum based on what the latest studies have proven. If they are to be true professionals, teachers have no choice but to follow the mandates laid down by experts. In this respect, teachers are sometimes compared to nurses. Their job is to administer the latest drugs (or curriculum) efficiently, not question whether these drugs are appropriate with their students.

A direct connection between the latest research findings and the practice of classroom teachers is the cornerstone of success to the authors of NCLB. Another statement from the *Parents Guide* makes this point clear:

> The key to helping all children learn is to help teachers in each and every classroom benefit from the relevant research. That can be accomplished by providing professional development for teachers on the use of scientifically based reading programs; by the use of instructional materials and programs that are also based on sound scientific research; and by ensuring accountability through ongoing assessments.[7]

Reading *instruction* is the most common part of the curriculum that is subjected to empirical studies of this type. The *curriculum* used in various reading programs, however, is typically not the focus of attention. The focus, rather, becomes the instructional methods, or techniques, that teachers use. Curriculum and teaching methods become separated. The most efficient (or "effective") reading teachers, based upon the assumptions embedded in NCLB, are those who pay careful attention to the most recent research produced by empirical researchers. Teachers should then take these latest findings and implement strategies accordingly so that curriculum and teaching can become increasingly systematic and efficient.

Systematic curriculists believe in only one kind of research, and the goal of that research is to produce theoretic knowledge that controls curriculum practice. Not every tradition, however, views the relationship between theory and practice in this way.

To provide teachers with the most efficient access to the latest studies, the U.S. Department of Education has set up a "What Works Clearinghouse." This clearinghouse evaluates the latest studies, publishes critiques of them through a "What Works" website, and allows teachers to build databases that include their favorite research studies. The U.S. Department of Education states that the What Works Clearinghouse was created "to provide a central, independent and trusted source of scientific evidence on what works in education for parents, educators, policymakers and anyone else who is interested."[8] Explanations of what the authors mean by such phrases as "what works" and "scientific evidence" are not given, but readers can assume that a study that "works" is one that makes whatever system teachers use more efficient or replaces their current system with a more efficient one.

The vision for what can be accomplished through the What Works Clearinghouse is nothing if not ambitious. The creators of the clearinghouse write:

> Over time, as the clearinghouse begins to produce its reports on these issues, parents will be able to ask their principal, teachers and school board members about the extent to which they select programs and curriculum that the research has determined to be effective. Under No Child Left Behind, educators are expected to consider the results of relevant scientifically based research—whenever such information is available—before making instructional decisions.[9]

The creators of the What Works Clearinghouse hope that all of the people mentioned above—parents, teachers, school board members, and the general public—will use the knowledge compiled in the What Works Clearinghouse to make sure that teachers teach a curriculum and use instructional techniques that have proven to be effective. The system that results in studies that make their way into the What Works Clearinghouse is bold in its vision for what can be controlled in the name of educational research.

Administrators are by no means immune from the NCLB system. They, too, must produce reports, read the latest research findings, implement strategies that have been proven effective, and comply with NCLB expectations if they expect their schools to survive. The NCLB system places principals in the position of midmanagers who are responsible for making sure that those underneath them—teachers and curriculum specialists—keep the system running efficiently. Assessment and accountability are two of the primary measures that NCLB uses to determine efficiency. NCLB envisions that principals will use test data to determine which part of their school plant is not operating as efficiently as it ought to be. In the words of the authors of NCLB:

> The point of state assessments is to measure student learning. A key principle of quality management is the

importance of measuring what is valued (e.g., production rates, costs of materials, etc.). Such measures enable
an organization to identify where and how to improve
operations. In the same manner, if schools and school
systems are to continuously improve, they must measure growth in student achievement.[10]

Based upon this language and the assumptions embedded
within it, the function of school administrators is to study
test data and make adjustments so that the system they manage produces at maximum capacity. The most ambitious principals are those who conduct their own research by designing
studies that adjust curriculum for one group of students but
not for another. If test results indicate that a new curriculum
arrangement produces higher test scores, then all teachers
must be required to use this new arrangement.

Most systematic thinkers tend to be Utopian in their views.
They have a high degree of confidence in what can be accomplished by treating education like a medical science. Systematic
thinkers seek to uncover a hidden piece of information—some
would say a panacea—that will unlock the gate to a world
of improved schools. Just like Jonas Salk cured polio, curriculum researchers of this type hope to discover treatments
that will cure educational ills once and for all. Whether they
state it this clearly or not, systematic thinkers seek to create a
perfect society in which teachers, school administrators, and
curriculum workers follow the research that has been collected through the What Works Clearinghouse.

Even though America's business community was deeply
influential in the writing of NCLB, not all systematic thinkers
come directly from the world of business. Support for NCLB
and the What Works Clearinghouse can be found in fields
throughout the modern social sciences, especially political
science and economics. The pinnacle of research of this type
is found in studies that prove a cause and effect relationship
between a specific instructional approach and student learning,
as measured by standardized tests. We find studies that make
claims such as "If teachers calibrate instruction to their views
of student ability, one could make accurate causal inferences
about instructional effects only by reconceiving and redesign-
ing instruction as a 'regime.'"[11] In this view of social science
as it applies to education, curriculum and instruction are separated and then studied separately to determine which instructional techniques and which curriculum schemes produce the

most powerful effects. In the words of the *Desktop Reference* to NCLB, "schoolwide and targeted assistance programs are required to use effective methods and instructional strategies that are grounded in scientifically based research. School improvement plans, professional development, and technical assistance that districts provide to low-performing schools must be based on strategies that have a proven record of effectiveness."[12] This same *Desktop Reference* emphasizes instructional methods more than it does curriculum. Like instructional methods, however, the best curriculum is one that has been proven to "work" regardless of the context in which it is taught, the teachers doing the teaching, or the students doing the studying.

An approach to systematic curriculum development that is both similar to and different from NCLB began to take flight during the early 1980s. What came to be known as "curriculum standards" has influenced schools profoundly ever since. We will now discuss this "curriculum "standards" movement and how it relates to a systematic view.

■ Curriculum Standards as a System

The main idea behind the creation of curriculum standards, whether state or national, is to establish what students "should know and be able to do" (a common phrase) within the various subject-matter fields. Few people can deny the value in setting up what students should be expected to learn at the various stages of the schooling process. The difficulty lies in identifying who should determine what these curricular goals ought to be, what they should include, and how they should be implemented once they have been established. These challenges, nevertheless, have not stopped reformers from attempting the task.

As the "standards movement" gained momentum during the 1980s and 1990s, a variety of people came to define "standards" in different ways, which makes characterizing the effort somewhat difficult. For example, some reformers like Diane Ravitch, who served as assistant U.S. secretary of education during the late 1980s and early 1990s, advocated an approach to curriculum standards that identified pieces of knowledge that students must learn but also recognized that standards documents are frameworks that are meant to guide teachers, not control them. Standards documents, to Ravitch, also must take school context and student interests into account. As Ravitch makes the point, "Whether standards are state or national, teachers *should* adapt and modify them to fit their own pedagogical skills as well as to take advantage of current events and student interests. The point is not to create uniformity of practice, but a challenging curriculum that is equally available to all students."[13] Ravitch's goal with the creation of standards was to increase educational opportunity by providing all students with access to a high-quality curriculum. Her work combines the positive effects of creating a system of curriculum expectations where none had existed before with respect for classroom teachers as well as sensitivity to the practical realities they face daily.[14]

Not everyone, however, approaches curriculum standards in the way that Ravitch does. For example, Fenwick English, a former public school administrator and professor of educational administration who has done as much as anyone in the last thirty years to apply business thinking to curriculum, brings the language of "curriculum alignment," "curriculum auditing," and "curriculum management" into the lexicon of school administrators and teachers. English's work merits attention not because he has been influential

---

Background on Curriculum Standards

Most people trace the idea of curriculum standards to the essentialist movement in education that began in the late 1930s. The "father" of essentialism is typically considered to be William C. Bagley, an educational philosopher and psychologist who was also a professor of teacher education at Teachers College, Columbia University. Bagley and several others, including Peabody College professor Michael John Demiashkevich and headmaster F. Alden Shaw of the Detroit Country Day School, joined together beginning in 1938 to argue for increased attention to curriculum in U.S. schools. They came to be referred to as essentialists because they made the case that the teaching of certain core subjects, for example, history and literature and mathematics, is essential for any curriculum to be considered sound. They maintained that American schools had grown weak—yes, this argument has been going on since then—because the progressive education movement had deemphasized curriculum standards, diminished the role of teachers, and fostered individualism. To counteract this problem, they insisted that states develop curriculum standards for each of the core subjects, standards that could then be used to compare how successful schools were at teaching these standards. At the same time, the essentialists were careful to argue for standards that did not seek to control teachers, but rather provided them with the guidance they needed to maintain consistency across core subjects and grade levels.

in the field of curriculum theory, but because his work has been popular with school administrators and curriculum directors. English has been advocating the application of business techniques to curriculum since the late 1970s. His book titles read as though CEOs, corporate board members, or accountants could have written them. Examples include *The Curriculum Management Audit, Educational Administration: The Human Science, Deep Curriculum Alignment,* and *Curriculum Auditing.*[15] English's work speaks directly to school board members and school administrators who pattern themselves after businessmen. He provides them with the tools they need to speak the language of corporate elites.

Curriculum is nothing if not a system to English. He believes the role of teachers is to implement the curriculum that has been written for them. He maintains that curriculum should control what teachers do. In his words, "The function of curriculum is to shape the work of teachers by focusing and connecting it as a kind of *work plan* in schools. It doesn't matter who 'develops' it, whether imposed top down or constructed 'bottom up,' the function of curriculum is to shape the work of classroom teachers."[16] Furthermore, when addressing the question of what he means by curriculum, English writes, "*Curriculum* is any document or plan that exists in a school or school system that defines the work of teachers, at least to the extent of identifying the content to be taught to children and the methods to be used in the process."[17] These two quotations provide a good bit of insight into how English views curriculum and curriculum making. The idea that curriculum is something that can be aligned, audited, and delivered reveals that he approaches curriculum from the perspective of an engineer. A good curriculum is efficient. It produces. It *causes* something to happen. A good curriculum *system* is one that identifies what pieces of information must be delivered at what stage and then establishes careful measures to determine whether this information has been delivered efficiently by the workers (i.e., teachers).

Speaking like an accountant, English and his followers have popularized the idea of "curriculum auditing." The idea is to "determine the degree to which the written, taught, and tested curricula are aligned and the extent to which all district resources are organized to support development and delivery of the curricula."[18] The process follows a step-by-step plan that includes the establishment of objectives, the formulation of plans, the measurement of outcomes and results, and the comparing of results and outcomes to the original objectives.[19] The process is intended to work in any school district in any state in any country. Fenwick contends that curriculum auditing can make any school district's curriculum more efficient. Nowhere is his vision more apparent than when he writes:

> The curriculum management audit assumes that school systems are "rational organizations." There is plenty of evidence that they must be. Increasing state legislation requires school systems and individual school sites to engage in the establishment of objectives, the development of plans to improve school operations and instructional processes, the utilization of measurement and testing to assess results, and prescriptive or diagnostic procedures to continually upgrade and improve operations and results.[20]

English speaks a language that resonates with businessmen. During the last fifteen to twenty years, his system of "curriculum alignment" has become popular nationwide. One reason is because school superintendents and board members view English's plan as "objective" and "practical." They also appreciate the opportunity to pattern themselves after businessmen.[21] Another reason English's system has spread is because it could be combined with state standards. Once state departments of education had set curriculum standards, school districts needed a plan for how to take their existing curriculum and align it—or completely redesign it—to match the new standards.

The assumptions with regard to teachers in English's work merit specific attention. He views teachers as frontline workers who have no choice (and should have no choice) but to implement the state-mandated curriculum. The best curriculum systems, in fact, are so tightly developed that teachers do not need to make decisions at all. Their job is to follow the scripted curriculum, which contains directions for not only the subject matter they must teach, but also the methods they must use. The job of teachers is not to question the curriculum that authorities have delivered, nor is it to exercise judgment. The role of teachers, rather, is to execute the required curriculum in an efficient, consistent, and unquestioning way.

Little known to many specialists in curriculum today, the roots of English's approach reach back at least to the early

1900s. Some attention to history can help us not only to understand how a systematic view came into existence, but also how it gains power at different times in American history. Views on curriculum change as events within the broader culture change. The first curriculum specialists, in fact, were systematic thinkers who rode the wave of the early 1900s as they sought to help America face the challenges of the time. These early curriculum "experts" grew out of English's field, educational administration, during the age of industrialization when factories popped up nationwide and the Ford Model T rolled off assembly lines by the thousands.[22] A closer look at two historic figures from the field of curriculum—John Franklin Bobbitt and W. W. Charters—allows us to gain a deeper perspective on the systematic tradition.

> Systematic teachers are often highly structured in the way they discipline students. They tend to use a variety of ways to count misbehaviors and then prescribe specific consequences for a clearly identified number of wrong actions.

■ Background on the Systematic Curriculum Tradition

Systematic curriculum has a long history. Economics and educational reform have gone hand in hand for decades, even centuries. Businessmen of course have a real stake in education, so they have a role to play in educational policy making and in deliberations about curriculum. Schools will always be closely tied to the economy. As a result, building relationships between members of the business community and educators is essential. The extent of this relationship, however, should be a constant topic of conversation.

The early twentieth century was a time of tremendous change for American education. Between 1890 and 1920, approximately thirty million immigrants came to American shores. Many of them, of course, were children. They came from eastern European countries like Romania, Yugoslovia, and Russia. Most of them did not speak English and were not prepared to begin the classics-oriented curricular track that dominated curriculum thinking during the nineteenth century.

In addition to immigration, industrialism began to change the way Americans viewed the purpose of schooling. Instead of attending school to become a learned or well-rounded person, many Americans began to see school as preparation for

> Many people believe that the application of business thinking to curriculum and teaching is a new idea that appeared only in the last twenty or thirty years. The reality, however, is that business thinking has had a tremendous influence on American curriculum for at least 150 years.

Taylor's Scientific Management

Frederick Winslow Taylor published a book in 1911 that was highly influential in many fields, including the development of systematic curriculum. Taylor, a mechanical engineer by training, wrote *The Principles of Scientific Management* primarily for plant managers who ran factories, but because the United States was enveloped in an age of efficiency, Taylor's "principles" became widely popular. His goal with *Principles of Scientific Management* was to show plant managers how they could get the most work out of their workers. Taylor brought the modern scientific techniques of observation, measurement, and standardization to bear on the problem of how to make factories more efficient. He argues that haphazard, rule of thumb methods had dominated business techniques for way too long, and the time had come to turn management into a legitimate science.

Perhaps the best-known aspect of Taylor's work is what came to be known as "time and motion study." The idea was for management scientists like Taylor to study every job scientifically in order to break it down into its component parts. Once every job had been analyzed and the most efficient methods for completing any particular task had been identified, those methods could then be generalized to all workers, thereby standardizing work and making a plant more efficient.

Taylor did not focus on education and curriculum, but many scholars of the time—including Franklin Bobbitt and W. W. Charters—saw obvious connections between Taylor's views and the fields of curriculum and teaching. The systematic tradition is heavily influenced by Taylor's views.

---

work. This change put further pressure on school districts to adjust their curriculum to meet the demands of the new industrial age. The "old" curriculum tied to Latin, Greek, classical literature, and mathematics was not viewed as "relevant" to many Americans who were convinced that a radically new age had dawned. To address these curriculum problems, in stepped John Franklin Bobbitt and W. W. Charters, both of whom fashioned themselves as curriculum "experts" who could help school districts revise their curriculum to meet the needs of the twentieth century.

John Franklin Bobbitt

In his effort to establish himself as a curriculum expert, John Franklin Bobbitt, a professor of educational administration at the University of Chicago, drew his inspiration from the fields of business and economics. Titled *The Curriculum* and published in 1918, Bobbitt published the first book ever written on curriculum in the United States. His trademark was applying the business thinking of his time to curriculum.[23] *The Curriculum* introduced educators to a new process—indeed a system—that Bobbitt argued should be used by educators at all levels to create curriculum. His process of curriculum making is worth discussing not only because of its influence during his career, but also because it is a model that has been copied countless times since Bobbitt produced it.

The core of Franklin Bobbitt's vision was that curriculum developers should look to the activities of adults for its material when deciding what should be taught. Rather than curriculum being dominated, if not completely controlled, by subject matter, Bobbitt argued that curriculum should serve communities in economic, pragmatic, and useful ways. The cornerstone of Bobbitt's curriculum-making process is what he calls "activity analysis." Activity analysis involves several steps. The first is to find the best workers in every profession throughout a community and then study those workers to discover what makes them so efficient. Next, empirically trained curriculum researchers should conduct observations of these workers. The goal of these observations is to collect data that results in large bodies of information. This information, according to Bobbitt, captures the essence of why each of these workers is so efficient. After the activities of the most efficient adults have been analyzed and catalogued, the next step is to identify those students who have the aptitude to fill each role in society. For example, students who have the mental aptitude and the inclination to become nurses should be matched with the body of information that has been derived through careful observation of the most efficient nurses. The body of "scientifically derived" information that results from activity analysis, therefore, becomes the curriculum for the students who fill the various jobs in any community. Future physicians get the curriculum designed through the analysis of physicians, bricklayers get the curriculum derived from observing bricklayers, and lawyers get the curriculum based on the daily activities of the most efficient lawyers.

Bobbitt's powerful insight was that curriculum developers should pay careful attention to the social activities of adults. In Bobbitt's words, "When the curriculum is defined as including both directed and undirected experiences, then its objectives are the total range of human abilities, habits, systems of knowledge, etc., that one should possess. These will be discovered by analytic survey. The curriculum-discoverer will first be an analyst of human nature and of human affairs."[24] In another of Bobbitt's highly popular books, *How to Make a Curriculum,* he continues this point by writing, "The first task [of curriculum making] is to discover the activities which ought to make up the lives of men and women; and along with these, the abilities and personal qualities necessary for proper performance. These are the educational objectives."[25] To Bobbitt, the proper subject matter for curriculum making is twofold: human nature and the social activities of adults.

Bobbitt was a social thinker, which placed him at odds with the "academic" mind-set that he frequently criticized. To Bobbitt, the academic view, which held great influence early in his career, resulted in nothing but reflection, useless philosophy, and "personal culture." This philosophy did not serve the community in any appreciable way, argued Bobbitt. He campaigned passionately that curriculum must serve the larger public welfare, albeit in an almost entirely economic way.

Bobbitt has been criticized for the narrowness of his vision.[26] He assumes that future occupations will be the same as they are in the present. His critics argued that his system offered little opportunity for curriculum to change with evolving conditions in the world of work. His philosophy also emphasizes the economy to such an extent that the moral dimension of curriculum is tied almost entirely to economic production. Nevertheless, Bobbitt does advocate for what he calls "occupational efficiency," which contains a moral dimension. The reason a person should become occupationally efficient is so that she can serve her community in an efficient way that produces the most for the community as a whole.[27] Bobbitt was both civic minded and democratic in his own way. He was civic in his concern for social welfare, and he was democratic in the way he argued that students should receive a curriculum that helps them find their economic place in society. Another prominent curriculum worker from Bobbitt's time also merits attention, not so much because he influenced K–12 curriculum, but because of his work at the university and college level.

Werrett Wallace Charters

Werrett Wallace Charters was a professor of education at the University of Chicago during the 1920s and later at Ohio State University until his retirement in 1942. Charters's views on curriculum are similar to Bobbitt's, but, unlike Bobbitt, Charters focused on teacher training curriculum, not curriculum in general.[28] Wallace took Bobbitt's activity analysis method and applied it to the profession of teaching. From 1925 to 1928, Charters directed the largest study ever on teacher training in the United States. Called the Commonwealth Teacher-Training Study and funded by the Commonwealth Fund, Charters's study involved hundreds of university professors and public school personnel. The idea was to determine the contents of teacher training curriculum by studying the activities of thousands of teachers from all states in the nation. Bobbitt had pioneered the activity analysis method that was used widely to create public school curriculum, but Charters took Bobbitt's method and used it to create curriculum for teacher education programs.[29] Charters witnessed many heated battles over what the content of teacher training curriculum ought to be. Through the Commonwealth Teacher-Training Study, he set out to end these controversies once and for all. He planned to use Bobbitt's task analysis method to take the politics out of teacher training curriculum. He also thought his work would bring status to teachers, the institutions that prepared them, and the teaching profession as a whole. His goal was to bring modern science, efficiency, and system to teacher training curriculum. Charters also made a direct connection between the results of the Commonwealth Teacher-Training Study and the growth of the American economy.

The mind-set that Charters brought to the Commonwealth study is evident in his numerous publications. For example, in *Curriculum Construction*, he writes, "The standards of our day demand that our courses of study be derived from objectives which include both ideals and activities, that we should frankly accept *usefulness* as our aim rather than *comprehensive knowledge*."[30] Charters makes a sharp distinction between knowledge and usefulness. The two do not relate to one another at all in his mind; in fact, Charters writes as if knowledge and utility are at war with one another. He elevates *usefulness* to the pinnacle of the curriculum-making process not only with what he argues for K–12 curriculum, but, perhaps more importantly, with what he does in the field of teacher training.

In the Commonwealth Teacher-Training Study, functionality and usefulness were the standards that Charters and his colleagues used as they observed teachers in action, catalogued their activities, and sought to "discover" the techniques that all teachers must use in order to be efficient. Based on three years of work, Charters's group developed a "Master List of 1001 Teacher Traits" that they argued must become the basis for teacher training curriculum throughout the country. This "Master List" reads like a catalog of every move that a teacher could possibly make both inside and outside of the classroom, including traits like "records pupils' results correctly," "smiles when the pupils do good work," and "keeps skin in healthy condition."[31] Charters's vision was that this information would be used to transform curriculum within teachers colleges as well as within the new departments and schools of education that were beginning to compete with teachers colleges at the time.

By bringing modern science and system to the construction of teacher training curriculum, Charters hoped to turn teaching into a "scientific" profession like medicine. This view is particularly evident, for example, when Charters writes, "To summarize, the first step in constructing curriculum for teacher-training institutions is to determine through market and plant analysis the types of teachers to be trained. . . . In this study we are exclusively concerned with the professional type of training."[32] Charters uses the term "professional" in a purely technical sense. Even though he sometimes makes reference to ideals and principles, Charters's vision of "professional education" is based on technical and not moral knowledge.[33] To him, teaching is a technical science and not an art.[34] Much like Bobbitt and Fenwick English, Charters wants teachers to become efficient technicians whose role is to implement the system designed by curriculum experts.

The approach to systematic curriculum making found in the work of Bobbitt and Charters is both similar to and different from a new approach that has gained popularity since the mid-twentieth century. The view that has been presented so far is best labeled "bureaucratic system," yet not everyone who views curriculum as a system has a positive view of bureaucracy. They have the opposite view, in fact. In the early twenty-first century, the term *bureaucracy* carries a somewhat negative connotation primarily because free-market advocates have had a major impact on public policy. Nonetheless, "bureaucratic system" still captures the ideas presented above. It is to a rather different view of system, this time a "free-market system," that the next section of this chapter will now turn.

■ The Free-Market System and Curriculum

No Child Left Behind, Fenwick English, Franklin Bobbitt, and W. W. Charters provide curriculum plans that result in large, typically government-funded institutions that are the foundation for curriculum. This bureaucratic system approach obviously has a favorable view of governmental involvement in curriculum and education. These writers see government as mostly positive in its effect. To thinkers like Bobbitt and English, governmental institutions, including curriculum, are the best route to solving society's problems.

Curriculum making based on the building of bureaucratic systems has been powerful since the early 1900s. Another view that also derives from the field of economics, however, has grown in popularity since the early 1960s. The term *free-market system* distinguishes this relatively new view from the bureaucratic systems perspective presented in the first half of this chapter. Popularized by works like Milton Friedman's *Capitalism and Freedom*, the free-market system uses many of the same terms as the bureaucratic system—for example, consumer, product, efficiency, effectiveness, accountability, and, of course, system—but it means something quite different with these terms.[35] Free-market advocates agree with bureaucratic curriculum makers that the purpose of schooling is to serve the economy. They disagree, however, on how to achieve this goal. For example, free-market proponents begin by criticizing the institutions that the earlier view of economics built. Instead of building large institutions based on the factory model, economists now say that the route to producing a perfect system is to replace public institutions with private markets.

Even though free-market proponents frequently criticize the idea of bureaucracy, they hold on to the idea that there is a system that will fix the problems of curriculum and schooling. Friedman's *Capitalism and Freedom*, published in 1962, launched a conversation about the privatization of public schooling that has remained provocative ever since. In his chapter on "The Role of Government in Education," Friedman, a professor of economics at the University of Chicago, made one of the first calls for school vouchers.[36] He and Rose Friedman later expanded their argument in *Free to Choose: A Personal Statement*. In their chapter on schooling, Friedman and Friedman present "the problem" and then follow it up with their "solution," which is a voucher system designed

The effort to introduce free-market ideas into American schooling is a relatively new phenomenon that began in the early 1980s. Free-market proposals directly challenge the idea that American students should learn a common core curriculum.

to privatize public institutions. Their enthusiasm for this vision is evident when they predict what will happen when vouchers control American schooling. They write, "As the private market took over, the quality of all schooling would rise so much that even the worst, while it might be *relatively* lower on the scale, would be better in *absolute* quality . . . ; many pupils who are among 'the dregs' would perform well in schools that evoked their enthusiasm instead of hostility or apathy."[37] To the Friedmans, good schools produce good students, whereas bad schools produce bad students. Curriculum and teaching need not be viewed as more complex than that.

Milton Friedman argues that public institutions, including public schools, have become so large that they stifle freedom, creativity, and competition. The solution, he argues, is to replace public schools with a privatized system that is based on competition, freedom, and choice. Modern economics, once again, becomes the discipline that controls curriculum and teaching. Friedman's views may be different from the early twentieth-century industrialism of Henry Ford, but his free-market capitalism remains a system that relies on institutions for efficiency. As Friedman sees it, the institutions that survive the pressures of free-market competition are the good ones, whereas those that die are the bad ones. Friedman's concept of system is a bit more elusive than the industrial system of the early twentieth century, primarily because he puts Adam Smith's famous "invisible hand" in charge of curriculum and teaching. He is, nevertheless, a systematic thinker. The "invisible hand" is not an institution in a conventional sense but rather a theoretic system that Friedman applies to all areas of society, not just curriculum. Like those who have followed him, however, Friedman makes no reference whatsoever to curriculum in *Capitalism and Freedom*, a point that should be remembered when the subject of discussion is curriculum.

Another book that has gained popularity in free-market circles is *Politics, Markets, and America's Schools* by John Chubb and Terry Moe.[38] Chubb and Moe share Friedman's disdain for contemporary public schools. They retain the "fix the problem" mind-set that predominates within the systematic tradition, but the solution they offer is for new institutions to be built, not for institutions to be eradicated altogether. In their words, "Because our institutional perspective reflects so poorly on the current system, and because it leads us to recommend a wholly different system—one built around school autonomy and parent-student choice rather than direct democratic control—our perspective will doubtless be met with disfavor."[39] They reject what they call a "one best system" approach, which is essentially the bureaucratic system of English, Bobbitt, and Charters. Like Friedman, Chubb and Moe want to bring choice, competition, and freedom to bear on public institutions so that the waste and inefficiency that has grown up within them can be eradicated. They advocate a voucher approach that puts demand from students and parents in control of which schools get money and which do not. As they put it, "schools that fail to satisfy a sufficiently large clientele will go out of business."[40] Like other systematic thinkers, Chubb and Moe accept the proposition that education—and everything that comes with it like curriculum—is a business and nothing else. For example, when encouraging the increased involvement of the business community in educational decision making, Chubb and Moe write, "Unlike the established players, the business community has strong incentives to take a coldly analytical approach to the problem, and thus to acquire the best possible knowledge about why the problem exists and what can be done about it."[41] To Chubb and Moe, the truly rational and analytical people involved in curriculum, teaching, and schooling are businessmen.

Using distinctions such as democratic control versus markets and hierarchical control versus freedom, Chubb and Moe see little middle ground behind public institutions and the freedom of individuals. Individual wants, desires, and the freedom of people to choose whatever they want become king in their system. They are convinced that competition, choice, and individual freedom will lead to an efficient system. As they put it, their work "is a proposal for a new system of public education, one that is built on school autonomy and parent-student choice rather than direct democratic control and bureaucracy."[42] They distinguish between a bureaucratic systems approach and their new free-market system when they write:

> A market system is not built to enable the imposition of higher-order values on the schools, nor is it driven by a democratic struggle to exercise public authority. Instead, the authority to make educational choices is radically decentralized to those most immediately

involved. Schools compete for the support of parents and students, and parents and students are free to choose among schools. The system is built around decentralization, competition, and choice.[43]

To Chubb and Moe, teaching a common curriculum would be an "imposition of higher-order values," not an act of introducing students to the traditions, cultures, and knowledge that bind a country or community together—as at least one other curriculum tradition would argue.

The application of free-market visions to education has engendered such enthusiasm in some circles that the idea has been presented as a panacea, by Chubb and Moe as well as others, that will cure the ills that beset public schools.[44] The more negatively that public institutions are presented in these arguments, the more attractive the panacea becomes. For example, in "Corruption in the Public Schools: The Market Is the Answer," Neal McCluskey argues that vouchers are *the solution* that will at last revolutionize schooling in America. He further argues that we must not taint the free-market panacea by watering it down with other initiatives. It will produce its cleansing effects when implemented only by itself. In McCluskey's words, "choice must be a single, stand-alone reform because it completely revolutionizes how education is delivered, making a system controlled by government into one controlled by consumers."[45] After praising the work of Chubb and Moe, McCluskey's dedication to a systems approach becomes evident when he writes, "Leaving education entirely to the market would likely provide the best, most efficient educational system possible."[46] McCluskey's free-market mind-set indeed appeals to those who want a "quick fix" that promises a perfect system. What, however, is missing from this view? What does he omit in order to present a simple vision?

■ What About Curriculum?

Although they write a great deal about education, free-market system builders ignore the most essential subject in any discussion of education: curriculum. Not one of the free-market-driven publications mentioned or quoted above makes even one reference to curriculum. Writers such as Friedman, Chubb, Moe, and McCluskey present themselves as if they were experts in education, but they have nothing to say about the question of what should be taught. Since this is a book about curriculum, the omission of curriculum by free-market system builders is not a minor point.

So why do free-market advocates ignore curriculum? One way to approach the question is to use the terminology of economists and use their distinction between macroeconomics and microeconomics. Microeconomics deals with the decisions that individual consumers make, whereas macroeconomics covers broader questions about the economy as a whole. Using curriculum as an example, one question that might be studied within microeconomics would be "Why do parents choose this curriculum within this particular school over another?" An example of a macroeconomic question would be "Will higher test scores translate into a stronger American economy?" When the distinction between micro- and macroeconomics is brought into view, it becomes somewhat easier to see how free-market thinkers can ignore curriculum, whether explicitly or implicitly, by categorizing it as a microeconomic issue and therefore not something that needs to be addressed (if, that is, they consider themselves macro-minded economists). Economists have a much easier time studying "education" as a macroeconomic process than they do curriculum. Free-market economists see little if any distinction between economics and education, leading them either to avoid the term *curriculum* or use it interchangeably with *education*. Free-market thinkers also tend to view both education and curriculum as subjects that belong in the realm of microeconomics. Not all economists, however, are pure free-market thinkers. For example, those who follow the views of British economist John Maynard Keynes tend to view curriculum (if they discuss it) from the perspective of macroeconomics, leading them to support broad level policies that are somewhat more in keeping with the views of Bobbitt and Charters.

Perhaps another reason free-market thinkers ignore curriculum is because they reject the idea of a common culture. Curriculum assumes there is a body of knowledge that all students must and should acquire as they complete their schooling and become citizens. Free-market proponents replace a common curriculum with *curricula* (presumably a different one for every student), leaving no body of common culture to hold a nation together. Once curriculum has been replaced with the free-market system, the only thing left to hold Americans together is a desire for personal gain, efficiency, and economic

Free-market thinkers would prefer to discuss education as opposed to curriculum. Curriculum brings up questions of ethics, purpose, and many other issues that free-market economists attempt to avoid.

growth. Curriculum becomes disconnected from community, citizenship, and the common good.

The difference between how bureaucratic system builders and free-market system builders approach curriculum is striking. Proponents of a bureaucratic system make controlling the curriculum essential to their plans, whereas advocates of the free-market system reject curriculum altogether. There appears to be no common ground between these two views. The field of economics, from which both derive, seems not to have the capacity to bridge the gap between individuals and institutions. Either institutions are the solution and individuals must be controlled by them (as in a bureaucratic systems approach) or personal freedom is the solution and institutions must be eliminated before the system can be fixed (as in a free-market systems approach). Both approaches leave out critical aspects of the curriculum-making process. A closer look at the systematic tradition through the eyes of the commonplaces uncovers both the strengths and the weaknesses of this view.

> Systematic curricu-lists want to compare the efficiency of one school (or school district) to another. Consequently, they look for commonality in curriculum, without which comparison is impossible.

■ Systematic Curriculum and the Commonplaces

Teachers

Teachers are essential to the systematic curriculum tradition. Regardless of whether the system is bureaucracy driven or free-market driven, teachers have a crucial role to play in producing learning. Teachers are viewed as frontline workers who should follow the dictates of their superiors, but they are nonetheless recognized as an irreplaceable link in the curriculum delivery process. System builders recognize that proposals for improving the efficiency of curriculum, instruction, and schools must go through teachers, who ultimately implement any new idea.

The emphasis that system builders place on teachers, however, also comes with a liability. The "cause and effect" thinking that prevails in the world of system building leads those who think in this way to assume that teachers *cause* learning. This overemphasis on the role of teachers forgets the fact that teachers do not control their students. Teachers influence their students, but they do not control them.[47] Learners have a role to play in the process as well. Both bureaucratic and free-market system builders often forget this point. We also can find an overemphasis on the power of teachers in rhetoric about "failing schools." Once again, underlying this phrase is the assumption that teachers and schools *cause* learning, when in reality they only increase the likelihood that learning will take place.

> Systematic curriculum tends to be highly practical to school administrators but not always to classroom teachers. Teachers focus on individual students and their needs, whereas administrators are forced to look at big picture questions that deal with schools and school districts as a whole.

Learners

Although they do not make learners the end of curriculum making, system builders often use the rhetoric of learning as the goal they are striving to achieve. Both bureaucratic and free-market systems are frequently justified on the basis of their ability to produce learning. To the extent that learners as individuals are considered, a bureaucratic system approach takes into account individual differences when matching future occupations to the talents of individual students. Efficient curriculum making, in fact, *must* use the aptitudes of students at the same time it studies adult activities. Without careful measurement of what learners likely will do upon graduation, curriculum cannot be linked with their future roles.

Free-market systematizers view learners, along with their parents, as customers. Their role is to choose the curriculum they want based on the available options. There is no set body of knowledge, or curriculum, that learners must acquire to become citizens. As a group, learners possess the power either to keep schools in business or destroy them based on their consumer choices. The individual differences and interests of students are taken into account when they, as customers, choose the school they want. The only part of the curriculum that remains consistent regardless of what school is chosen is the point that learners must become efficient producers for the economy.

Subject Matter

System builders almost invariably speak of content and not subject matter. Nevertheless, I will use subject matter to remain consistent with the language of the commonplaces. True subject matter to system builders must be derived through empirical analysis. Bobbitt uses empirical methods when he completes his task analysis, the end result of which is subject matter that becomes the basis for curriculum. Subject matter, in this respect, is not based on traditional subjects like mathematics, philosophy, or history. Rather, it is a collection of activities and experiences that empirical researchers have discovered through inductive means. When using the language of "content," systematizers also privilege knowledge from the traditional disciplines, but only knowledge that has been derived using empirical methods. Thus, knowledge in the physical sciences is regarded as more valuable than knowledge in humanities fields like literature, poetry, and art.

> Systematic curriculum makers want consistency between schools so that a third grader who transfers midyear between schools will be able to do so without any gaps in his curriculum, even to the point of not missing a chapter in his textbook.

A free-market approach to subject matter is somewhat more difficult to grasp. Since there is no body of subject matter that all students should learn, the subject matter commonplace is deemphasized compared to the commonplaces of teachers and learners. The subject matter (or "content" as systematizers put it) that is prized in the free-market system approach is subject matter that, once again, is based on empirical research and that has been produced using randomized trials. All curriculum must be proven to work based on randomized studies that demonstrate conclusively that one subject matter arrangement is more efficient than another.

Context

In some respects, systematic curriculum builders disconnect entirely from context. In other ways, however, they place a high value on it. The side of systematic curriculum that elevates above context is found in the example of No Child Left Behind. NCLB is a system designed to produce effects in every state, city, and school in the nation. Studies within the What Works Clearinghouse are predicated on the assumption that the results are universal, context-free, and applicable in any classroom. Context is reduced to a level even lower than the commonplace of subject matter. The curriculum alignment system of Fenwick English is another example of a procedure that some believe will fix curriculum problems in all schools regardless of context. All schools need to do is align their curriculum so that it can be delivered more efficiently. The idea that some schools may not need to work on curriculum alignment or that work of this type may in fact harm a specific school rather than improve it is not part of English's plan.

Free-market advocates also tout a system they believe will "fix the problems" with schools regardless of the social and political context in which a school exists. Competition, choice, deregulation, and accountability are mechanisms that will improve curriculum, teaching, and learning in any school. All schools, the free-market systematizers assume, can (and should) benefit from the power that choice and competition bring to the equation.

Within the bureaucratic system-building tradition, however, there is a recognition that context must be taken into account. For example, Bobbitt argues that curriculum must be based on the activities of the adults within the community where the school is located. The system that Bobbitt sets up is acontextual in the sense that he argues it can be applied in all circumstances. Nevertheless, within the procedure he creates for curriculum making, local community context is taken into account when curriculists study the activities of local adults. In this respect, Bobbitt's bureaucratic system approach, due to its use of activity analysis, elevates context to a level higher than individual learners.

Curriculum Making

Curriculum making is viewed differently in the bureaucratic system approach compared to the free-market system. Curriculum making is crucial to the former but rejected by the latter. Bobbitt, Charters, and English make curriculum making the centerpiece of their efforts. They define curriculum making as the task either of engaging in task analysis to create curriculum or aligning already existing curriculum to state or national standards. Curriculum making, to bureaucratic systematizers, is about bringing expert, universal knowledge to bear on schools and school systems regardless of context. Good curriculum makers provide expert advice that helps curriculum systems run more smoothly.

Free-market system advocates, however, present themselves as experts in education and rarely, if ever, tackle the subject of curriculum. Curriculum making is not the kind of language used by economists like Friedman, Chubb, and Moe. They presumably view curriculum making as something that is not rooted in theory or science, making it unworthy of their attention. Perhaps curriculum making is something that individual teachers or school administrators do as they put together the day's lessons, but curriculum is not the kind of subject that requires in-depth analysis and planning.

■ Conclusion: Strengths and Weaknesses of Systematic Curriculum

The strengths of a systematic approach are found in its emphasis on measurement, efficiency, and universality. Without a reasonable amount of attention to system, any curriculum loses its coherence. A curriculum is something that learners complete as they move through an educational institution. Without system, learners—and indeed the general public as a whole—will never know when they have completed the necessary requirements to receive a degree from a given institution. Measuring to determine whether learners are completing an institution's requirements is an obvious step to determining whether students have grasped what they should be learning.

The systematic tradition also makes a powerful point when it insists that curriculists look to local communities for subject matter. Bobbitt made this point originally in *The Curriculum*. When accepted in moderation, it makes good sense. Any school's curriculum must answer to a public constituency. If a curriculum changes to such an extent that the general public does not view it as relevant, the school that offers that curriculum will lose its support.

Bobbitt also makes a related point about human nature, one that bears emphasizing. He argues that curriculum specialists must begin not only by looking at community activities, but also by studying human nature. This point sounds similar to an appeal that has been made by political philosophers (for example, Plato and Aristotle) for centuries. The starting point for good politics is human nature, argue these ancient Greeks, so it is only reasonable to start with human nature when making curriculum. Contemporary teachers and curriculum makers may not agree with Bobbitt's view of human nature, but his point that human nature is foundational to curriculum making is nonetheless insightful.

Attention to system within curriculum also provides a public face for the institutions that offer education. Ideas like "kindergarten," "first-grade reading," "sixth-grade social studies," or "freshman English" are understood universally by the public because of the underlying system that provides the foundation for these curricula. For example, just about all Americans complete first grade; as a result, people understand the idea of "first grade." They recognize that "first grade" means a curriculum that revolves around learning to read, learning how to count and do arithmetic, and learning to write letters and words. The same holds true for curriculum constructs like sixth-grade social studies or freshman English. If curriculum loses its systematic dimension, it also loses its universality.

At the same time, too much system can lead to an unnecessary amount of abstraction. It can result in theoretic visions for what curriculum can or should do without sufficient attention to what may be accomplished within specific schools and school districts. Systematic thinking about the curriculum has a valuable role to play, but when taken too far, it forgets the human dimension of curriculum. A significant problem for a systematic view is that a humanistic perspective matters considerably to practitioners like teachers and administrators. The human element of teaching is what draws and keeps most people in the profession.

Another objection that can be raised is that the business leaders who take on the challenge of educational reform know little, if anything, about curriculum, yet they claim to be experts in education. They make a sharp distinction between "education" and "curriculum" and then declare that their knowledge has to do with improving the process of "education" but not the content of curriculum. Their business expertise, in other words, classifies them as experts in "education" but not curriculum. In making this distinction, business-minded systematic thinkers dismiss the subject of curriculum as something that is either secondary to the systematic process of education, or at best a lesser extension of it. Curriculum and education, however, are impossible to separate. If curriculum is the foundation for education as many curriculum scholars and practitioners contend, then how can free-market advocates sell themselves as experts in education and simultaneously ignore the subject of curriculum? Speaking of education without attention to curriculum is like discussing politics without addressing human nature.

Another problem is that systematic thinkers sometimes appear to be philosophically confused. For example, we find proponents of the free-market system who are also advocates of No Child Left Behind.[48] One view seeks to eliminate (or at least radically reduce) the role of bureaucracy in the administration of schools, whereas the other uses federal governmental intervention to an extent never seen before in American history. How is it possible for people to be both supporters of No Child Left Behind and advocates of a free-market system?

One final weakness that can be identified with a systematic view is one suggested previously. Systematic curriculum thinkers tend to forget that a curriculum is a human institution created by people for people. There is no way to eliminate the human element from curriculum. Viewing curriculum (or education) as a "problem" to be "fixed" ignores the complexities involved in teaching and curriculum making. Curriculum is not a Ford truck that curriculists, or anyone else, can "fix" by changing a flat or replacing a broken hose. Curriculum is about human beings as much as it is about systems. Working with human beings is not the same as working with Ford trucks, and a systematic perspective too often forgets this distinction. Systems, by definition, are abstract, impersonal, and disconnected from individual people, whereas curriculum cannot be created without regard to the teachers who will teach it and the learners who will learn it.

Chapter 3 turns to address a tradition that in many respects corrects the extremes of a systematic view. This second perspective, referred to as existentialist, has been powerful for many years and is often attractive to those who take a more individualistic approach to curriculum making. Like a systematic view, the existentialist tradition has strengths and weaknesses, both of which will become apparent in the next chapter.

■ Discussion Questions

1. Why is *system* an appropriate term for this tradition?

2. What is the relationship between research and practice within a systematic view?

3. Why are school administrators frequently attracted to a systematic view?

4. What is the process of "task analysis" and how does it result in a curriculum?

5. How does the author distinguish between a "bureaucratic system" and a "free-market system"? How are these two types of system both similar and different?

6. How is a systematic view essential to curriculum concepts like "first grade" or "sixth-grade social studies" or "freshman algebra"?

7. What does a systematic view omit that many people believe is essential to a well-rounded curriculum?

CHAPTER 3

Existentialist Curriculum

SOME PEOPLE view curriculum as a personal journey. They are not particularly concerned about system and authority but prefer to concentrate on the unique characteristics of individual students and the process of personal meaning making, which they believe is the goal of curriculum. As Maxine Greene, a nationally known educational philosopher who writes from this perspective, has written, "Authority and dignity are both unthinkable if the individual agrees to subordinate himself to a system or to define his belonging by locating himself in a hierarchy."[1] A professor of educational philosophy at Columbia University's Teachers College, Greene stands as a contemporary proponent of a long tradition of curriculum thinkers who make individual desire and personal choice the end of education. Any curriculum, from this perspective, must connect with students on a deeply personal level. Without that, a curriculum is useless, if not downright harmful. Existentialist thinkers like Greene assert that young people will never become fully human unless they choose their studies for themselves. Personal choice is paramount. Curriculum is an individual, not a communal creation. In the words of Alfie Kohn, a popular speaker and reformer who also fits within this perspective, "If the child is deprived of any opportunity to decide what happens to her, the parents' unity amounts to an alliance of them against her. Again, choice is the decisive issue."[2] Whereas systematic thinkers make planning, structure, and efficiency the essential components of a good curriculum, existentialist reformers take an opposite approach and propose that randomness, individuality, and personal freedom are the most important characteristics in a curriculum. Individual needs, not institutional responsibilities, take center stage.

The goal of this chapter is to provide an introduction to an existentialist approach. The chapter then connects this tradition to the curriculum commonplaces discussed in chapter 1. Alfie Kohn, Maxine Greene, and Elliot Eisner serve as contemporary figures who represent an existential perspective, whereas G. Stanley Hall and William Heard Kilpatrick provide historical background. Like the other traditions, existentialist curriculum has its strengths and weaknesses, which are discussed at the end of the chapter.

■ Alfie Kohn and Curriculum for Personal Choice

Alfie Kohn is one of the most outspoken contemporary critics of curriculum standards, competition, and accountability. A former high school teacher, Kohn has published more than half a dozen books with titles like *Punished by Rewards, No*

Maria Montessori

Maria Montessori (1870–1952) was an Italian-born physician and educator whose work fits within an existentialist perspective. She completed her medical degree in 1896 and soon thereafter began to work as a psychiatrist at the University of Rome. While working in this capacity, she became increasingly interested in helping students with special needs learn to become effective members of society. She then took advantage of an opportunity to work with about fifty children in one of the poorest parts of Rome known as San Lorenzo. In San Lorenzo, she established her school known as Casa dei Bambini, or "House of Children." The method that grew out of Montessori's work at Casa dei Bambini emphasizes the use of objects, manipulatives, and other devices to engage students on a tactile level while at the same time encouraging them to follow their own interests. Montessori was part of the explosion of interest in child study and developmental psychology that took place during the early years of the twentieth century. Like other existentialists, Montessori believed that curriculum should follow the interests and needs of learners. In some respects, Montessori schools are highly structured in the types of materials they use to engage students' interests. At the same time, teaching in Montessori schools is highly individualized because students choose what they want to study and pursue their own interests at their own pace. Although Montessori's methods have been applied at many age levels (including high school), her work was mostly with children ages two to six.

Contest, What to Look For in a Classroom, and *The Schools Our Children Deserve.*[3] Kohn argues that school reformers are obsessed with competition, productivity, and measurement. These trends, to him, have damaged schools and caused them to veer from their true purpose, which, to Kohn, is to meet the needs and interests of learners.

Kohn began his teaching career after completing his BA at Brown University. He then earned a master's degree at the University of Chicago. During his years of teaching, Kohn became disenchanted with the system that was forced upon him. He decided to take his argument for school reform to the public through books, articles, and essays. He has become well known not so much because of his contributions to curriculum philosophy in a scholarly sense, but because he has published books and articles that appeal to parents, especially those, of course, who share his existentialist viewpoint.

Reggio Emilia

Sometimes mistaken for a person's name, Reggio Emilia is an approach to teaching young children that grows out of a community known as Reggio Emilia in northern Italy. Founded by Loris Malaguzzi following World War II, Reggio Emilia schools have grown in popularity in the United States during the last fifteen to twenty years. The Reggio Emilia approach embodies all of the characteristics of existentialist curriculum. Lessons are project centered, teachers pay careful attention to the developmental stages of children, and students are always encouraged to follow their own interests and choose what it is they want to learn. The concept of experience is also crucial to "Reggio" schools. Learners are viewed as bundles of potentiality that are shaped powerfully by their senses of touching, feeling, hearing, smelling, and tasting. Teachers work to create activities and establish environments that stimulate all five of these senses. Reggio schools also stress partnership with parents more than some existentialist philosophies. Parents are viewed as colearners in the educational process, partners who direct the learning experiences of children at home just like teachers do at school.

Another hallmark of Reggio schools relates to the forms of language that children use to communicate. Writing and speaking are of course two ways that students communicate, but Reggio schools also recognize that some children would prefer to communicate using other means. Consequently, children are encouraged to express themselves in any way they choose, including through art, puppetry, role-playing, drama, and music. These various arts of expression are viewed as "symbolic languages" that allow students freedom and creativity when deciding how to express themselves.

Kohn professes the common position that teachers should be *guides* who direct student learning, not lecturers who tell students what to know. A good classroom, to Kohn, is one in which students are actively engaged in pursuing projects that interest them. These classrooms can be loud, haphazard, and even confusing, so long as students engage in creating something that interests them. In Kohn's words:

> The best teachers are vitally active and involved, but not in propelling students toward right answers. Not in filling them full of facts. Not in giving them worksheets that consist of naked numbers, or disconnected sentences in which the point is to circle vowels or verbs. The teacher starts with the kids and then gently challenges them, subtly disorients them, throws them off balance with new ideas that the students have to struggle to reconcile with the way they'd been looking at things.[4]

Existentialist curriculum tends to be popular in the United States because it appeals to the individualistic spirit that drives many Americans.

One of the hallmarks of existentialist teaching is that teachers must not have a prescribed curriculum. They are to allow students to create their own answers, regardless of whether these answers are correct. Existentialist teaching (or constructivist teaching as some refer to it today) must begin by drawing upon the immediate interests and instincts of children—not subject matter, future occupations, or the needs of society.

Kohn's perspective is often viewed as democratic because it eradicates the authority of teachers by placing them on the same level as students. In an existentialist classroom, everyone assists the other members of the class in the pursuit of their own learning. In the words of Kohn, "A curriculum geared to the needs of learners requires of the teacher an enormous amount of flexibility, a high tolerance for unpredictability, and a willingness to give up absolute control of the classroom."[5] Connecting students with a common curriculum is much less important than cooperating with them as they pursue the subjects they want to study. Subject matter is secondary; students' personal interests are primary.

Kohn bolsters his personal choice viewpoint with an implicit view of human nature that is positive and social. In contrast to a view like that of Thomas Hobbes who sees human beings as competitive and self-interested, Kohn believes that human beings are cooperative and civil. He believes that our society's obsession with competition is the result of how we have socialized children, not the inevitable result of an innate desire to compete. In *No Contest,* Kohn spends more time critiquing a competitive view of human nature than he does presenting his own position, but a reasonable conclusion to draw is that Kohn believes human nature is highly malleable. He contends that we create competitive, selfish children by surrounding them with a culture that rewards these behaviors.[6] Inundating them, instead, with a culture of community and self-reliance will produce better children and ultimately a better society. This elastic view of human nature is consistent with an existentialist philosophy. Existentialists seldom discuss the subject of human nature, preferring instead to believe that people are the product of their surroundings and nothing else.

When we accept the assumption that culture produces students, an existentialist approach begins to make more sense. To authors like Kohn, curriculum is not so much the subject matter or the plan that we put before students, but rather the environment we create around them. Curriculum making is about surrounding students with interesting possibilities, not producing a plan for what they must learn or who they should become. All children are interested in something, existentialists assume, and the role of teachers is to create an environment that builds upon their innate desires. The opposite from a teacher-planned curriculum is a curriculum designed by students. This kind of curriculum, Kohn argues, is what truly motivates students to learn. They will never engage a curriculum that is designed by people they perceive to be their superiors. A self-directed curriculum, on the other hand, leads to the kind of powerful learning that will remain with students for a lifetime.

> Existentialist teachers allow students to choose whatever topic they wish for a research paper.

Kohn does not advocate a radical position that completely turns curriculum over to students, but he does insist that students must have a say in what they learn. Student input, to him, is every bit as important as teacher input during the curriculum-making process. In Kohn's words:

> No one ought to be required to memorize the elements— or for that matter, the state capitals. But there are aspects of learning that require hard work, and it is here that

talented teachers really shine. They arrange for students to be part of a community of learners who help each other do their best. They embed the task in a question or context to which students resonate, and they help make the connections to the questions clear. They give students choice about how they will approach a task and a reasonable rationale for what they are being asked to do.[7]

This argument exemplifies an existentialist approach in several ways. First, Kohn argues that teachers "arrange" for students to be part of a community. At the most, he wants teachers to take an indirect approach to curriculum, not a direct one. Second, he stresses choice. He believes students will never learn anything unless they choose the material themselves. Internal choice must be the starting point for all learning. Third, teaching is about asking questions and leading students to multiple answers, not guiding them to supposedly correct answers. To existentialists like Kohn, there are no right or wrong answers, just more questions. The audience for Kohn's work is a certain portion of the general public that is drawn to the emotional side of curriculum and teaching. This constituency includes many teachers and parents who seek an alternative to the systematic view. Another author who recognizes that we live in a systematic age and wants to change it is Maxine Greene. Unlike Kohn, however, Greene directs her work toward an academic audience. There are many consistencies, nevertheless, between the perspectives of Kohn and Greene.

■ Maxine Greene and Existential Curriculum

Maxine Greene's approach to curriculum is much less about political engagement and more about releasing imagination. Her work draws upon literary theory, women's studies, and existential philosophers like Jean-Paul Sartre to challenge people to become more fully human. To do this, she argues, human beings must reflect upon their innermost desires. If Kohn's existentialism aims at political engagement, Greene's stresses psychological transformation.

Although she sometimes uses the term *curriculum*, Greene is much less concerned about curriculum than she is about personal fulfillment. Nowhere does she describe what should be included in a common curriculum for a school or university, preferring instead to allow learners to create their own curriculum in a creative way. She wants teachers to create individuals who rebel against institutions, not citizens who see themselves as members of a community. In her words:

> The teacher, having identified himself as a lover of art and freedom, can only offer possibility. He can only try to free his students to love in their own way. If he succeeds, if they dare to chance the jungle river and the underground and the void, there will be interior journeys taking place in the classroom. There will be movements towards meaning, assertions of freedom. People will be learning to rebel.[8]

Greene does not expand on what students should rebel against or the goal toward which they should rebel, but she does challenge them to defy the status quo. Good teachers, to Greene, foment revolution, but the revolution takes place internally and with the end of transforming a person's internal life through the release of imagination. Teachers do not offer curriculum or knowledge in a traditional sense but rather possibility, deliverance, and a heightened sense of personal awareness. As Greene puts it, "The teacher's object can only be to launch the student on his own journey, to goad him to his own action and his own choice, to confront him with possibles."[9]

Personal freedom is an end in itself to Maxine Greene. Learning is the means to internal liberation. What students learn is much less important than their becoming autonomous, self-sustaining actors who are in charge of their own lives. In Greene's words, "To be autonomous and independent: This seems to many to be the American dream."[10] To Greene, learning is an intensely emotional act, one that culminates in poetic living. Lives are created like poetry. To Greene, there is no human nature that exists prior to the choices we make. Human beings have the power to create whatever kind of life they wish. Human nature is the product of individual choices, but of course those choices are influenced by the environment in which we live. Traditional discussions of human nature that emphasize an eternal soul or the ultimate purpose of man are passé to existentialists like Greene.

Greene rarely if ever discusses curriculum in any significant detail, preferring to use terms that allow her to remain at a high level of abstraction. For example, she writes, "If we are to educate for mindfulness and critical understanding in its manifold forms, we need somehow to enable the young to recover themselves, to recover what might be called a lost spontaneity. By that I mean to help them regain contact with their original landscape, their original sense of horizon, of the not yet."[11] Like other existentialists, Kohn included, Greene is optimistic about how human beings can re-create themselves in a positive way, despite the many problems she sees in the world. Greene's view of human nature is similar to what French philosopher Jean-Jacques Rousseau proposed when he declared in his novel *Emile* that children are born perfect and society corrupts them.[12] In Greene's view, if educators can return to the original perfect state in which children were born, they (meaning both the educators and the students) can reform society for the better. The present state of curriculum and teaching surrounds perfect children with corrupt institutions. To recover their sense of creativity, children must be sheltered from flawed institutions so that they can be cleansed by the influence of pure nature.

A third contemporary figure who fits within an existentialist perspective is Elliot Eisner. An emeritus professor of art and education at Stanford University, Eisner has been active in the fields of art education and curriculum for more than four decades. A closer look at his views on curriculum, specifically his concept of "forms of representation," broadens existentialist curriculum to include the field of art and the unique approach it contributes.

■ Elliot Eisner and Artistic Existentialism

Elliot Eisner completed his PhD in education at the University of Chicago in June of 1962. He joined the faculty at Stanford University's School of Education soon thereafter, where he taught until his retirement in 2005. Eisner has consistently called for reform in education that de-emphasizes test scores and places a greater emphasis on helping learners to make a personal connection to the curriculum they study. Eisner's work shows great respect for science, but he also argues that the fine arts offer the richest way to make sense of human experience.

Like other existentialists, Eisner views human beings as malleable creatures who are shaped entirely by their experiences. He views teachers and curriculum makers as directors of learning experiences who attempt to liberate students

Artists are often drawn to existentialist curriculum because of its emphasis on creativity, personal meaning making, and self-expression.

by offering them meaningful experiences that connect with them on a deeply personal level. Eisner contends further that a high-quality curriculum encourages students to demonstrate what they have learned in a public way that allows them to choose a variety of forms in which to communicate. Eisner is concerned that certain types of knowledge—for example, intellectual skills in mathematics and writing skills in English—have been significantly overemphasized, to the detriment of other ways of sharing experiences such as music, dance, and theater. To break out of the straitjacket of traditional representations of knowledge, Eisner has introduced his concept of "forms of representation." Like other existentialists, Eisner believes that all knowledge derives from experience and that all experiences originate with the five senses. He makes no distinction between knowledge and experience.

Eisner's idea of "forms of representation" has to do with the way in which learners take in experiences and then share them with other people (in other words, share them with the public). Eisner's most succinct description of "forms of representation" can be found when he writes, "Forms of representation are the devices that humans use to make public conceptions that are privately held."[13] We engage in a form of representation anytime we take a piece of knowledge and share it with other people. Writing and speaking have been two traditional forms of representation, but Eisner has sought for many years to move the field of curriculum—as well as professional education as a whole—toward multiple forms of representation, especially those that take into account affective modes of experience that acknowledge the role of emotions in learners' lives. In addition to cognitive or intellectual forms of representation, Eisner maintains that a good curriculum must connect with students who excel in areas such as dance, poetry, music, and other fine arts. These forms of representation open up new avenues for learners to pursue as they share their experiences with a public audience.

The existentialist aspect of Eisner's work becomes especially evident when he argues, "Education ought to help the young learn how to create their own meanings through these forms (of representation). Schools cannot accomplish these aims unless the curriculum they provide offers students opportunities to become, for want of a better term, multiliterate."[14] The concept of students "creating their own meanings" is a distinctive feature of an existentialist view.

To existentialists like Eisner, every student will make sense of a curriculum in a different way. Teachers and curriculum makers, instead of trying to get all students to have the same experiences, should embrace the reality of "multiliteracy." This means encouraging learners to share what they have experienced using forms of representation that grow out of their individual interests and abilities. Eisner acknowledges that the notion of forms of representation shares many similarities with Howard Gardner's work on "multiple intelligences." The main difference between these two ideas can be found in the fact that Gardner's multiple intelligences concern primarily the way students learn, whereas Eisner's forms of representation address not only how students learn but also how they share their experiences with others.

Even though his work is complex and he has been influenced by many different traditions, Eisner's views fit best within the existentialist tradition for at least three reasons. First, teachers, to Eisner, are not successful unless they make a personal connection with students, a connection that goes well beyond the intellectual aspect of curriculum. Second, Eisner belongs within this tradition because, like all curricular existentialists, he insists that curriculum makers must learn to adapt curriculum to individual students. From design to evaluation, Eisner wants teachers, as well as school-level administrators, to create a curriculum that impacts students in emotional and affective, not just intellectual, ways. The only way to do this, he contends, is if teachers and school administrators create a climate in which students feel comfortable sharing their views. Eisner does not emphasize adapting curriculum to developmental stages as some existentialists do, but he does insist that teachers and school administrators find ways to adapt their curriculum to the emotional needs of learners. Third, and finally, Eisner fits within an existentialist perspective because he rejects the objectivity that serves as the foundation for a systematic view. The false quest for objectivity, as he sees it, grows out of the desire that educational researchers have to pattern themselves, inappropriately that is, after scientists in fields like chemistry and physics. In Eisner's words, "The model of natural sciences on which much educational research is based is probably inappropriate for most of the problems and aims of teaching, learning, and curriculum development."[15] Just like he wants students to find personal meaning in the curriculum they study, Eisner wants researchers to acknowledge that their research is impacted by their personal views. This "personalization" of research is another key feature of an existentialist view.

Compared to other curriculum traditions (for example, a systematic view), Eisner's artistic existentialism is relatively new within the field of curriculum. The existentialist tradition traces to the late nineteenth and early twentieth centuries, whereas the roots of systematic curriculum extend at least to the materialism of eighteenth-century philosopher Auguste Comte. A closer look at the early days of an existentialist view within the field of curriculum enables us to understand this perspective's strengths and weaknesses.

■ Background on Existentialist Curriculum

G. Stanley Hall and Developmental Curriculum

One of the most enduring aspects of the existentialist tradition is its focus on child development. This component of existentialist curriculum is found somewhat in the works of Kohn, Greene, and Eisner, but it is not their primary emphasis. Another educational reformer pioneered the idea that curriculum should be adapted to learners' developmental stages. His name was G. Stanley Hall, a psychologist who made a significant impact on American curriculum. He completed the first American doctoral degree in psychology in 1878 at Harvard, after which he enjoyed a highly successful career as a professor at Antioch College in Yellow Springs, Ohio, and later at the Johns Hopkins University in Baltimore, Maryland. He then served as president of Clark University in Worcester, Massachusetts, from 1888 to 1920. As early as the 1880s, Hall began to argue for revolutionary changes in American education, specifically the idea of curriculum differentiation.

One of Hall's earliest publications was "The Contents of Children's Minds on Entering School."[16] To collect the data that served as the foundation for this article, Hall devised a survey that was given to hundreds of students throughout the country. His goal was to determine the "contents of children's minds," meaning, he wanted to know which subjects naturally interested students at the various stages of their development. He also wanted to know what information students from the various grades possessed in their minds when they began school. He asked children questions about their favorite book, color, animal, and game. He also gave them lists of terms and then asked them to provide definitions. Hall believed that once he had determined the interests that students possessed at the various stages of development, teachers and curriculum developers could use this information to differentiate curriculum for individual students as well as for groups. His idea was that curriculum could be made more interesting to students if teachers introduced the right pieces of subject matter at the right time, which to Hall meant the time when students were developmentally ready for each piece of information.[17]

Another dimension of Hall's work concerns what is sometimes referred to as "prior knowledge." In contemporary usage, prior knowledge means the knowledge that students possess before they begin a new class or otherwise attempt to learn something new. The greater the distance between students' prior knowledge and the new material being presented, the more difficult the learning process will be. In Hall's words, "If children are pressed to answer questions somewhat beyond their ken, they often reply confusedly and at random."[18] The insight that teachers should be aware of students' prior knowledge, which is an extension of the point that teachers should begin their lessons with students' interests, is a significant contribution to the curriculum field by existentialist thinkers. Almost everyone has experienced a class in which the teacher presents material that flies over the heads of the entire class, yet the teacher remains unaware that this is happening. An existentialist viewpoint corrects this problem by challenging teachers to think first about the knowledge that students possess and only secondarily about subject matter. Hall's emphasis on children and their developmental needs coincided with the early years of the twentieth century, often referred to as the "century of the child."[19] This identification of children and their individual needs as the end of curriculum led to contentious, often titanic battles between competing sides. These two sides pitted advocates of subject matter against proponents of children's needs. Hall was squarely on the side of the developmental needs of learners, as was one of his successors, the charismatic William Heard Kilpatrick.

William Heard Kilpatrick and Project-Based Curriculum

William Heard Kilpatrick espoused a philosophy of curriculum that was similar to Hall's but also different in notable ways. Kilpatrick was a professor of education at Teachers College, Columbia University, from 1912 to 1937. He wrote dozens of books and was a disciple of John Dewey, emphasizing the "child-centered" aspects of Dewey's thought. Kilpatrick criticized the idea of a formal curriculum, especially if it emphasized subject matter. Kilpatrick ridiculed the notion of "subject-matter-set-out-to-be-learned" in favor of allowing students to choose what they want to pursue.[20] In his book *Remaking the Curriculum,* Kilpatrick insists that teachers must privilege learners' needs, not subject matter. As he wrote:

> The child must for us come before subject matter as such. This is the everlasting and final condemnation of the old curriculum. It put subject matter first and it bent—or if need be, broke—the child to fit that. . . . Subject matter—if any reader be concerned for it—will be called this way better into play than is usual now, and more of it, but probably not the precise subject matter of the customary school and most certainly not in the usual order.[21]

Kilpatrick was more than willing to enter into battle against traditional conceptions of curriculum. Many traditional educators overemphasized subject matter to the detriment of learners' interests. Kilpatrick, on the other hand, was sometimes criticized for going to the other extreme and overemphasizing learners' needs, thereby neglecting subject matter.

Kilpatrick became well known in 1918 when he published an essay entitled "The Project Method: The Use of the Purposeful Act in the Educative Process." With this essay, he injected the idea of "project-based learning" into elementary and secondary schools. The idea has remained powerful ever since. Kilpatrick's point in "The Project Method" is that students learn material best when they use it to do something that interests them, when they have chosen the activity for themselves, and when the project engages their full range of desires. Above all, Kilpatrick wants knowledge to be useful and meaningful to students on an intensely

Any project that encourages students to express themselves, whether that means drawing a picture or writing a poem, is an indication that a teacher or a curriculum designer is operating from an existentialist perspective.

personal level. He seized upon the idea of a "project" as the end or culmination of curriculum. He argues not for an organized or planned curriculum, but for classroom activity that is centered around projects that arise from what students want to do. As Kilpatrick's subtitle indicates, "The Use of the Purposeful Act in the Educative Process," his work possessed an element of purposefulness. Even though "The Project Method" may have been purposeful at first glance, it was not teleological, however, in the sense that it addressed questions about the ultimate purpose of curriculum and teaching. The project method was only teleological in the way it focused students on the solution of immediate problems. To Kilpatrick, there is no end beyond present problems. Teaching students to solve problems through the use of projects is an end in itself to Kilpatrick. He was able to use the language of purposefulness and teleology without providing answers to truly teleological questions.

Kilpatrick argues that this project-based approach is more effective, more meaningful, and better prepares students for life. In his words, "Any plan of educational procedure which does not aim consciously and insistently at securing and utilizing vigorous proposing on the part of the pupils is founded essentially on an ineffective and unfruitful basis."[22] Kilpatrick contends that learning is most effective when teachers use projects that engage students wholeheartedly, meaning it connects to them physically, emotionally, mentally, socially, and with all five senses. This argument culminates in classroom projects that, for example, use a theme like learning about apples. Teachers will have students read a book about apples, then taste apples, visit an apple orchard, make applesauce, perhaps bob for apples, and finally bake an apple pie. A series of lessons of this sort is designed to engage students with their entire being, not just mentally, socially, or physically.

Like Hall, Kilpatrick wants curriculum to meet the developmental needs of learners. He stresses that learners should produce something tangible if they expect their learning to last for any considerable length of time. Like Kohn, Greene, and Eisner today, Kilpatrick argues that personal choice is foundational to good curriculum making. If authorities—for example, teachers or school principals—establish curriculum standards without substantial input from students, their curriculum will fail. Instead, Kilpatrick insists that student choice must be the first step—not the last—in curriculum making.

There should be no single curriculum for a school but rather multiple *curricula* that allow every student to pursue his own path. The existentialist dimensions of Kilpatrick's views are evident when he writes, "It is what the self accepts and how thoroughly it accepts that counts. Education becomes thus the process of helping the self to rebuild itself to ever higher and finer levels by helping it to think and choose better than otherwise it would."[23] To Kilpatrick, the preeminent concern in all curriculum making must be the wholehearted purposeful choice of the learner. Such an emphasis on learners' needs has its benefits. It can help curriculum makers to counteract the excesses of a systematic view, which deifies institutions. It also reminds us of the emotional side of curriculum, teaching, and learning. On the other hand, viewed in light of the curriculum commonplaces, an existentialist perspective turns out to have shortcomings that need to be offset by other traditions.

■ Existentialist Curriculum and the Commonplaces

Teachers

The existentialist tradition severely alters traditional conceptions of teaching and the role of teachers. Existentialists refer to teachers as guides who suggest what students might want to learn, as opposed to subject matter specialists who introduce learners to time-tested knowledge. An existentialist view diminishes the teacher commonplace by placing teachers in a secondary role to learners. Every member of a community or school becomes a teacher because each person is responsible for teaching herself. One person cannot teach another in a traditional sense. Teachers can only make suggestions that indirectly influence the people around them. If there is a stronger view of the teacher commonplace in the existentialist tradition, it is found in those who emphasize curriculum differentiation that is designed to meet learners' developmental needs. Still, however, this secondary aspect within existentialist thinking places the learner commonplace ahead of teachers. The starting point for curriculum remains the characteristics of the learners to be taught.

> Existentialist teachers allow students to present research projects in a variety of ways, such as with a traditional research paper, a PowerPoint presentation, artwork, or an oral presentation.

Learners

The learner commonplace is where existentialist curriculum places its emphasis. The age-old declaration "I teach children, not subjects" is a common rhetorical device used by existentialists (whether they recognize it or not). Learners become the beginning, middle, and end of curriculum making. The idea of balancing the five commonplaces is not in the language of this tradition. Existentialists assume that if the learner commonplace is respected and given its appropriate (and vaulted) place within the curriculum-making process, then the other commonplaces will take care of themselves. A good curriculum is assumed to be one that cleanses learners psychologically. There is no such thing as an objective curriculum that exists outside of the subjective desires of individual learners. Much like the dream of objectivity dominates in the systematic view, subjectivity reigns supreme in the world of existentialists. Learners and learning are ends in themselves, and there is no need to discuss goals or purposes beyond the subjective choices that learners make.

> There is a tension within existentialist curriculum that revolves around the question of freedom for students compared to freedom for teachers. Existentialists combine a strong emphasis on individuality for students with highly prescribed methods of teaching for teachers.

Subject Matter

Like the teacher commonplace, subject matter takes a backseat when existentialists control curriculum. Many battles have been waged during the last century between advocates of the subject matter and learner commonplaces. The two are set against one another so often that astute followers of educational rhetoric can predict the points that advocates of the two sides will make. Existentialists redefine the nature and purpose of subject matter. To them, subject matter is no longer confined to the traditional academic subjects. From an existentialist view, the proper subject matter for students to study is life. The traditional disciplines are of course part of life, but they are only useful if they help us to meet our daily problems. Teachers and learners must learn to transgress the traditional subject matter boundaries by focusing on projects, activities, problems, and forms of representation that serve as the focal point of curriculum. Subject matter must not be seen as an end in itself but only as a source of experiences that learners should draw upon as they construct their lives.

Context

Because of its emphasis on individual learners, an existentialist view, at least at first glance, appears to take into account context in a unique and powerful way. Upon further reflection, however, just the opposite turns out to be the case. By placing learners at the top of the curriculum hierarchy, existentialists assume there will never be a school or community context in which one of the other commonplaces should take priority. Regardless of the school or students involved, existentialists assume that focusing on the needs of learners will make for a good curriculum. The idea of individual needs is therefore abstracted to the point that it becomes decontextualized—even deified—as the only commonplace to be considered.

This tendency raises important questions. What if the emphasis on the individual needs of learners leads to a classroom in which teachers have no control? What if students are following their interests in, for example, a mathematics class, yet the answers they construct are incorrect? What if graduates of a "learner-centered" high school have become so accustomed to following their own desires that they cannot function in a workplace where their supervisor expects them to follow strict rules? Due to their neglect of context, existentialists have difficulty answering these questions. Personal context is taken into account from the perspective of existentialists, but community context is severely diminished, if not rejected outright.

Curriculum Making

Existentialists want curriculum to be personal. They emphasize curriculum as lived experience, not as objectified subject matter or as a framework for moral virtue or as the occupational skills needed to perform a job. Existentialists who take a psychoanalytic approach see life as one big process of curriculum making. Each of us makes our own curriculum, they contend. Our choices determine who we become and the possibilities we create. Good curriculum makers must recognize this internal, personal side of curriculum. Curriculum making that does not inquire into the internal desires of learners is not curriculum making at all.

Several representative questions arise when this perspective is used as the basis for curriculum making. For instance, what novels should teachers choose if they want to connect with this student who is confronting these personal challenges at this time? How can teachers create a writing assignment that prompts students to begin the process of personal reflection and exploration? How can curriculum makers design a history curriculum that connects each student with his or her family's story of immigration? These types of questions, all of which emphasize personal connections, are of utmost significance to existentialist curriculum makers.

A more developmentally oriented approach to existentialist curriculum focuses on stages of childhood growth and development. Good curriculum making is a process of differentiating subject matter and skills so that both correspond to the natural instincts of learners. The personal desires of students are important, but even more significant are empirical studies that demonstrate what subject matter will connect with students at different times in their lives. Do third graders really want to learn cursive? At what point do teenage boys become interested in music? What types of books are naturally interesting to middle school boys? Questions such as these begin with the interests of students, but they emphasize classes of students, not individuals. The goal of existentialist curriculum making, nevertheless, is for teachers to connect with students on a personal level. *How People Learn,* published by the National Research Council, is a popular book that captures this developmentally focused approach to existentialism. Books like this borrow from a systematic perspective to buttress their credentials as works grounded in empirical science, but, in the end, learners and their developmental stages reign supreme.[24]

■ Conclusion: Strengths and Weaknesses of Existentialist Curriculum

Existentialist curriculum has clear advantages. It reminds us of the *who* in the curriculum-making process. The point that learners remember lessons best when they *choose* what it is they want to study is a significant contribution this tradition makes to curriculum. Without active choice on the part of students, no lesson can be successful. Existentialists like G. Stanley Hall made a powerful contribution when they taught curriculum specialists that learners pass through developmental stages. Planning a curriculum for second graders is not the same thing as planning a curriculum for college sophomores. There was a time when this point was revolutionary. Adapting curriculum to the developmental stages of learners has become a commonplace due to the success of existentialist reformers. Existentialists also enrich the field of curriculum by reminding us that the purpose of schooling is much broader than test scores or the accumulation of subject matter. To existentialists, the end of education is personal growth, sometimes referred to as self-actualization. This is the kind of goal that can be pursued for a lifetime, one that will never be captured with a paper and pencil test.

These strengths, however, also come with weaknesses. For example, the existentialist tradition's focus on the learner commonplace—nearly to the exclusion of all others—leads to multiple *curricula*, not a unified *curriculum*. As a result, existentialists will never provide curriculists with a truly liberating curriculum. If, as existentialists want, every student pursues her own curriculum, then the idea of a coherent curriculum serving as the foundation for community is impossible. An overemphasis on the individual needs of learners also leads to individualism. Preparing students for citizenship is difficult if learners consistently experience teachers who adapt everything they teach to learners' individual needs.

Young students also do not inherently know what it is they ought to learn. Each generation of adults has the responsibility to introduce children to the knowledge, practices, and traditions they must know in order to keep their communities flourishing. Children may have tendencies toward natural goodness, but, like all humans, they are also prone to capriciousness, shortsightedness, and wrongdoing. Without guidance from educated adults, learners will choose to pursue a curriculum that does not have lifelong value. In this respect, the role of curriculum makers is to put learners in touch with eternal knowledge that helps them to overcome their capricious inclinations.

As suggested earlier, the primary weakness of existentialism is its neglect of the subject matter commonplace. Its extreme emphasis on the individual needs of learners leaves little room for organized bodies of knowledge to be taught in a coherent way. This rejection of subject matter leads to a curriculum that disconnects learners from their cultural heritage. Most students are not naturally interested in Latin, calculus, or British literature, but that does not mean that teachers ought not to require students to study these subjects. Traditional forms of subject matter are repositories of our cultural past. Failing to connect students with this knowledge does them a disservice, one that ultimately traps them in a life spent satisfying their own desires as opposed to one spent seeking to comprehend the world around them.

Liberation becomes impossible if learners are taught to pursue only what their emotions tell them to learn.

Despite these shortcomings, the points raised by an existentialist viewpoint are essential if a liberating curriculum is to be achieved. Good curriculum makers can use the positive aspects of existentialist curriculum while at the same time control the effects of its shortcomings. A third tradition, referred to as radical in the next chapter, shifts our attention to a paradigm that is known not for its focus on the individual needs of learners but for its emphasis on social transformation. A radical approach concentrates not on building efficient systems or on connecting with learners' desires, but rather on battling against the political status quo. The following chapter considers this perspective in detail.

■ Discussion Questions

1. What is unique about the existentialist tradition?

2. Why is "personal meaning making" such a critical aspect of existentialist curriculum?

3. Why do existentialists reject the distinction between "knowledge" and "experience"? Why does the rejection of this distinction matter?

4. How do existentialists view human nature and how does it impact the way they see curriculum?

5. How does an existentialist viewpoint change the traditional role of teachers?

6. Which of the commonplaces is considered most important to existentialists and why?

7. In what way (or ways) does an existentialist viewpoint emphasize curricula instead of curriculum?

8. Are there any subjects within the curriculum that you think would be taught best using an existentialist view?

9. What does an existentialist viewpoint omit that many people believe is essential to a well-rounded curriculum?

CHAPTER 4

Radical Curriculum

I N SHARP CONTRAST to systematic and existential curriculists, radicals view their work as inherently political. Systematic curriculists present a view of curriculum—and curriculum making—that they believe is neutral, objective, and apolitical. Radical curriculists, on the other hand, embrace the political nature of curriculum work. They see politics and curriculum as inseparable. In the words of one radical reformer, "Neutrality with respect to the great issues that agitate society, while perhaps theoretically possible, is practically tantamount to giving support to the forces of conservatism."[1] This rejection of neutrality and the acceptance of political advocacy lead radical curriculists to take positions that differ markedly from the other traditions. Whereas systematic thinkers stress efficiency and existentialists emphasize personal freedom, radicals concentrate on resistance, revolution, and strict adherence to a political vision. Radicals promote service to the common good, whereas existentialists stress individuality and personal freedom. Political action is by no means the primary goal of existential curriculists, whereas radicals thrive on making an impact on the world politically.

Radicals contend that changes in curriculum must keep the goal of equality in mind at all times, even if achieving this goal means sweeping change or revolutionary action. To these thinkers, almost every school's curriculum is a source of cultural oppression, one that serves to keep minority students in positions of inferiority while at the same time providing a pathway for privileged students to gain a leg up in society. In the words of Michael Apple, an author of many books and a leading figure in the radical tradition, "The study of curriculum . . . provides one area through which we can examine the cultural and economic reproduction of class relations in unequal societies."[2] A radical view sees curriculum work from the perspective of race, class, and gender analysis. Those who adopt this view seek to understand how curriculum, and the work of curriculum developers, contributes to the reproduction of economic and social inequalities. The most common modes of analysis used by radical curriculists include sociology, economics, phenomenology, qualitative forms of research, and, in almost all cases, a distinctively left-leaning approach to politics. Of the five curriculum traditions included in this book, the radical tradition adheres most strictly to one political perspective. Apple makes no attempt to conceal his political views, for example, when he writes, "I was one of the first to reestablish the neo-Marxist cultural tradition in the early '70s in the United States."[3] Apple has been working for almost forty years to turn a marginal political perspective into a dominant one.

"Radical" is an appropriate term for curriculum thinkers like Apple because they advocate changes that are immediate, wholesale, and far-reaching, not piecemeal or gradual. They are driven by a sense of urgency, by a conviction that society is deeply unjust, and by an allegiance to the vision that society must change and change quickly. They contend that immediate actions must be taken in order to battle against class-based injustices.

To represent the radical paradigm, this chapter has three main goals. First, it introduces readers to two contemporary thinkers who have influenced radical curriculum thought and practice: Michael Apple and Paulo Freire. Second, it provides background on the radical tradition by discussing the work of George S. Counts and Harold Rugg. Both were prominent radical curriculists from the twentieth century. Finally, as in chapters 1 through 3, we will use the five commonplaces to analyze radical curriculum philosophy before concluding with the strengths and weaknesses of this tradition. A reasonable place to begin with this tradition is with Michael Apple, one of the most prolific authors whose work fits within this perspective.

> Radical curriculum typically gains adherents during decades when the political Left is in power, for example, during the 1930s and the 1960s.

■ Michael Apple and Radical Curriculum

Michael Apple is a professor of curriculum and instruction at the University of Wisconsin, Madison. He has published actively in the field of curriculum since the early 1970s. He is primarily a sociologist who analyzes curriculum in order to determine its effect on society. He has offered a blistering critique of American educational institutions, especially curriculum, for at least forty years. Since the time he completed his dissertation, Apple has reiterated the point that America's educational institutions are not just broken but positively harmful and in need of radical transformation. In Apple's words from his dissertation, "There is at least a vocalized belief by many members of minority groups that the schools have failed. They have not met the needs of the people they supposedly serve. The schools are not 'relevant.' They are not personally meaningful. What they are is 'brutalizing.'"[4] To Apple, there is almost nothing positive to report about America's educational institutions. He assumes a priori that all educational institutions are in need of radical reform, if not revolution. He contends that American schools are damaging to all students, but they are particularly "brutal" toward minority students who are sorted, unwillingly, into jobs and other social positions that are inferior to those held by white students who come from higher classes.

Official Knowledge

Apple has published books that speak to school practitioners as well as other titles that have university professors in mind as their audience. One example of the former is *Official Knowledge,* published in 1993. The purpose of the book is to analyze "struggles over curriculum, teaching, and policy at a variety of levels."[5] Apple argues that "the forms of curricula, teaching and evaluation in schools" are always the result of "compromises where dominant groups, in order to maintain their dominance, must take the concerns of the less powerful into account."[6] The idea of taking the less powerful into account that Apple has in mind is critical of the status quo and the institutions that support it. More powerful groups take less powerful groups into account not to listen to their concerns but to devise ways to control them.

The "official knowledge" that Apple describes is the institutionalized curriculum that powerful groups maintain dominion over so that they can control lower classes, especially minority groups. To Apple, what becomes official knowledge (and hence part of the official curriculum) is inherently biased against African Americans, Mexican

Americans, and other historically disadvantaged groups. In the face of this problem, critics like Apple seek to subvert the status quo. They teach courses, write scholarship, and engage in conversations that strive to "awaken the consciousness" of oppressed groups. Because many if not all of these oppressed groups are unaware that they are being controlled, the oppressed are by default reliant upon radical reformers like Apple to awaken them to new possibilities. Oppressed groups could pursue a multitude of new possibilities if they would overthrow the institutions that keep them down. If Apple and other radicals can persuade these groups to battle their oppressors, they will rise up and demand that their knowledge become part of the official curriculum.

In Apple's view, conservative politicians have used the tools of government to keep minority groups in positions of inferiority. Apple is critical of anything that resembles a conservative political position. He bases his writing on the assumption that "progressive" policies are always right and "conservative" policies are always wrong. He explains the opposition between "conservatives" and "progressives" in stark terms when he writes, "The conservative alliance has clearly attempted to transform what education is for and what our policies and practices over curriculum and teaching will look like."[7] Elsewhere, Apple distinguishes between conservative politics and other views by writing, "We face what . . . I call conservative modernization. This is a powerful, yet odd, combination of forces that is in play in education; a combination that many educators, community activists, critical researchers, and others believe poses substantial threats to the vitality of our nation, our schools, our teachers, and our children."[8] Apple frequently speaks of "conservative modernization" or the "conservative restoration" when describing the destructive influence he believes conservative policies have had on curriculum and teaching. In Apple's mind, conservatives are the bad guys, and he and other radical curriculists are the good guys. He argues that the conservative movement, which he also refers to as the New Right, is driven by a sense that conservatives have lost control over their lives economically, politically, and culturally. He thinks conservatives are particularly motivated by a sense that their views of morality, knowledge, history, and politics no longer hold the same influence they once did in American culture.[9]

The counterattack that Apple proposes in the face of "conservative restoration" consists of "grass-roots movements that seek to expand the space created by the new accord and whose educational and social visions suggest a different course for teachers, administrators, students, and community members to take."[10] Given Apple's assumption that every curriculum and teaching act is political, he sees no need to limit the role of politics in curriculum and teaching. Once this step is taken, the issue becomes the nature of the politics that teachers and school leaders should take with them into schools, not whether politics should be part of what they do. Apple wants teachers to promote a left-leaning politics that furthers the agenda he has in mind, whereas critics of his approach question whether teachers should espouse a political position in their classrooms.

Instead of foundational curriculum questions such as "What should we teach?" or "What should we include in the curriculum?" radicals propose that curriculists should emphasize the "who" aspect of curriculum. This means they want curriculists to ask "Whose curriculum should we teach?" or "Whose knowledge is of most worth?" or "Whose knowledge is present in the curriculum?" Apple frames one of these questions in *Official Knowledge*, "Whose curriculum is this anyway?"[11] This seemingly subtle, yet powerful shift in questioning reveals essential aspects of the radical approach. First, the who dimension of curriculum becomes more prominent than the what, how, or why. Subject matter becomes viewed as a tool that is used by powerful classes to subjugate the less powerful who are forced to learn the curriculum created by those in power. Apple wants to upset this balance by awakening dominated groups to their oppressed status. Second, emphasizing *who* leads curriculists to concentrate on analyzing the people behind the curriculum-making process. As a result, analysis frequently takes the place of creating a real curriculum. In addition, the radicals' strong emphasis on the people behind curriculum diminishes the importance of the students who do the learning. There is much emphasis in the radical view on liberating oppressed peoples, but the community vision of what society must become is most dominant. The views of individual students are reduced significantly in importance.

Finally, while often criticizing the free-market idea that curriculum is a private good, radical curriculists admit this same point when they raise questions about whose curriculum is most worth teaching. They assume that interest groups control curriculum. At the same time, however, they reject the position that schools should teach a common body of knowledge (in the form of a curriculum) that binds communities together.[12] To raise questions about whose curriculum is worth teaching is to assume that one group's knowledge will always win and another group's will always lose. The prospect of compromise, wherein different groups find common ground, is rarely present in Apple's work.

Apple's language is sometimes difficult for uninitiated practitioners to penetrate, even in works like *Official Knowledge* that were written, at least in part, for teachers and other school-based leaders. Another one of Apple's books, however, is directed almost entirely to university professors. *Ideology and Curriculum* provides deeper insight into what Apple tries to do at a theoretic level. Looking at the arguments in *Ideology and Curriculum* enables us to contrast his views with those of other radicals and, of course, curriculists from other traditions.

Ideology and Curriculum

Apple begins *Ideology and Curriculum* with a chapter entitled "On Analyzing Hegemony." The use of "hegemony" signals that the target audience for this work consists of people who are already in tune with a radical vision. Terms like *hegemony* and *conservative modernization* are tied to a specific language that is rarely used by teachers, school-level practitioners, or district-wide curriculum directors. *Ideology and Curriculum*, however, does speak to some university professors in fields such as curriculum and teaching, sociology, economics, and political science.

Radical curriculists would analyze a school district's curriculum to determine whether it pays sufficient attention to women and minorities. If it does not, they would likely offer practical steps that can be taken to rewrite the curriculum, or they may pressure those in power to make the changes themselves.

Apple has three main tasks with *Ideology and Curriculum*: to encourage readers to examine the assumptions they hold about education, to bring about a distinctly political approach to the reproduction of class relations, and, finally, to scrutinize the overt and hidden curriculum that Apple sees embedded in American schools. Apple then compares this overt and hidden curriculum to the commonsense assumptions that teachers and other educational leaders bring to their work.[13] Apple seeks to achieve these goals by drawing upon a "tradition of neo-Marxist argumentation" that he contends offers "the most cogent framework for organizing one's thinking and action about education."[14]

The concept of "hidden curriculum" is central to Apple's argument in *Ideology and Curriculum.* The term plays a prominent role in almost all writing within the radical tradition. By "hidden curriculum," radicals mean those attitudes, values, and beliefs that are conveyed to students as part of the overall school culture but are not explicitly stated in curriculum documents. Elements of the hidden curriculum can be found, for example, in the way teachers treat students of different races, the manner in which school administrators respond to students who are misbehaving, and the interpretation of American history that is taught in social studies classes. Hidden curriculum can be found in other subjects as well, for example, mathematics. When teachers assume that boys will be more successful than girls, they will sometimes respond to questions more eagerly from boys or in general pay more attention to the work they do.

The Null Curriculum

The concept of the null curriculum is also useful to radical curriculists. The idea is similar to the concept of the hidden curriculum, but also different. In short, the null curriculum is what is not taught as opposed to what is. The idea behind the null curriculum is that schools shape the way students think not only by what they include in the curriculum, but also by what they omit. Central to the idea of the null curriculum is the recognition that no school or teacher can teach everything. Any curriculum, therefore, requires choices, and choices mean priorities. For example, if a school or a state chooses to eliminate the Pledge of Allegiance from each morning's routine, that decision sends a message to students that reciting the pledge is not as important as other activities or parts of the curriculum. Another example can be found in English literature curriculum. Schools send a message by what books they include on reading lists. J. D. Salinger's *Catcher in the Rye,* for example, is found in the English literature standards for some states but not for others. The fact that the book is not found in the standards for some states tells us something about those states. The types of books omitted tell us as much as the ones that are present. Some states, for example, emphasize only contemporary books, while others include classics as well as more recent works. Analyzing a curriculum using the idea of the null curriculum can teach us a great deal about the people who design a state's or a school district's curriculum.

The idea of "hegemony" is crucial to understanding hidden curriculum. Apple describes hegemony as the unspoken but nevertheless present societal rules that serve "to organize and legitimate the activity of the many individuals whose interaction makes up a social order."[15] Hegemony is somewhat like the hidden curriculum, except that hegemony exists throughout society, not just in schools. By hegemony, Apple means those power structures that allow certain people within society to rise (especially white males), while at the same time keeping other groups in lower-class positions (for example, minority females). To radicals like Apple, hegemonic powers must be uncovered, interrogated, and dismantled. Decentering hegemonic powers opens up spaces for oppressed groups to rise in power, thereby redefining culture and making society more just. That, in a nutshell, is the theory for how societal transformation must and should work.

Apple's work appeals to some researchers within fields such as sociology of education and curriculum theory. For practicing schoolteachers and administrators, however, his message often seems esoteric. Like many other radicals, Apple is concerned about action. The theoretic nature of his critique, however, makes it difficult for teachers to comprehend the action he wants them to take. Many years of graduate schooling are often required for classroom teachers to be transformed into the revolutionary reformers that Apple has in mind.

A second radical curriculist is worth considering not only because he is a prominent figure within the radical tradition, but also because his views on curriculum differ in notable ways from Apple's. Paulo Freire was a Brazilian-born educational reformer who is considered a hero to many who write within the radical tradition. Apple agrees that Freire is an icon. He writes, for example, "There are few people I am willing to sit at the feet of, and Freire is one of them."[16] Even though Apple holds up Freire as a seminal figure, the two differ in the sense that Apple's views are secular, whereas Christianity is pivotal to Freire's work. Discussion of Freire's influence within radical curriculum provides additional background into this tradition while at the same time demonstrating how the Christian faith can coexist with a radical view.

■ Paulo Freire and Radical Curriculum

Paulo Freire is not known for his work on curriculum, but he is recognized as a formidable figure within what has become known as "critical pedagogy" or "critical theory." Freire spent much of his life as a revolutionary reformer in Brazil. He helped to educate thousands of peasants to read so that they could play a more active role in Brazilian politics. When he observed poor literacy levels and the lack of empowerment in communities of Brazilian peasants and others throughout South America, Freire became determined to do something about this problem. In doing so he created his own unique educational philosophy.

The book that made Freire famous is *Pedagogy of the Oppressed*.[17] He wrote it while he was a visiting professor at Harvard University in the late 1960s and early 1970s. Freire's emphasis on "pedagogy" as opposed to "curriculum" turns out to be significant. *Pedagogy of the Oppressed* does not address curriculum, or what should be taught, even once. Freire's lack of attention to curriculum, however, has not kept him from becoming a frequently cited figure in radical curriculum literature. Freire's pedagogical views are mainly theoretic; he writes a great deal on radical pedagogy but ignores curriculum. The popularity of Freire's work, nevertheless, merits attention.

Pedagogy of the Oppressed

In *Pedagogy of the Oppressed*, Freire presents his own unique pedagogical language. Becoming schooled in Freirean pedagogy is similar to learning a new language. He uses terms and phrases like "the banking concept of education," "conscientization," and "dialogics" to argue for an approach that liberates oppressed classes by awakening them to a new reality, one that shows how they have been controlled by the social, economic, and political structures that surround them. To Freire, the "banking concept" is present when teachers do nothing other than deposit inert, objective facts into students' minds without teaching them to think, challenging them to struggle against power structures, and liberating them from their oppressed state. In the banking view of teaching that Freire critiques, teachers expect students to accept these deposits of information as right, true, and unassailable. Oppressive teachers use the banking model to keep students in place, forcing them to remain in lower-class positions. In Freire's words, "The capability of banking education to minimize or annul the students' creative power and to stimulate their credulity serves the interests of the oppressors, who care neither to have the world revealed nor to see it transformed."[18] Freire believes this banking model must be eradicated because it keeps teachers and students from becoming truly free, as he understands freedom. Teachers who use the banking model do not teach real knowledge; therefore, students never learn anything of real value from the teachers who use it.

As opposed to the corrupt banking model, Freire contends that educators should practice what he calls "dialogics." He wants teachers to initiate conversations with students about their status in the world. Dialogics requires simultaneous reflection and action. Freire contrasts dialogical teaching with antidialogical teaching. Antidialogical teachers fail to engage their students in revolutionary conversations. They instead attempt to remain objective purveyors of information. To Freire, this goal of objectivity is not only impossible, but dangerous. Supposedly neutral teachers hide behind their professed objectivity in order to force students to accept the political status quo. As Freire puts it, "The antidialogical individual, in his relation with others, aims at conquering them."[19] In sharp contrast to teaching that seeks to conquer students, Freire wants discussion leaders to engage in teaching that has the effect of personal and societal transformation. To Freire, the only kind of teaching that is truly pedagogical is that which is based on dialogue and that which transforms students emotionally, socially, politically, and economically. Teachers not only have the capability, but indeed the responsibility, to raise questions that lead to personal and societal transformation.

Radical Christian Curriculum

Despite the fact that Freire is one of the most frequently cited authors in critical pedagogy literature, the Christian aspects of his philosophy are seldom discussed. Faith, however, is foundational to what he wrote and did. His views cannot be understood without addressing the way his revolutionary pedagogy relates to his faith.

One of the more insightful articles in this regard is an essay Freire published in 1984 entitled "Education, Liberation, and the Church."[20] Central to the essay is Freire's point that no church can be truly neutral with regard to social and political affairs, a common beginning point by writers in the radical tradition. Here again, Freire argues that churches that attempt to be neutral only contribute to political and economic oppression. To argue for his "theology of liberation," Freire divides churches into three types: traditional, modernizing, and prophetic. He writes specifically of Latin American churches, but his views can be extended to other countries as well.

Traditional churches espouse a theology similar to the banking concept of teaching. To Freire, traditional churches do not seek to liberate their members. Instead, they seek to satisfy "the fatalistic and frightened consciousness of the oppressed at a certain moment of their historical experience."[21] They achieve this goal by making a sharp distinction between the heavenly world and the political world. Traditional churches teach members that the political world is evil and therefore should be rejected in favor of the divine. This redirection of attention to the heavenly world only further isolates oppressed classes by teaching them to ignore political realities. To Freire, the Christian story, at its essence, is a revolutionary message that has theological *and* political ramifications. By ignoring the political implications of Christ's teaching, Freire argues that traditional churches offer a theology that has a "masochistic emphasis on sin, hell-fire and eternal damnation."[22] This shallow, false theology does not offer Christians a path to liberation but rather leads them toward catharsis, alienation, and "salvation without knowing liberation."[23]

Modernizing churches, on the other hand, fare somewhat better in Freire's analysis, but they also fail to offer the kind of teaching he wants. Modernizing churches differ from traditional churches in that they teach members to accept the status quo but without diverting all of their members' attention to the world of the divine. Modernizing churches are heavily influenced by industrialization, a force that brings about inevitable changes that require elites to rethink their views on economics in general and social classes in particular. Elites can no longer ignore the inequality that surrounds them. To address this problem, churches of the modernizing type institute reforms that appear to benefit all classes but in fact only reinforce the class-based dominance that pervades society. Modernizing churches create additional bureaucracy that allows them to engage in "do-goodism," as Freire calls it, but the poor remain poor and the elite remain in power. As Freire argues, "Like the traditional churches, of which they are a new version, they (modernizing churches) are not committed to the oppressed but to the power elite."[24] The church, therefore, instead of serving as a revolutionary force, ends up reinforcing class structures by making cosmetic changes that appear to address the problem of inequality but do nothing to resolve it in any substantive way.

The third and final type of church is the kind Freire wants to multiply. He calls these churches "prophetic." Frequently attacked by both traditional and modernizing churches and ridiculed by the power structure that is reliant upon class structures, prophetic churches reject "do-goodism and palliative reforms" and instead commit themselves "to the dominated social classes and to radical social change."[25] Prophetic churches make no apology for the fact that they exist to further the cause of revolution. They are explicitly political. Potentially Protestant or Catholic, prophetic churches must be prepared for military responses to their actions. In Freire's words, "revolution is seen as the means of liberation for the oppressed people, and the military coup as the reactionary counter-move."[26] Prophetic churches have moved beyond the idealistic aspect of Christianity, which Freire argues is dominant in the other two modes of churches. The prophetic church, as a result, is more dialectical than idealistic. The ideals embedded in Christ's message must come into contact with the economic and political realities that people face. Similarly, economic and political challenges must transform the ideals that Christ embodied. These two entities—ideals and economic realities—must interact in order to form a new vision of what society can become. Prophetic churches, moreover, embrace Freire's point that neutrality is impossible, pointing out that no church can exist outside of a historical, sociological, and political context. Prophetic churches, therefore, must become a home for oppressed people who are looking for, to use Freire's phrase, "a new Exodus."[27]

Freire's vision differs from that of other radicals because he argues that revolutionary change cannot take place in a secular context. To Freire, an underlying theology is essential to pedagogical liberation. Freire contends that discussing secularization or trying to figure out whether secularization is good or bad is a waste of time that should be spent on liberating oppressed classes.[28] Instead, he wants a curriculum that is an "instrument of transforming action" and that results in "permanent human liberation."[29] The Christian position that Freire has "always attempted to hold" is one in which faith is deeply embedded in local community action. Freire sees Christ as the embodiment of this work, writing, "He was himself the Truth, the Word that became flesh."[30] Each of us has the potential to practice a liberating pedagogy, but we first must liberate ourselves as either an oppressor or one of the oppressed. Once we have taken this step, we can begin a dialogue with others who are at different stages of the liberation process. Throughout this evolution, theory and practice must constantly interact with one another in a dialectical process that culminates in revolution.

Even though their writing has appeared in the late twentieth century, the work of Freire and Apple grows out of a tradition that has deep roots. To provide this broader historical and philosophical context, we will now concentrate on the work of two writers from the early twentieth century. Considering the work of George Counts and Harold Rugg helps us to understand some of the background behind the radical tradition, enables us to recognize how the radical tradition relates to the others, and shows how the radical tradition has gained or lost power at different stages in American history.

> For radical curriculists, liberation through curriculum and teaching is as much a political process as it is an intellectual one.

■ Background on Radical Curriculum

George Counts

George Counts became prominent in the early 1930s when he helped to chart a new path for the Progressive Education Association (PEA) when it was experiencing difficult times due to the onset of the Great Depression. The "child-centered" wing of the PEA, referred to as existentialist in the previous chapter, faced criticism because many people believed that radical individualism had contributed to the economic collapse. The child-centered philosophy placed the individual child at the center of teaching. It simultaneously ridiculed curriculum, at least in the subject matter sense in which curriculum had been understood for decades. In addition to neglecting subject matter, child-centered advocates diminished the civic goals of curriculum, preferring instead to concentrate on fulfilling the desires of students. Those, at least, were the arguments that PEA members had to address in the early 1930s.

With the economic collapse that began with the stock market crash of October 1929, the PEA needed a new direction. Counts stepped up to the challenge. He had the background needed to connect with K–12 teachers and university faculty. He grew up in Kansas, earned a BA degree at Baker

University, taught high school for a few years, and then served as a high school principal. Counts chose to continue his education by attending the University of Chicago where he earned a PhD in education in 1916. Like Apple and others in this tradition, Counts was interested in how schools can be used either to reproduce societal inequalities or to reform culture. These interests led him to the study of sociology, a common subject for radical thinkers who place a high priority on the social sciences. Counts completed several classes with Albion Small, a prominent member of the Chicago sociology department.

After completing his PhD degree, Counts went on to hold numerous positions as an education professor at Harris Teachers College, the University of Washington, Yale University, and, finally, Columbia University's Teachers College. Counts spent the majority of his academic career at this final stop, where he was on the faculty from 1927 to 1956. By the time he began to reshape the PEA in 1932, Counts had published several books and numerous articles, mostly in the fields of educational sociology and comparative education. It was this latter field, comparative education, that nourished Counts's fascination with Russia. Immediately following the stock market collapse, Counts published two books on Russia, *A Ford Crosses Russia* and *The Soviet Challenge to America*.[31] Counts's broad goal with both books was to provide a new economic and political vision for America during these troubled times, a vision that was heavily influenced by what Counts had learned from Russia. In a twist that was relatively new at the time, he placed teachers, not subject matter or the interests of students, at the forefront of his philosophy.

The event that brought national recognition to Counts was a speech he delivered at the 1932 annual meeting of the PEA. Entitled "Dare the School Build a New Social Order?," Counts ridiculed child-centered progressives on three counts. First, he said they neglected a social purpose for education. Second, he claimed they reduced moral education to nothing but meeting the whimsical needs of individual learners. Finally, he criticized child-centered progressives for contributing to classism instead of battling it. His speech shocked the PEA, prompting them to cancel the remainder of the meeting to discuss his message. Counts published the address a few months later as a book under the same title.[32] Since its publication, *Dare the School* has served as a foundational text for those who adopt a radical vision.

Similar to others who write within this tradition, Counts rarely uses the term *curriculum*. Much like Freire's *Pedagogy of the Oppressed*, *Dare the School* makes only one reference to curriculum, and then only in passing. Avoiding the language of curriculum allows Counts, like Freire, to remain at an abstract level that steers clear of the specific, application-oriented questions that are essential to curriculum. Nevertheless, there is an implicit view of curriculum found within *Dare the School* that merits attention.

Dare the School Build a New Social Order? and Curriculum

Counts begins *Dare the School* by launching into a critique of existentialist[33] curriculum by asserting that advocates of this view have been too narrow in their conception of what education can and should do. Counts acknowledges the importance of taking individual students into account but contends that child-centered progressives have considered "but one-half of the landscape."[34] They have forgotten the need for education to take students in a social direction, one that imbues them with a sense of purpose, vision, and service to the common good. Counts puts the point forcefully when he writes, "The weakness of Progressive Education thus lies in the fact that it has elaborated no theory of social welfare, unless it be that of anarchy or extreme individualism."[35] Critique of individualism was in the air, and Counts knew how to capitalize on the zeitgeist.

The closest Counts comes to addressing curriculum is when he discusses the role of teachers. He wants teachers to seize power over schools, take control of curriculum, and use their influence to create a society in line with a radical political vision. He writes, "Teachers should deliberately reach for power and then make the most of their conquest. . . . To the extent that they are permitted to fashion the curriculum and the procedures of the school they will definitely and positively influence the social attitudes, ideals, and behavior of the coming generation."[36] Counts does not discuss what subject matter should be taught while teachers fashion the next generation, but he does hold firm to the conviction, held by other radicals, that politics does and should pervade all areas of the curriculum. Counts recognizes that teachers are only one constituent group that should influence the curriculum; however, he wants teachers to expand their influence considerably, admonishing them to use their "power fully and wisely and in the interests of the great masses of the people."[37] Like Apple and Freire, Counts wants teachers to become social revolutionaries who look for opportunities to seize power and further the goal of radical transformation.

Another place Counts deals with curriculum is when he discusses the relationship between moral and intellectual knowledge. Unlike thinkers in the systematic tradition, Counts makes the case that moral and intellectual curricula are inseparable. Just like teachers must have a broad social goal in mind when they teach, any piece of intellectual content must have moral direction. Thus, Counts differs from existentialists and systematizers when he criticizes the tendency to treat education in a purely intellectual way disconnected from morality. He makes this point, for example, when he writes that "the educational problem is not wholly intellectual in nature."[38] He chides the "intellectual class" for its "fallacy" of treating education as purely intellectual by writing:

> Here, in my judgment, is one of the great lacks in our schools and in our intellectual class today. We are able to contemplate the universe and find that all is vanity. Nothing really stirs us, unless it be that the bath water is cold, the toast burnt, or the elevator not running; or that perchance we miss the first section of a revolving door. . . . We are moved by no great faiths; we are touched by no great passions. . . . In my opinion this is a confession of complete moral and spiritual bankruptcy.[39]

More than anything else, Counts wants to cultivate educators who are driven passionately by their work and who place the good of their communities above their private, personal interests. To achieve this ideal, he wants teachers to integrate his political vision into their curriculum regardless of the subject matter they teach, the students they serve, or the community where they work. Central to Counts's task is the challenge of convincing teachers to adhere to his vision. With the support of teachers, he is convinced that a new economic, social, and political order is attainable. In his words, "I should say that teachers, if they could increase sufficiently their stock of courage, intelligence, and vision, might become a social force of some magnitude."[40] This charge resonated with those teachers who were already inclined to infuse politics into their classrooms, but that portion of the teaching population has always been small. Most teachers prefer to remain neutral or avoid politics altogether.

Beyond the points that curriculum should serve a larger purpose, that teachers should take charge of curriculum, and that the moral and intellectual aspects of curriculum cannot be separated, Counts has little to say about either the content of curriculum or the curriculum-making process. We can extrapolate from Counts's vision, nonetheless, and presume that once the economic revolution has taken place, the new political regime will set up a structured, even systematic curriculum that will reinforce the moral and political views that Counts has in mind. Because Counts concentrates so much on fomenting revolution, however, he dedicates no time whatsoever to the postrevolutionary world. This lack of attention to the world beyond revolution is a weakness in the radical view that is explored toward the end of this chapter; first, however, a closer look at one additional figure helps us to see how the radical perspective rises and falls with the times.

> A radical view of curriculum is attractive to some people because, unlike the systematic or the existentialist view, it offers a social and moral vision of what society ought to look like.

Harold Rugg and Radical Social Studies Curriculum

The final figure to be discussed in this chapter is Harold Rugg. Rugg began his career as an engineer, completing undergraduate and master's degrees at Dartmouth University in 1905 and 1906, respectively. After working for a railroad company and then teaching engineering courses for a short time (his master's degree was in civil engineering), Rugg became interested in the new science of education that was developing in the early years of the twentieth century. After completing his PhD in educational psychology at the University of Illinois in 1915, Rugg began a career as an educational testing expert at the University of Chicago. He left the University of Chicago after four years, however, to join the star-studded faculty at Columbia's Teachers College. While at Teachers College, Rugg left his interests in testing and engineering to focus on the new field of "social studies" that sought to integrate the traditional subjects of economics, history, political science, and geography. Rugg also became increasingly interested in how society could be radically transformed if educators would begin to reconstruct the curriculum, especially the social studies curriculum, based on a "progressive" vision of society.[41]

Given his background as an engineer, Rugg has strong tendencies toward a systematic perspective. Following World War I, however, Rugg's systematic inclinations became secondary to his concern for reconstructing society. Rugg remained a systematic thinker, but he became convinced that radical reform must come first. As early as 1926 in an article he coauthored with Counts, Rugg criticized school-level leaders for their hesitant approach to curriculum reform. Instead of piecemeal changes based on local and district-level problems, Rugg called for the radical transformation of American society. In his words, "Partial, superficial, and timorous 'revision' rather than general, fundamental, and courageous reconstruction characterizes curriculum making in the public school."[42] As opposed to an apprehensive approach, Rugg argued for a "systematic reconstruction of the curriculum" that relied upon local school leaders who understood that "the machinery of curriculum making in school systems must guarantee that the curriculum of the schools keep pace . . . with the ceaseless change of American life."[43] The systematic aspect of Rugg's thinking is evident in these statements. They show that radical curriculists have a tendency toward system and institution building, but of course the institutions they seek to build must reflect the social, political, and economic assumptions they hold.

Rugg became famous in the 1920s and 1930s when he published a series of social studies textbooks that were adopted by hundreds of school districts nationwide. Over a fifteen-year period, the books sold more than two million copies. The vision for social studies curriculum that Rugg advances in the series is one in which students are taught to challenge America's economic and political institutions. In the words of Ronald Evans who has published a book on Rugg's work, Rugg's textbooks "were, decidedly, oriented toward raising serious questions in the minds of students about the social and economic institutions of the nation."[44] Rugg's goal was to use the textbooks to persuade students that traditional forms of capitalism were corrupt and that a new economic order, one based on a planned society, must be established. Rugg made no bones about the fact that he believed in a collectivist society. He was highly critical of laissez-faire economics, preferring to advocate, both implicitly and explicitly, for an economic order in which a political and economic elite controls the means of production. The only way to achieve this society, Rugg became convinced, was to teach students, preferably in social studies classes, how to reform the corrupt institutions that he believed were destroying America. To do this, Rugg wanted a curriculum that emphasized social problem solving, student activism, and the integration of all social science subjects with a progressive vision of America's future. Rugg did not believe that there was a fixed body of knowledge that all students must learn, whether it is found in mathematics, history, science, or literature. Instead, he maintained that knowledge is constantly changing; therefore, the curriculum should evolve as well. However, even given the emphasis that Rugg placed on "social improvement" and a social mission, he never explained the kind of society he wanted to build. In the words of Evans, "Though the direction of social improvement was never explicitly defined, much of the content of the Rugg pamphlets and textbook series left little doubt as to the progressive drift of Rugg's worldview."[45]

Rugg's message of radical social change found a wide audience during the Depression, when the desire for reform was great. During the late 1930s and throughout World War II, however, the popularity of his textbooks declined sharply. The reasons for this decline are numerous, but one factor was the controversy that arose when Rugg's books became the subject of widespread protest. Groups like the Daughters of the American Revolution, the American Federation of Advertising, and the American Legion disagreed with Rugg's negative presentation of America, specifically his views on free-market capitalism. These and other similar groups pressured school boards to ban Rugg's books. They succeeded at getting the books banned in at least twelve cities, including Cedar Rapids, Iowa; Glen Rock, New York; and San Francisco, California.[46] These criticisms and the subsequent banning of Rugg's books led him to publish an autobiographical response defending his claims.[47] Criticism from conservative groups, however, was only one factor in the decline of Rugg's textbooks. Books by other social studies educators, for example, Paul Hanna of Stanford University, became more popular partly because they did not present a view of America as negative as Rugg's. In addition, Rugg was unable to keep up with the many revisions that were needed to keep his textbooks relevant to high school students.[48]

The Rugg story on curriculum is instructive for at least two reasons. First, the story shows how the various curriculum traditions rise and fall based in large part on the social and political context in which curriculum exists. Second, Rugg's work matters because of the assumptions he brings to curriculum thought and practice. He agrees with other radicals that no curriculum can or should be neutral. He adheres to the assumption that traditional curriculum, which to him means a curriculum rooted in history and geography, was irretrievably flawed. To Rugg, the goals of curriculum can and should be much more revolutionary than merely passing along bodies of knowledge. Rugg also maintained that his proposed curricular changes needed to take place across the nation, in every school and in every classroom.[49] Only radical action against the dominant institutions could improve the woeful curricular situation he found in American schools. Rugg then takes his argument one step further and contends that just about every other American institution is defective, not just curriculum. Radical transformation must take place throughout society.

Another assumption of Rugg's has to deal with his choice of language, which reveals his underlying political views. In keeping with radical writers like Apple and Freire, Rugg uses terms that identify "progressive" as always good and "conservative" as always bad. Curriculists are therefore left with the choice of either agreeing with Rugg and his larger collectivist vision or face being labeled "conservative," a signifier that automatically carries negative connotations to people like Rugg. Radicals like Rugg operate under the assumption that to disagree with their political views is to join the masses of Americans who, often through ignorance, lack the capacity to grasp their political vision. This sharp separation of the public into "progressive" and "conservative" camps ultimately obscures more than it clarifies. It also results in a curriculum that takes the views of some members of the public into account, but not others.

Now that we have considered contemporary and historical writers from the radical tradition, this chapter will now follow the pattern of the others and evaluate the radical tradition using the framework of the commonplaces.

■ Radical Curriculum and the Commonplaces

Teachers

The teacher commonplace is the most powerful in the radical tradition. To radicals, this commonplace is not equal to the others. No vision for reconstructing society can be achieved without the active participation of teachers. Whether the vision comes from Michael Apple, Paulo Freire, or Harold Rugg, radicals place a heavy emphasis on the transformational power of teachers. They are the ones who have the power, or at least the opportunity, to redirect any nation in a more socially just direction. To achieve this goal, however, teachers must buy into—and indeed comprehend—the class-driven critique that radicals offer. This is a difficult task for radicals to achieve because teachers tend to come from middle- and upper-middle-class families that do not necessarily share a radical vision of social transformation.

Beyond that, whether teachers think in terms of social transformation or not, they tend to be attracted to an existentialist or a systematic perspective. Many teachers are naturally attracted to an existentialist view because they enjoy working with children, and an existentialist approach places great stress on personal relationships with learners. In addition, systematic curriculum attracts many teachers because it claims to discover panacea-like teaching techniques that are presumed to be "practical," claim to be based on objective research, and are presented as if they will "solve the problems" that teachers face. Radical curriculum, however, makes none of these claims. Instead, it places demands on teachers to become moral and intellectual "change agents" both in the classroom and in their communities. Radicals want to attract people into teaching who will look beyond their classroom walls and find ways to connect their schools to the problems that communities are facing. Ultimately, radicals want teachers who will awaken a transformation in their communities through the power of their teaching and social activism.

> Radical teachers will find assignments that challenge students to see how those who are less fortunate in their community are forced to live. Examples include poverty simulations that are experience based, role-plays that focus on racial prejudice, and history lessons that uncover race and gender discrimination.

All of the authors highlighted in this chapter place great stress on the role of teachers, but there are slight differences that show variability within the radical tradition. George Counts, for example, pays little attention to curriculum itself, and instead makes teachers the centerpiece of his vision. Rugg, on the other hand, began his career by emphasizing teachers but began to place more emphasis on textbooks and curriculum materials later in his life. He began to think that teachers could only create a transformational experience if they had the right textbooks to guide their work. Nevertheless, the success of Rugg's plan to transform society remained dependent upon teachers using his textbooks in the way he wanted.

Like Counts, Freire does not address curriculum, nor does he believe that the best route to a liberating pedagogy is through institutions. Instead, Freire places his faith in individual conversations that take place in homes, schools, churches, or anywhere in which liberated teachers can begin a dialogue with oppressed classes. Like the others, Freire's vision of liberation for subjugated groups is only possible through the transformational work of teachers. Apple continues this trend by stressing the work of teachers, but he places additional emphasis on the analysis of curriculum using the tools of sociology.

Learners

Due to the emphasis on a revolutionary vision through the power of teachers, the commonplace of learners takes a backseat in the radical approach. Too much emphasis on the learner commonplace, in fact, is what led to the rise of a radical vision in the 1930s and again in the 1960s. This does not mean that the individual needs of learners are ignored. It does, however, mean that learners are seen as potential converts to a social vision, and not necessarily ends in themselves. Learners need to be awakened, or released from their "false consciousness," so that the revolutionary vision can be achieved. Learners can choose to reject the radicals' class-driven analysis and instead embrace free-market capitalism, but they will be seen as naive contributors to an oppressive social order.

As far as human nature is concerned, radicals see learners as malleable creatures who are not constrained by an eternal aspect of existence. They believe that learners are dramatically influenced by their surroundings. The notion of social reproduction assumes culture produces, or reproduces, students. This dialectical view of human nature, to which radicals adhere, leaves some room for learners to mold their own futures, but the power that individual learners possess is frequently lost within the overwhelming stress that radicals place on the production of inequality. When this view is pushed to its extreme, learners are discussed as if they have no power of individual agency. They become viewed as pawns who are produced by culture, not free agents who shape culture as much as it shapes them. The power that culture has over learners is one of the main reasons why this tradition places tremendous faith in teachers. Teachers are assumed to be the prime force that creates culture within a school, and learners are viewed as products of that culture.

Subject Matter

In the radical tradition, subject matter is a means, not an end. Consequently, subject matter is not on par with the other commonplaces. The traditional subjects are at best a distant second to the commonplace of teachers. Even still, however, not all subjects are created equal. The radical vision is inherently social, so subjects broadly categorized as belonging to the "social studies" are of natural consequence for this tradition. Sociology, politics, economics, and anthropology, for example, take precedence over less socially oriented subjects like chemistry, physics, and literature.

In this tradition, moreover, there is no such thing as an objective, value-free subject. This belief has considerable ramifications for curriculum. Even the most empirical of subjects (chemistry, for example) is taught by someone who holds social and political views. These views cannot be divorced, for example, from a chemistry curriculum. Given this reality, teachers, at the very least, should acknowledge that the subject matter they teach is influenced by their social perspective. Better still, they should use their subject matter as a tool to achieve the vision to which radicals adhere. Of course, some subjects lend themselves to social interpretation more than others. History is a subject that can be infused quite easily with a social justice agenda. Teachers can use examples of injustice from the past to highlight inequities that remain prevalent today. Looking at people who fought against injustices and were martyred for their efforts can identify new heroes to include in a revised history curriculum.

To other radicals (for example, Freire), the teaching of language is significant. Learning a new language, or learning to use one's native tongue more effectively, can be a powerful force for liberation when combined with a revolutionary political vision. All teachers in the radical tradition become teachers of politics, regardless of the subject they are expected to teach. Politics becomes the preeminent subject.

Context

Because of the somewhat complex nature of the relationship between theory and practice within the radical tradition, the role of context is not altogether easy to comprehend. On one hand, radicals place great emphasis on context when they seek to understand how class relations are reproduced. When understanding is the goal, context is crucial. To see how class relations are maintained, for example, radicals scrupulously analyze factors such as the actions teachers take, the textbooks students study, the history that has shaped a school or a school district, and the overall environment in which a school exists.

On the other hand, when the goal is to make a decision about what should be done, the radical vision rejects the notion of context by assuming, a priori, that students are failing due to power structures in society. In this respect, context becomes problematic if contextual experiences on the ground conflict with the assumptions built into the radical vision. Radicals already know what must be done to improve schools—battle social and economic injustices—before they consider what is taking place within a particular school or classroom. Knowledge drawn from specific contexts is welcome so long as it does not clash with the radicals' vision of social transformation.

Curriculum Making

Curriculum making is not highly emphasized in the radical view. We find evidence of this point in the fact that many who write from this perspective avoid the term *curriculum*, instead preferring to write on pedagogy, critical theory, or critical pedagogy. Even for those in this tradition who use the term *curriculum*, they almost invariably see it as something to be analyzed with the goal of understanding the sociology behind how schools reproduce inequality. Radicals almost never move beyond discussing curriculum as an institution to addressing specifics about what subjects should be taught, whether these subjects might differ depending upon context, how the subjects taught should be influenced by the learners involved, or the issue of what process schools should use to make curriculum decisions. Without additional attention to these issues, we can only assume that once the revolution has taken place, radicals believe that curriculum making should be done by the people who have seized power. We can only assume further that this new curriculum would then be disseminated, in systematic fashion, to teachers whose job is to implement it in a way that is consistent with the revolutionary movement that just seized power.

Another reason radicals avoid the subject of curriculum making is because it assumes teleology, or an ultimate end. Radicals are seldom interested in discussing ultimate ends. They would prefer to use broad terms like reform and transformation, thereby avoiding the question of ultimate goals. To radicals, society is in a constant state of flux. As a result, discussing ultimate ends is either naive or a waste of time. In the end, however, the radical tradition does not provide curriculists with enough information to evaluate how it views the subject of ultimate ends.

■ Conclusion: Strengths and Weaknesses of Radical Curriculum

The radical tradition has numerous strengths and weaknesses. Perhaps its greatest strength is the passion it generates in its followers. Defenders of the work of Michael Apple or Paulo Freire, for example, passionately advocate their views while pursuing the goal of social justice. This passion has led radicals to achieve great successes in battling injustice. Successes to which a radical vision of curriculum have contributed include school desegregation, equal rights for women, and the increased visibility of minority groups in subjects like history and literature. Many of the advances that have been made toward greater equality could not have been achieved without the perspective brought by the radical tradition.

Radicals also deserve credit for the critique they provide of the educational tracking that often takes place through the school curriculum. Apple, for example, challenges us to face the idea that knowledge is not neutral. Some groups, moreover, shape knowledge more than others. Apple wants to challenge those in power to acknowledge that they shape what is taught while at the same time awakening less powerful groups to make their demands known to those who write and teach curriculum.

Another strength of the radical view is the emphasis it places on the social purpose of schooling. It serves as a strong counterweight to the individualism inherent in the existentialist view. Especially in America, individualism is a powerful force, and radicals have a role to play in reminding curriculists that the curriculum they create must serve communities as a whole if it expects to flourish. This emphasis on social purpose relates closely to another strength of this tradition, which is the point that any curriculum must be built on an underlying moral philosophy. In works like *Dare the School*, Counts insists that ethics and intellect cannot be separated. He provides a merciless critique of the idea that curriculists can pay attention to intellect without regard to moral formation. Counts's point that curriculum must shape students morally *and* intellectually seems right on target.

What attracts many students, especially graduate students, to the radical approach is that it presents a moral message. The vision of Counts, Freire, and Apple has moral content, whereas the systematic tradition rejects the moral aspect of curriculum altogether. Teachers and curriculists who are driven by the moral impact they can have on society find little to attract them to a systematic view, but the radical perspective offers a vision that is quite appealing. Existential curriculists address morality, but not in a community-oriented way. Radicals, however, present their vision in the context of community, which is quite attractive to some teachers and curriculists. After reading the radicals' critique of intellect divorced from ethics, curriculists can reasonably disagree with the moral philosophy offered by this tradition, but it becomes increasingly difficult to defend the idea of a strictly intellectual curriculum. The issue becomes, what moral philosophy ought to guide our curriculum? not *whether* moral philosophy ought to be included at all.

Despite these considerable strengths, the radical tradition brings with it weaknesses, some of which have come to light in the analysis above. Radicals strive to produce theoretic explanations that describe how society became and remains unjust. This penchant for descriptive analysis can lead radicals away from curriculum and toward fields that are more purely theoretic, for example, sociology, economics, anthropology, and critical theory. Critical theorists can spend so much time criticizing institutions that they forget the purpose of theory is to provide a basis for sound practice. This difficulty with the proper relationship between theoretic knowledge and practical action has been at the heart of debates within the radical tradition for decades. This issue leads adherents of the radical view to rush between two extremes. One extreme places all of its faith in action and rejects theoretic explanations, the other abstracts entirely from practicality and instead places its emphasis on producing critical theory research. This problem with rectifying how knowledge and practice should relate to one another has not been lost on Michael Apple. For example, in his typical Right versus Left style, Apple writes:

> Perhaps the most important [problem within the field] to note is the danger of losing our political soul on the altar of grand theorizing. A large part of what is called "critical educational studies" has tended to be all too trendy. It moves from theory to theory as each new wave of elegant meta-theory (preferably French) finds its way here. . . . At times the perspectives of, say, post-modernism and poststructuralism have been appropriated in ways that make them into simply the cultural capital of a new elite within the academy; so concerned about academic mobility and prestige that some individuals have lost any sense of "real" political issues over culture and power in schools. For some, it is almost as if elementary, middle, and secondary schools hardly exist at all. Everything becomes so "meta-meta." And, in the meantime, the Right has a field day.⁵⁰

Apple identifies several problems with the radical tradition that keep it from offering a truly persuasive vision for curriculists. An emphasis on grand theorizing may be fine for fields like anthropology or sociology, but, in an application-oriented field like curriculum, a richer foundation for how knowledge and practice ought to relate to one another is essential. Apple is different from others within the radical tradition because he combines his production of theoretic knowledge with practical political action within his community. Nevertheless, the tendency within the radical tradition to theorize without taking action in a practical way is strong.

Another weakness in the radical tradition is that it appeals almost exclusively to one portion of the political spectrum: a progressive one. It is virtually impossible to hold conservative political views and espouse a radical vision. As a result, radicals, by definition, can draw upon only a limited portion of the public when it comes to deliberations on curriculum.

People interested in curriculum are forced to choose between converting to the views held by radicals or risk being labeled one of the oppressors. Paulo Freire, for example, offers only two options when he presents his critique of the "banking model" of pedagogy: either we adhere to a mechanistic view of curriculum making (as he describes it) or we subscribe to his revolutionary vision. This dichotomy, however, is false. There are other ways in which to view the relationship between curriculum and teaching, possibilities that make Freire's vision one alternative among many.

Another drawback inherent in a radical view is found in the expectations that radicals have for teachers. They admonish teachers to espouse revolutionary, left-leaning views in the classroom, all in the name of social justice. This demand on teachers, however, raises questions. What if teachers hold conservative views? Should they espouse those in the classroom? What if teachers are passionate about hot-button political issues for conservatives like abortion, gay marriage, or stem cell research? Would Apple, Freire, and Counts be comfortable with teachers actively arguing against abortion, gay marriage, and stem cell research? Should they integrate these views throughout their curriculum? If not, why is it acceptable for teachers to promote some political views and not others? How are teachers and curriculum makers supposed to decide which political views to express? Once decided, how should these views be expressed in practical classroom action? It is one thing to recognize that curriculum is inherently political; it is another to encourage the advocacy of one perspective to the exclusion of all others. A curriculum should teach students to think for themselves, which may include disagreeing with either a pro-life position or a neo-Marxist interpretation of history. Teachers should encourage students to develop their own sense of reason, politics, right, and wrong. There is a way for teachers and curriculists to create classrooms in which opposing political views are expressed in reflective, thoughtful, and deliberative ways. A radical vision for curriculum, however, does not provide the kind of moral philosophy needed to make this happen.

Radical curriculists also can be criticized for a tendency they have to espouse what can only be described as a conspiracy theory. Given the emphasis on social injustices, radicals spend a great deal of time criticizing those in power. These criticisms can become so driven by emotion that they blame those in power for every problem that arises. When this happens, radicals begin to talk as if those in power—meaning those who are "in the know"—are behind the scenes in a smoke-filled room plotting to oppress certain members of society. There is no doubt that powerful groups have oppressed minorities in the past and will do so in the future. At the same time, it is exceedingly difficult for one group to amass the power needed to control the future in a complex democracy. What radicals see as a conspiracy theory derives more from the organic, contradictory, and even confusing nature of a democratic society than it does from a covert political plot designed to exploit minorities.

Radicals also merit critique on the basis of how they relate to the business community. They so strongly reject the connection between curriculum and business that they alienate a powerful constituency within any society. America, for example, exists in a capitalist society, and that reality is not going away. Deliberations about curriculum cannot ignore men and women who own businesses and believe in free-market capitalism. They are an important part of the constituency that curriculum must serve. They employ high school graduates, pay taxes, serve on school boards, and vote for the politicians who have a powerful impact on schools and curriculum. Curriculists ignore right-leaning businessmen at their own peril. To acknowledge that schools should serve an economic purpose is not to give in to the idea that economics should drive curriculum. Our goal should be to take economic ends into consideration while balancing all of the other factors that must be weighed when making curriculum. It is possible to consult members of the business community without allowing them to dominate.

Finally, a consistent criticism that has been leveled against radicals for many years has to do with the kind of society they want to build. The problem is that they spend so much energy on fomenting revolution that they devote little time to the type of society that should be established once the revolution has taken place. Should they create a democracy based on the principles of, say, John Locke and the Federalist papers? Or should they establish a socialist or even a communist society built on the political views of Karl Marx or Che Guevara? Chances are many radicals would prefer the second option that, when put into effect, turns radicals into systematic curriculists as soon as their political views have gained power. Perhaps the only difference between radical and systematic curriculists is the issue of who currently holds political power.

Instead of specifics that would help us to decide which of the above two options is preferable, however, radicals offer generalizations, emotion-driven claims about social justice, and promises of social improvement but then fail to offer an end that can be used to judge whether improvement has been made. Ronald Evans recognizes this problem, for example, when he writes, "The rationale for Rugg's curriculum led to the goal of social improvement" but "the direction of social improvement was never explicitly defined."[51] Without more explicit attention to the question of what social improvement means, the radical tradition will always be limited in what it can offer curriculum.

There is yet another perspective on curriculum that differs from those that I have discussed so far. It merits attention not so much because it offers a well-defined tradition, but because it is found throughout American culture as well as in Europe. What I will call pragmatic curriculum draws upon the other traditions but does so in a manner quite different from the deliberative tradition, which is the subject of chapter 6. Pragmatists care less about achieving a social vision than they do about working through an immediate problem that has arisen. They are the quintessential problem solvers, but not for the sake of an ideal. They prefer to solve problems for the sake of making things work.

■ Discussion Questions

1. What is the relationship between politics and the radical curriculum tradition?

2. What are some of the benefits that the radical tradition has brought to American schooling?

3. According to radicals, how is curriculum a source of oppression for students and society in general?

4. Why do some radicals, for example, Paulo Freire, write a great deal about pedagogy and educational philosophy but not much about curriculum?

5. How does faith inform Paulo Freire's views?

6. How did the early 1930s provide a unique opportunity for George Counts to espouse a radical curricular vision?

7. What was controversial about Harold Rugg's textbooks?

8. Which of the commonplaces in the radical tradition becomes most significant and why?

9. Why is the relationship between theory and practice a difficult issue for radicals?

10. In what way (or ways) can radical and systematic curriculists be considered quite similar?

CHAPTER 5

Pragmatic Curriculum

SOME PEOPLE view curriculum as a process of fixing problems. Those who do so tend to be solution-oriented people who want a curriculum that helps students figure out what works within a given context. Pragmatic curriculists are not the kind of people who discuss ultimate goals or broad ideals. They prefer to focus on the immediate needs of an individual or a community, toward the end of fixing problems through empirical means. Pragmatic curriculists want ideas to produce results. In the words of William James, a principal founder of the distinctly American school of philosophy known as pragmatism, "That new idea . . . makes itself true, gets itself classed as true, by the way it works."[1] Although this quotation does not deal specifically with curriculum, it does indicate the general viewpoint taken by pragmatic curriculists.

Pragmatic curriculum is perhaps the most difficult to capture because it defies straightforward categorization. The whole purpose of the pragmatic perspective is to avoid definite answers, allowing solutions to remain workable regardless of how circumstances change. Pragmatists create a curriculum that emphasizes a variety of subjects, is based on a wide range of assumptions, and is used for a host of different ends. The workability of an idea matters more than consistency. A pragmatic curricular philosophy is held together by a commitment to achieving goals such as effecting change, making a difference in students' lives, producing empirical results, or, as James puts it, "working" to perform its function. This view of curriculum may be difficult to capture, but it is quite

Pragmatic Philosophy

Pragmatism is known as America's unique contribution to philosophy. Writers who are typically included within the pragmatic tradition include Charles Sanders Peirce, Ralph Waldo Emerson, John Dewey, William James, George Herbert Mead, and Richard Rorty. Pragmatists assert that an idea is true if it is determined to be successful in practice. In other words, truthfulness does not exist in an ideal world separate from our daily actions, as idealists such as Plato believed.

One way to make sense of the pragmatic notion of truth is to think of a specific question, for example, "What is 13 divided by 4?" Mathematically speaking, the answer, of course, is 3.25. To a pragmatist like John Dewey, however, the answer to this question is not automatically 3.25. Our answer changes when we shift from idealistic notion of truth to one that focuses on results in practice. For instance, if a teacher has a class of thirteen students and wishes to divide them into four groups, the answer to "What is 13 divided by 4?" is not 3.25, but rather three groups of 3 and one group of 4. In the real world of experience, Dewey maintains, there is obviously no way to have one-quarter of a child.

To some people, this answer to "What is 13 divided by 4?" may seem like a sneaky way to avoid a straightforward question, but pragmatists are no doubt serious about their answer. Pragmatists maintain that ideas are nothing until they have become instruments in the solution of practical problems. Because of our nation's history, Americans are action-oriented people who are frequently attracted to the pragmatists' views on truth, knowledge, and morality.

---

attractive, especially to Americans who often disdain dogma and have little patience for philosophical reflection.

There are at least three reasons why a cohesive pragmatic tradition is more difficult to identify than those described in previous chapters. First, pragmatists distance themselves from tradition, making the recognition of a tradition inherently challenging. Second, pragmatism is relatively new compared to the other traditions. It arose as a separate school of philosophy only in the late nineteenth century following the work of Charles Sanders Peirce. Consistent with the American mind-set that gave rise to it, pragmatism stresses means and methods, not ends or customs. Third, the major thinkers within pragmatism often disagree on what a uniquely pragmatic philosophy is and ought to be, so the tradition has a thin orthodoxy—if it may be called that at all—at its core. Even though these factors make the identification of an explicit tradition difficult, there are several unique aspects to pragmatic thinking, at least when it comes to curriculum, that

> Pragmatic curriculum looks different in just about every context in which it is found. As a result, common elements within pragmatic curriculum are difficult to find. Nevertheless, pragmatists share a common method of solving problems using empirical verification to determine effectiveness.

have been influential for more than a century. These distinct characteristics can be categorized, at least loosely, as a tradition within the field. The writers who exhibit these characteristics and, as a result, will be discussed under the heading of pragmatic curriculists include Ted Sizer, Harry K. Wong, John Dewey, and Ralph Tyler. Even though he is not the most well known of the pragmatists included in this chapter, the best place to begin when making sense of the pragmatic tradition is with the contemporary work of Sizer.

> Pragmatic teachers place students in circumstances that require them to solve problems or figure out solutions on their own using trial and error.

■ Ted Sizer and Pragmatic Curriculum

One prominent educator who stands firmly within a pragmatic curricular tradition is the late Ted Sizer. Sizer, who passed away in 2009, was a dean of the Harvard Graduate School of Education, an author of many books on education, and the founder of an educational reform initiative known as the Coalition of Essential Schools. The Essential Schools movement began with the publication of *Horace's Compromise: The Dilemma of the American High School.* Published in 1984, the book was the first report Sizer produced following a comprehensive study of American high schools. Sizer and others conducted the study during the early 1980s on behalf of the National Association of Secondary School Principals. *Horace's Compromise* is an example of pragmatic curriculum for two main reasons. First, even though the book is a report about high schools, Sizer exhibits many of the characteristics of a pragmatic curriculist. He does not claim to have discovered the "one right answer" for how to improve schools; he supported a wide variety of curricular initiatives throughout his long career. Sizer believed in finding "what works" and then spreading this idea (or cluster of ideas) to as many schools as possible, and he is known (even after his death) as a non-ideological contributor to a host of reform initiatives. The second reason *Horace's Compromise* serves as a good example of pragmatic thinking is found in a composite character that Sizer presents in the book. After conducting many interviews with high school teachers from throughout the nation, Sizer chose to create a composite character, Horace Smith, for whom he named the book. Horace is indeed instructive when it comes to understanding pragmatic curriculum.

Horace Smith's Compromised Curriculum

Horace is a high school English teacher who has been forced to make compromises during his challenging career of twenty-eight years. Sizer uses Horace not just to explain what many high school teachers are like, but to hold up Horace as a hero who has managed to make a continuous impact on students' lives despite the unsettling and in many respects contradictory compromises he has been forced to make. Sizer presents Horace as someone he agrees with on matters of curriculum and teaching, at least in the way curriculum and teaching must take place given the current context of schooling. Sizer does not disagree with the compromises that Horace has had to make, but rather acknowledges them as realistic, even smart reactions to a difficult context. Sizer is less interested in attempting to influence what Horace is doing than he is in describing the realities of Horace's teaching life.

Horace began teaching high school English at the age of twenty-five. Now fifty-three, he has had many opportunities to watch teachers come and go, observe countless school reform proposals, and otherwise learn the "tricks of the trade." Despite many challenging days, Horace loves teaching, is well respected by his fellow teachers, and works hard at his job. He has struggled, however, to get his students interested in plays like Shakespeare's *Romeo and Juliet* or *Macbeth* as well as literary classics like *The Great Gatsby* and *All the King's Men*. Horace has high standards, but due to circumstances beyond his control, he has been forced to lower his standards. He has compromised for the sake of survival. He has been overwhelmed by low expectations from parents, a crushing number of students to teach (more than 120 per day), and a barrage of extracurricular activities. The curricular idealism that brought Horace into the profession more than twenty years ago has been sucked out of him by the pragmatic realities of his job. Horace constantly finds himself compromising what he thinks students ought to learn with the realities of what his circumstances allow him to teach.

One example of Horace's propensity to compromise can be found in his teaching of writing. Horace believes strongly that all of his juniors and seniors should be writing multiple short essays of at least two pages per week. Furthermore, he believes that, as their teacher, he should read and critique all essays weekly to improve their writing so that they can communicate successfully through prose. The reality, how-ever, is that Horace faces dozens of students per day, many of whom are low achieving. In addition, students and teachers alike have many distractions within and outside of school—such as pep rallies, athletic events, classroom announcements, state test days, and a torrent of outside-school activities that usurp the time Horace and his students have to improve their writing. These realities force Horace to require students to write only one or two paragraphs per week. Horace's ide-alism has been sacrificed at the altar of survival. He has a reasonable chance of success at convincing students to write one or two paragraphs, whereas an assignment of four to five pages would yield little to no work at all. Horace also knows that he has the time to grade 120 papers if they consist of two paragraphs or less. This situation is less than ideal, but it is workable given the pragmatic circumstances that he and his students face. Horace has made compromises not because he likes them but because he wants to survive. He has at times contemplated leaving the profession, but he loves the students and the life of teaching too much to consider that option seriously.

At the root of Horace's dilemma is a gap between the ideal of what many outside the profession want teachers to accom-plish and the reality of what Horace faces each day. Horace is easily irritated by the constant stream of idealism—frequently combined with criticism—that rains down on the teaching profession, almost always from people who have no under-standing of what he does. Using Horace as a prototypical example of a high school teacher, Sizer explains:

> Most jobs in the real world have a gap between what would be nice and what is possible. One adjusts. The tragedy for many high school teachers is that the gap is a chasm, not crossed by reasonable and judicious adjustments. Even after adroit accommodations and devastating compromises . . . the task is already crush-ing, in reality a sixty-hour work week. For this, Hor-ace is paid a wage enjoyed by age-mates in semiskilled and low-pressure blue-collar jobs and by novices, twenty-five years his junior, in some other white-collar professions.[2]

This attitude toward teaching and curriculum is not one rooted in system or in constructing individualized lessons or in a radical vision for social change. Instead, Horace's philosophy, if that term is appropriate for it, is one of drawing upon whatever resources are available to make it through each day. Horace is much less interested in long-term thinking than he is in how to fix the immediate problems in his classroom. He has little inclination—or indeed time—to reflect on the ideal ends of a school's curriculum. His desire to achieve lofty goals has been drained out of him by the daily grind of difficult students, the monotony of correcting the same grammar mistakes every week, and the contradictory demands placed upon him by a public uncertain of its respect for the teaching profession. In the face of hearing the news of yet another high-sounding reform initiative, Horace is often heard reminding new teachers that the latest fad will never work, that the most recent "new idea" is really very old, and that everyone would be better off if they would just leave him alone. Just give it time, Horace says, and yet another "reform" initiative—this time with a new name—will come along claiming to fix everyone's problems in one fell swoop. Nothing, however, changes. Nothing ever works, except the compromised curriculum that Horace has cobbled together within the four walls of his classroom. A workable curriculum—not a liberating one—is the only conceivable course of action to Horace. Survival has become an end in itself.

Sizer presents Horace Smith not in order to criticize him but to make the case that those who make educational policy should not force Horace to make these compromises. Rather, they should change school structures so that Horace has a reasonable number of students to teach, is not overburdened with duties outside of teaching, and is given respect by the general public for the role he plays in American culture. What is most central to the purpose of this book, however, is not so much the plan for school reform that Sizer presents, but rather the views of curriculum that undergird his work. Sizer presents Horace as someone who is effective given his circumstances and who should be admired for making things work. In addition, when Sizer moves beyond his depiction of Horace to providing his own vision for curriculum, many of the pragmatic tendencies found in Horace are also present in Sizer's own views.

Sizer's Pragmatic System

Sizer rejects the systematic thinking that he contends has led to many, if not all, of Horace's problems. Sizer blames the obsession with system building on progressive reformers from the early twentieth century who sought to "fix" all educational problems with efficiency, measurement, and bureaucratic control. He argues that school bureaucracies have crushed the idealism that brought Horace into the profession. Teachers have little time left to foster creativity within themselves or their students because "twentieth-century Americans' breathless belief in *systems* to run their lives tilts the scale markedly toward predictable order. . . . Progressive reformers placed great faith in 'scientific management.' Rational, politics-free system, driven by dispassionate professionals, was their cure for the country's ills of chaos."[3] Sizer goes on to acknowledge that system and bureaucracy have a role to play, but he also maintains that their overemphasis has had a crippling effect on high schools.

Sizer discusses numerous defects that arise from systematic thinking, all of which relate in one way or another to the inability of systematic thinkers to recognize the specific needs of local schools. In other words, systematizers forget conditions on the ground, precisely the factors that govern (indeed control) Horace's life. Sizer ultimately presents readers with a pragmatic versus systematic choice that leaves little doubt which approach he thinks is best. Sizer wants systematic thinking to be replaced with highly contextualized decision making that keeps schools operating effectively, even if the larger ideals of the school must be surrendered in the name of curricular exigency.

Despite Sizer's criticism of systematic thinking, he ultimately ends up presenting his own systematic "solution" to improving high school curriculum. In the 1992 edition of *Horace's Compromise*, for example, he lays out nine principles that must and should serve as the foundation for improvement. These nine principles are the basis, indeed the system, for Sizer's Coalition of Essential Schools. Sizer draws upon all three traditions presented previously—an approach common to pragmatists—to argue for what should make up twenty-first-century high schools. He insists that these nine principles are not a "plug in program" that simply can be "installed" but goes on to make the case that all good high schools embody these nine principles. He lists them as follows: a focus on helping adolescents to use their minds well, simple curricular goals organized around the development of skills, universal goals that meet the needs of all students, personalized learning (and curriculum), students as workers instead of teachers as deliverers, the requirement that students only earn diplomas if they complete an "exhibition" that demonstrates what they have learned, an attitude of trust and high expectations, a staff of principals and teachers who view themselves as generalists first and specialists second, and a school budget that makes plenty of room for collective planning on behalf of the entire school.[4]

These nine principles are difficult to reject because they are so broad. At the same time, what is clear is that they do indeed constitute a system, a pragmatic one that emphasizes individual circumstances. A pragmatic system is one that is highly flexible, avoids the subject of ultimate ends or ideals, and claims success by the way it "works" to produce results. Sizer's principles exhibit all of these characteristics. He is less concerned with meaning than he is with utility. The meaning of these nine principles is clouded not only by their lack of specificity, but also by the fact that their general nature allows them to be implemented in hundreds if not thousands of ways. For this reason, a pragmatic curricular philosophy can be popular without necessarily adding coherence or direction to a curriculum. For example, who could disagree with the statement that high schools should focus on helping students to use their minds well? Everyone involved in the improvement of curriculum, of course, subscribes to the idea that students should learn to use their minds. The difficulty lies in making sense of what this statement means—in both theory and practice—when a school attempts to create or revise its curriculum. A reasonable question for Sizer and other pragmatic curriculists to answer is: *what* should students study as they seek to use their minds well, and *to what end* are they studying?

The most explicit discussion of curriculum that we find in *Horace's Compromise* is found in Sizer's conclusion. After pointing out that his nine principles have frequently been criticized for their ambiguity, Sizer raises the issue of curriculum when he acknowledges that critics often respond by saying: "What of the course of study? You are as vague about the curriculum as you are about standards."[5] Sizer's response to this critique is that ambiguity is not only inevitable when creating curriculum but should be embraced as essential to good curriculum making. Sizer touches upon several, although not all, of the curricular commonplaces when he writes, "Care should be taken to remember both that the details of any curriculum must reflect the community and the students served and that any 'course of study' represents only one point on the triangle of student, teacher, and subject. Alter any one and the others shift—or the triangle breaks."[6] Sizer's framework using the "triangle" offers an opportunity to show similarities and differences between the deliberative and pragmatic traditions. There are of course only three elements to Sizer's triangle, whereas a deliberative tradition operates with five commonplaces. The two commonplaces missing in Sizer's presentation are the commonplaces of context and curriculum making. Context is such a dominant factor in pragmatic curriculum, however, that the entire framework for pragmatic thinking assumes that curriculum must be rooted in context. Context is so essential that there is no need for Sizer to mention it. That leaves the curriculum making commonplace, which Sizer ignores completely. To his credit, he places the three elements of student, teacher, and subject matter in relationship to one another, but he does not address the issue of how curriculum decisions should be made. He also does not tackle the question of the ultimate end of curriculum. Both of these latter two issues—how decisions should be made and ultimate ends—are essential within a deliberative perspective. Sizer's triangle ends up either floating in the air without connection to practical decision making, or it becomes embedded so deeply within a unique context that it fails to move a school toward the ideal of a liberating curriculum for all.

Sizer published a number of books in addition to *Horace's Compromise,* all of which embody his pragmatic, non-ideological approach. At one point, Sizer states the basis for his views most plainly when he writes, "My critique and the plans of the Coalition are the result of common sense and experience."[7] Pragmatists value empirical results and experience, while at the same time de-emphasizing reflection, purpose, and ideals. Sizer's pragmatic viewpoint is especially evident in the title of his third book published in the Horace series: *Horace's Hope: What Works for the American High School.*[8] During his long career, Sizer searched for "what works" so that he could replicate these procedures on a large scale. Like many pragmatic curriculists, Sizer addresses curriculum only as a subset of the larger task of educational administration. This de-emphasis on curriculum as the guiding factor in school improvement leads to a situation in which Sizer stresses different curriculum commonplaces (or parts of his curriculum triangle) at different times depending upon which commonplace is useful in making the argument he wants to make. This strategy does not necessarily lead to an all-encompassing curricular philosophy, but it can produce popular results. We will now turn away from Sizer to a second pragmatic curriculist who has learned this lesson of popularity better than most.

■ Harry K. Wong and Pragmatic Curriculum

A second example of a pragmatic curriculist may come as a surprise to some readers because he is not necessarily well known as a curriculum writer, nor is he popular within the university environment. Harry K. Wong, however, has become nothing less than famous in the world of K–12 schooling, especially among classroom teachers. A former middle school science teacher and now a popular speaker on the education circuit, Wong earned his EdD degree at Brigham Young University in 1980 after completing a study on the usefulness of behavioral objectives.[9] Wong became a national figure after he and his wife published *The First Days of School: How to Be an Effective Teacher,* in 1990. Now in its fourth edition, *The First Days of School* has sold more than three million copies worldwide. Wong has crisscrossed the nation during the past fifteen years giving speeches on how to become an "effective teacher." He directs his work primarily to first year teachers, but his speeches and how-to oriented publications appeal to teachers regardless of their experience. The speakers bureau that promotes Wong bills him as "the most sought after speaker in education today, booked from two to four years into the future."[10] Wong is tapping into a widespread impulse within the teaching profession. Not only teachers, but also school administrators, are drawn to Wong's work because he presents his ideas as a set of solutions. The most frequent subjects that Wong addresses are teaching and learning, but his views on curriculum are implied in *The First Days of School.* To Wong, the success of a teacher's first year has everything to do with classroom management techniques, research-based procedural skills, and the efficient use of instructional time.

Wong provides useful tips to teachers as they navigate their first year. From the perspective of curriculum, however, *The First Days of School* leaves many unanswered questions. He presents positions that sometimes do not proceed logically. For example, in his introduction to *The First Days of School*, Wong writes, "This book does not contain a plan.

Nor is this a model."[11] During the chapters that follow, however, he presents dozens of plans and models, supported with research studies, that tell teachers what they must do in order to be effective. Wong eventually turns his "This book does not contain a plan" statement completely on its head when he writes, "To do anything in life successfully, you simply follow the procedures. Student success or achievement at the end of the school year is directly related to the degree to which the teacher establishes good control of the classroom procedures in the very first week of the school year. It is the procedures that set the class up for achievement to take place."[12] Considering these two statements side by side raises a number of questions, especially given the popularity of Wong's message. Why does he switch from criticizing the idea of plans and models to presenting his own? Does Wong reject or support uniform procedures for teachers to follow? Is the popularity of his book somehow tied to his willingness to offer his own model of effectiveness?

One answer to the first question is that Wong realizes the desire first year teachers have for specific procedures. Their lack of experience leads them to latch onto whatever model "experts" present as the way teaching "must be done," especially if these methods are presented under the guise of "scientifically based" research. One way to answer the second question is to say that Wong presents a model, but it is one that is pragmatic as opposed to systematic. He wants enough system so that his methods appeal to busy teachers but not so much that his solutions shackle teachers to the point of neglecting unique classroom circumstances. Some attention to system provides his work with "scientific credibility" but without so much emphasis on system that all teachers must implement the proposed panacea in the same way. What is not addressed in *The First Days of School* is how system and circumstance should relate to one another. Wong rejects the idea of a "one right model," moves forward to provide his own, and then shifts to providing pragmatic techniques without discussing an overall purpose for schooling.

Pragmatic curriculists like Wong use ideas from the other traditions, but they often do so not to draw upon the strengths of the other traditions but to appeal to a broad audience. Wong is nothing if not successful with his rhetorical techniques. He is especially adept at delivering lines that make teachers think positively about the teaching profession. He writes, for example, "When you look at truly effective teachers, you will also find caring, warm, lovable people" and "The depth of your heart determines the height of your dreams."[13] Statements like these attract teachers because they sound good. As a basis for good curriculum, however, they do not provide the kind of substance that many people desire. Wong frequently appeals to an existentialist population with his views and rhetorical flourishes, but that does not make him an existentialist. In keeping with his background, he also sounds systematic at times. He understands how to appeal to teachers' emotions on the one hand and their desire for scientifically based systems on the other. He can sound like the most systematic of thinkers in one sentence, but then embrace what can only be described as an existentialist view a few pages later.

Wong's systematic tendencies are most conspicuous when he discusses the utility of behavioral objectives. He has no hesitation setting up a system, for example, when he writes, "To teach for accomplishment, you must have a series of sentences that clearly and precisely state what is to be accomplished. These sentences are called objectives. . . . Each sentence must begin with a verb that states the action to be taken to show accomplishment. The most important word to use is a verb, because verbs show if accomplishment has taken place or not."[14] Directions like this can be helpful to teachers who find themselves in schools where behavioral objectives are expected for every lesson. Wong, however, changes dramatically and flips these views around to embrace a child-centered philosophy more commonly found in the work of existentialists. For instance, he writes, "Children get excited about everything in the world . . . ; there is nothing they cannot do, even though they cannot read, write, or spell. Yet they are ready to do anything you want them to do."[15] He also makes a classic statement within an existentialist tradition when he encourages teachers to take the position "I do not teach history; I teach students."[16] Wong seems to be more interested in identifying phrases, statements, and "tricks of the trade" that will have wide appeal than he is with offering a long-term vision for curriculum and teaching.

Some attention to the most powerful term in Wong's repertoire—*effectiveness*—merits discussion because it is at the heart of his message. In classic pragmatic fashion, Wong identifies effectiveness as the ultimate end for curriculum. *Efficiency* was the word of choice for pragmatists of an earlier age, but Wong prefers *effectiveness* now that efficiency carries less appeal. The idea that teachers should be "effective" is, of course, impossible to reject. Nobody wants to be ineffective. Disagreeing with effectiveness is somewhat like disagreeing with goodness. There is, of course, a difference between goodness and effectiveness, but not in the work of Wong. Moving beyond the rhetoric of effectiveness to inquiring about what effectiveness is *for* helps curriculum makers find the deeper issues that divide the public on matters of curriculum. Wong, however, avoids moral matters by focusing on effectiveness, not goodness, as the end he wants to achieve. As his book's subtitle indicates ("How to Be an Effective Teacher"), Wong's ultimate concern is with questions of how, not questions of why.

The use of effectiveness as the end for curriculum allows Wong to avoid the subject of ultimate goals (teleology), while at the same time providing teachers with tips, skills, and methods that he presents as "scientifically based" and "practical" in a quick and easy way. Wong's language allows him to concentrate on "training" teachers to be "effective" without requiring them to agree with him or with each other about the purpose of schooling. Part of Wong's success rests in the fact that teachers can use his techniques to achieve whatever ends they have in mind. The book is a technology somewhat like e-mail. E-mail is effective at allowing users to communicate, but what they communicate *about* and *for* is irrelevant to the technology. They can use it however they wish.

Curriculum, however, is not just a technology. Curriculum begs the question not only of subject matter, but also the goal to which this subject matter should be taught. Perhaps these reasons provide insight into why Wong rarely discusses curriculum. He prefers to remain in the realm of strategies, techniques, skills, and procedures without venturing into the issue of what should be taught. This is classic pragmatic curricular philosophy, which, ironically enough, has the effect of avoiding curriculum almost entirely.

Wong's *The First Days of School* is only one recent manifestation of the pragmatic tradition within curriculum. The highly adaptable pragmatic approach has a history that includes some of the most prominent of American philosophers. Wong is more concerned with appealing to a contemporary audience than he is with providing a detailed philosophical foundation for his views. This latter goal, however, is one that John Dewey and Ralph Tyler addressed frequently in their work on curriculum. Attention to the scholarship of these two thinkers provides additional background to pragmatic curriculum. It also reveals how a pragmatic tradition differs from those discussed in previous chapters.

■ Background on Pragmatic Curriculum

John Dewey and the Philosophical Roots of Pragmatic Curriculum

John Dewey dominated American educational thought during the first half of the twentieth century. He has the reputation of writing a great deal about curriculum, but the reality is that most of his work pertains to educational philosophy in general and does not address curriculum specifically.

John Dewey is a notoriously difficult person to categorize, although few scholars would disagree that he fits squarely within a pragmatic tradition—however that tradition may be understood. Dewey accepts empirical science as the basis for his views, he acknowledges ideas only if they "work" to produce observable results, he rejects teleology while focusing exclusively on problem-solving skills, and, when it comes to curriculum, he values subjects only if they can be shown to solve material problems. All of these characteristics are unique to a pragmatic tradition.

Dewey's views on curriculum did not remain consistent throughout his life. Of course, no person's views can remain completely unaltered during a long career, but Dewey was remarkably versatile as culture changed around him. His views on curriculum and teaching mirrored the culture in which he taught and wrote. When religion was a powerful force in American culture during the 1880s, Dewey accepted Christianity as the foundation for his curricular views, even while he searched to reconcile his faith with Hegelian philosophy.[17] As a philosophy professor at the University of Michigan, Dewey actively participated in the work of the Student Christian Association and the First Congregational Church, his local congregation.[18] Robert B. Westbrook, Dewey's biographer, writes that Dewey "taught Bible classes and lectured students on such topic as 'The Search for God,' 'The Motives of the Christian Life,' 'The Obligation to Knowledge of God,' and 'The Place of Religious Emotion.'"[19] Works such as these fit the context of the University of Michigan in the 1880s. Michigan, like many other universities at the time, was a religious institution even though it was under the auspices of the state.

By the late 1890s, however, Dewey had undergone a dramatic transformation. He jettisoned the Christian faith in favor of the new psychology that was sweeping the country. By the turn of the century, Dewey had left Michigan for the University of Chicago. As a Chicago professor, he began to argue against traditional views of curriculum, including those rooted in religion. Instead, he began to place children's interests at the heart of his philosophy. Dewey led a revolt against the subject-oriented curriculum that dominated K–12 schools until the early 1890s. Dewey and William James worked to undercut traditional conceptions of curriculum that were rooted in the humanities. Dewey was a philosopher, but he valued nonhumanities fields, specifically the social and physical sciences, more than he did the humanities. He made his case for a "child-centered" curriculum by drawing upon the new empirical psychology that grew exponentially between 1890 and 1900.[20] As was his custom, Dewey shifted as American culture evolved. He began to place his trust in developmental psychology, not the faith that guided his life previously.

To illustrate the pragmatic, even chameleon-like, nature of Dewey's views on curriculum, the following section analyzes works that Dewey produced at three distinct times in his career: the late 1890s, the mid-1910s, and the mid-1930s. These examples illustrate how a pragmatic approach can lead to strikingly different curricular views depending upon the context in which curriculum decisions are made.

Dewey in the 1890s

The first example from Dewey's work comes from a book he published in 1899, *School and Society*. The book is well known to Dewey scholars, who often portray it (rightfully so) as a revolutionary document. Dewey intended for the book to incite a revolution against conventional views of curriculum. A battle was waging between the traditional view of curriculum, which emphasized subject matter, and the "new" view that prioritized children's developmental stages and de-emphasized curriculum, specifically subject matter. In *School and Society,* Dewey more than takes the side of the new view. He sets up a famous metaphor, indeed an opposition, when he draws upon the Copernican revolution to make the case that learners, not subject matter, must become the center of curriculum. Dewey is wrestling with two of the five curricular commonplaces when he writes:

> I may have exaggerated somewhat in order to make plain
> the typical points of the old education: its passivity of

attitude, its mechanical massing of children, its uniformity of curriculum and method. It may be summed up by stating that the center of gravity is outside the child. It is in the teacher, the textbook, anywhere and everywhere you please except in the immediate instincts and activities of the child himself. . . . Now the change which is coming into our education is the shifting of the center of gravity. It is a change, a revolution, not unlike that introduced by Copernicus when the astronomical center shifted from the earth to the sun. In this case the child becomes the sun about which the appliances of education revolve; he is the center about which they are organized.[21]

Dewey knew the power of this metaphor in the minds of the public. His argument demotes subject matter while at the same time places children's interests on a pedestal. These two commonplaces are not equal in Dewey's mind, at least not at this point in his career.

We can find evidence of the 1890s child-centered Deweyan position in another of Dewey's writings, this one published in 1898. Again siding with child-centered advocates, Dewey launches an attack on the teaching of reading and writing in elementary schools. In "The Primary-Education Fetich," Dewey ridicules the traditional practice of ensuring that all six-, seven-, and eight-year-olds will learn to read and write in a systematic fashion. He argues that radical shifts in science and industry had created a culture in which reading and writing were no longer essential. He argues that subjects such as manual training, nature study, and science should replace reading and writing as the primary focus of elementary school curriculum. Reading and writing, he contends, can wait until students show a developmental interest in these subjects. Dewey supports his case against the "fetish" of reading and writing with evidence from recent scholarship in psychology and physiology. He contends these new sciences had "proven" that young children were not emotionally or physically prepared to learn to read and write. As Dewey puts it:

There is . . . a false educational god whose idolaters are legion, and whose cult influences the entire educational system. This is language study—the study not of foreign language, but of English; not in higher, but in primary education. It is almost an unquestioned assumption, of educational theory and practice both, that the first three years of a child's school-life shall be mainly taken up with learning to read and write his own language. . . . It does not follow, however, that because this course was once wise it is so any longer.[22]

A new, wiser path, Dewey argues, should be to teach children manual training skills, not how to read and write. Dewey makes the case for radical curricular change based on new conditions in American culture during the 1890s. In both of the above works, Dewey builds his case on the point that teachers should look first to the needs and interests of students when establishing a curriculum—not to tradition, religion, the economy, the needs of society, or subject matter. This new view he began to espouse was in keeping with the mood of the times. Part of the reason Dewey's work became popular is because he had an unmatched ability to sense the mood of the public and shift his views accordingly.[23]

With writings such as these, readers may come to the conclusion that Dewey fits better within an existentialist tradition than a pragmatic one. What makes Dewey a pragmatist instead of an existentialist, however, is that he shifts his views away from child-centered existentialism to a different perspective as American culture changes. By 1916, Dewey supports a quite different view.

Dewey in 1916

The industrial age had a firm grip on American culture by 1916 when Dewey published *Democracy and Education*. He wrote the book during a time when the child-centered views that he espoused in the 1890s had given way to concerns for vocational training. President Woodrow Wilson formed a commission in 1914 to pursue the subject of how the federal government could further curriculum for vocational purposes, specifically in the areas of agriculture and industry. The work of Wilson's commission resulted in the passage of the Smith-Hughes Act in 1917, a law that brought unprecedented funding to states that agreed to create vocational curricula.

Significant portions of Dewey's *Democracy and Education* fit squarely within the curricular views promoted by the Smith-Hughes Act. Dewey downplays the point that curriculum should meet students' needs. Instead, he argues that all teaching should be centered on "occupations" designed to prepare learners for a life of work. Dewey writes, for example, that "education *through* occupations consequently combines within itself more of the factors conducive to learning than any other method. It calls instincts and habits into play; it is a foe to passive receptivity. It has an end in view; results are to be accomplished."[24] The kind of curriculum Dewey advocates in *Democracy and Education* is one that is oriented toward *social* (specifically economic) ends, not individual ones. Individual needs now should be subordinated, Dewey contends, to the needs of the group, specifically those that further the growth of America's economy. Dewey argues the point further when he writes, "The only adequate training *for* occupations is training *through* occupations."[25] Instead of placing individual children at the center of curriculum, Dewey wants schools to prepare students for lives of work through a curriculum rooted in manual occupations.

To further the cause of vocational training, Dewey makes an argument that is part historical and part philosophical. He asserts that all education, even that of the higher "liberal" type, has been vocational training all along, regardless of whether this education has been called "liberal" by upper-class elites. As Dewey puts the point, "many a teacher and author writes and argues in behalf of a cultural and humane education against the encroachments of a specialized practical education, without recognizing that his own education, which he calls liberal, has been mainly training for his own particular calling."[26] Dewey successfully eradicates any distinction between liberal and vocational curriculum. The consequence of this collapse is that all curriculum becomes vocational. Dewey helps to usher in a major change that transforms the older conception of liberal arts curriculum into a course of study tied to economic needs, problem solving, and the production of empirical results.

Dewey goes on to provide five reasons why policy makers should prioritize a vocational curriculum and not the traditional liberal one. Three of these reasons seem most salient. The first is that manual labor had increased significantly in prestige, indicating Dewey's ability to read the changing cultural circumstances and adjust accordingly. Dewey writes, "There is an increased esteem, in democratic communities, of whatever has to do with manual labor, commercial occupations, and the rendering of tangible services to society."[27] Dewey extends this theme in his second reason, when he makes the point that industrialists now run America, so Americans should adapt public school curriculum to meet their needs. In Dewey's words, "Those vocations which are specifically industrial have gained tremendously in importance in the last century and a half. . . . The manufacturer, banker, and captain of industry have practically displaced a hereditary landed gentry as the immediate directors of social affairs."[28] Dewey does not criticize this change in power; rather, he states that the shift has taken place and curriculum should change accordingly. For his third reason, Dewey points out that industrial occupations have grown to the point that they now have their own substantial intellectual content. In his words, "Industrial occupations have infinitely greater intellectual content and infinitely larger cultural possibilities than they used to possess. The demand for such education as will acquaint workers with the scientific and social bases and bearings of their pursuits becomes imperative, since those who are without it inevitably sink to the role of appendages to the machines they operate."[29] Arguments like these from Dewey, who by the mid-1910s was a leading public intellectual, provided a powerful political and intellectual boost to arguments for vocational curriculum. Dewey's support was music to the ears of industrialists who needed justification to use public schools to train workers.

Dewey rejected a narrow utilitarianism that reduced curriculum to nothing but training in job skills. Not everyone, however, shared Dewey's somewhat larger vision for what training through occupations could achieve. Instead of spreading a broader vision that combined liberal and vocational curricula as Dewey sometimes sought to do, his advocacy for vocational training provided justification for narrow trade training. His support for vocational curriculum resulted in the kind of class-based tracking that he hoped to avoid when he sought to bring democracy and education together. As one of many popular "social efficiency educators," Dewey contributed to the view that a good curriculum is one that trains students to serve the economic ends of society.[30] He was firmly in the mainstream of American curricular thought by 1916. Through his promotion of "social efficiency" and vocational curriculum, Dewey no longer supported the view that the child should become "the sun about which the appliances of education revolve, . . . the center about which they are organized."[31] Instead, he now made the case that economic ends should trump individual desires.

During the height of what is known as the efficiency era, Dewey began to sound similar to the systematic curriculists described in chapter 2. In keeping with a pragmatic approach, however, Dewey's support of industrialism did not last. His curricular views transformed yet again as culture evolved. He rethought his earlier positions following the stock market collapse of 1929 and the Great Depression that ensued. The two primary views on curriculum that Dewey had espoused previously (meeting the individual needs of students on the one hand and training students to serve society's economic ends on the other) now had far less support from the general public. Dewey changed accordingly.

Dewey during the Great Depression

For a third and final example of how Dewey's curricular views depend heavily on the context in which he was writing, the focus changes to his work during the mid-1930s. Radical curricular visionaries like George Counts (see chapter 4) were calling upon teachers to reconstruct society based on a revolutionary political vision. Dewey at one time supported a view opposite of this, one that supported the work of industrialists who argued for vocational training. By 1933, however, capitalism was under attack. Dewey began to ride the wave of political change that Counts and others put into motion. Dewey began to offer his support of a curricular vision that emphasized social ideals, the common good, and radical action by classroom teachers. Dewey's concern with the vision of radicals like Counts was not that their views might be wrong but that their focus on ideals would keep them from being truly effective. Dewey's views supporting the work of radical curriculists can be found throughout his scholarship from the early to mid 1930s. For instance, in a special section called "Dewey's Page" published in the *Social Frontier* (the primary journal for radical curriculists), Dewey writes:

> If the teacher's choice is to throw himself in with the forces and conditions that are making for change in the direction of social control of capitalism—economic and political—there will hardly be a moment of the day when he will not have the opportunity to make his choice good in action. . . . I believe there are enough teachers who will respond to the great task of making schools active and militant participants in creation

of a new social order, provided they are shown not merely the general end in view but also the means of its accomplishment.[32]

By 1934, Dewey is in complete support of the position that teachers should use their power to advance a radical agenda. Dewey changed from promoting a curriculum that serves capitalism through vocational training to supporting a curriculum that situates capitalism within a larger structure of social control rooted in a revolutionary vision. Until this point in his career, Dewey had avoided any discussion of ends when it came to curriculum philosophy. During the 1930s, however, he reversed his position. He began to make the case that curriculum must and should be part of a vision of what society should become. Twenty years previously, he focused exclusively on process. Now, he contends that teachers must attend to ideals if they want to succeed. For one example from twenty years before, Dewey writes, "Our net conclusion is that life is development, and that developing, growing, is life. Translated into its educational equivalents, that means (*i*) that the educational process has no end beyond itself; it is its own end, and that (*ii*) the educational process is one of continual reorganizing, reconstructing, transforming."[33] As far as Dewey was concerned, growth was a sufficient end for curriculum in 1916. By 1934, however, Dewey writes something quite different:

> Teachers are unfortunately somewhat given to wanting to be told what to do, something specific. But is it not true that understanding of forces at work, of their direction and the goal to which they point, is the first prerequisite of intelligent decision and action? What will it profit a man to do this, that, and the other specific thing, if he has no clear idea of why he is doing them, no clear idea of the way they bear upon actual conditions and of the end to be reached?[34]

To Dewey in 1934, "growth" is anything but a sufficient end upon which to build a curriculum, yet it satisfied him twenty years before. Unlike his position in *Democracy and Education,* Dewey now insists that teachers must begin with a social ideal if they expect to succeed. His new position is that the ambiguity that comes with "development" or "growth" has to be eliminated.

What accounts for these shifts in Dewey's curricular views? How can he justify moving from a position that exalts individual student desires, to one that places the needs of businessmen first, to one that encourages teachers to reconstruct the social order? The way that Dewey worked around this problem is to say that context is everything. Situations change, so curricular views must change as well. Context is everything to pragmatic curriculists like Dewey. No aspect of a curriculum ever exists (or should exist) outside of a tangled web of social and political constructs. Logical consistency is less important than creating a curriculum that solves the context-specific problems a community or nation faces at a particular time in history. This effort to solve problems within a unique context is evident in each transformation that Dewey made during his long career. Many of these same characteristics can be found in a pragmatic curriculist whose work came a generation later than Dewey's, but someone who nevertheless knew Dewey's work well.

Ralph W. Tyler is often portrayed as a systematic thinker. Compared to the other traditions presented in this book, however, he fits best within a pragmatic view. The following section draws primarily on Tyler's *Basic Principles of Curriculum and Instruction* to show why he is more concerned with a pragmatically effective curriculum than he is with a systematic one.

Ralph Tyler and Pragmatic Curriculum

Ralph Tyler completed his PhD in education at the University of Chicago in 1927. Curriculum played a significant role in his dissertation, but he looked specifically at the subject of teacher training curriculum, not K–12 or college curriculum.[35] Tyler's graduate training prepared him to launch a successful career as an educational statistician. He knew how to measure the effects of curriculum and teaching, a specialization that made him popular during a time of intense interest in testing and measurement. Tyler became a national figure in the 1930s when he served as the lead evaluator for the Eight-Year Study, a major effort that compared different types of curricula in U.S. high schools.[36]

The book of Tyler's that has become most well known is *Basic Principles of Curriculum and Instruction*. Published in 1949, *Basic Principles* is perhaps the most frequently cited book on curriculum ever published in the United States.

Many people think that the drive for testing and measurement during the last decade is a new development. The reality, however, is that the first half of the twentieth century was also a time of intense interest in measurement, efficiency, and test score production.

The Eight-Year Study and Curriculum

The Eight-Year Study was an effort launched by the Progressive Education Association in 1930 to achieve several goals. First, the study addressed the problem of college entrance requirements. Almost all colleges and universities expected incoming freshmen to have completed a traditional college preparatory curriculum. The Eight-Year Study was designed to discover whether different types of curricula could prepare students as well as the traditional curriculum did. At least 250 colleges and universities agreed to suspend their conventional entrance requirements for students who attended one of the approximately thirty high schools that participated in the Eight-Year Study. A second purpose of the study was to compare the effectiveness of high schools that taught a traditional curriculum with those that were more experimental in their outlook. A third purpose was to design more nuanced forms of assessment that took into account types of learning that were not considered worthy of attention in most high schools of the time. Examples include social, emotional, and vocational forms of learning.

As the name implies, the study was designed to last eight years, but instead it lasted twelve. Wilford Aikin, the study's lead author, concluded that students who attended experimental high schools were equally as well prepared, and in many cases better prepared, than those who attended schools that taught a more traditional academic curriculum. By assessing students from both types of schools, Aikin, Ralph Tyler, and many of their colleagues concluded that students from the nontraditional schools often performed better in college than those who completed a strictly college preparatory track. Nevertheless, the results reported and the methods used to produce them have been a source of disagreement and controversy ever since the results of the Eight-Year Study were published. No other similar study, at least of this scope and size, has ever been conducted.

Tyler built the book around four leading questions that he contends should serve as the heart of curriculum making:

1. What educational purposes should the school seek to attain?
2. How can learning experiences that are likely to be useful in attaining these objectives be selected?
3. How can learning experiences be organized for effective instruction?
4. How can the effectiveness of learning experiences be evaluated?[37]

Despite the way this Tyler Rationale (as it has come to be known) has been described by some curriculists, Tyler did not intend for these questions to serve as a rigid model that curriculum developers must follow. He argues, rather, that any attempt to reform curriculum must address these questions in one way or another.

One important point to keep in mind when considering Tyler is that he is agnostic when it comes to the purpose of curriculum. He designed his rationale to be used by anyone who does curriculum work regardless of the goals they seek to attain. The first question of the rationale, "What educational purposes should the school seek to attain?" assumes there is no overarching goal that should tie schools together. Tyler's agnosticism is particularly evident when he writes:

> Another question with which the school's philosophy will need to deal can be stated, "Should there be a different education for different classes of society?" If the answer is "yes," then the practice of setting up different objectives for children of lower social classes who leave school early to go to work may be justified. On the other hand, if the answer to this question is "no," if the school believes in a common democratic education for all, then in place of having differentiated objectives for different classes of youngsters in the school an effort is made to select common objectives that are personally and socially significant and the school tries to develop ways of attaining these common objectives with a wide variety of types of young people.[38]

Using his neutral language, Tyler does not take a position on whether a common curriculum is a good idea. Rather, he leaves this decision up to individual curriculum makers within individual schools and districts. This quotation reveals, in keeping with a pragmatic tradition, that Tyler does not care what ends are pursued, so long as the curriculum "works" to achieve the goals set forth by the planning group. One school might design a curriculum to train students to write computer software, another might create a curriculum to cultivate literary scholars, and another might build a curriculum around athletics. Tyler does not privilege a social ideal or the economy as the end of curriculum, nor does he privilege a literary, humanistic end. His method is best understood as a technology that places the neutral goal of effectiveness as its end, thoroughly in keeping with an empirical, pragmatic approach.

The second reason Tyler's views are pragmatic is because Tyler, like Dewey, places great emphasis on context. Curricular goals must arise from the unique contextual circumstances that surround each school. Tyler identifies four main "sources" (to be discussed shortly) that should be consulted when developing curriculum, but he always preferences *context*. He is not the kind of curriculist who would support broad national or even state standards (he uses the term "objectives") if these standards did not pay careful attention to the context in which a school exists. The closer curriculum decisions are made at the individual school and classroom level, the better. Tyler's emphasis on context is particularly evident when he argues:

> In one school, participation by the staff in a program of child study may provide an entering wedge in studying the learner, in another school the results of a follow-up of graduates may focus attention upon identifiable inadequacies. . . . In another situation, the deliberations over a school philosophy may provide an initial step to an improvement of objectives. . . . The purpose of the rationale is to give a view of the elements that are involved in a program of instruction and their necessary relations.[39]

Another place in *Basic Principles* where Tyler stresses context is when he discusses the creation of objectives based on contemporary life outside of schools. He does not argue that contemporary social problems should be the only basis for curriculum, but he does contend that any curriculum will only be effective if it takes into account social problems. This point is particularly significant, Tyler asserts, when it comes to the subject of health. Since no two communities face the same health problems, any health curriculum must (and should) be built on unique community needs. In Tyler's words:

> Another illustration might be the examination of health data within your community. Analyze the morbidity and the mortality statistics. Find out whether any public health surveys have been made in your area and any studies of nutritional status. With such data as you can obtain in this fashion . . . attempt to infer educational objectives and see what problems are involved in doing so.[40]

The transformation of the field of psychology during the last 150 years has had a tremendous influence on curriculum. Psychology was once closely tied to humanistic disciplines like philosophy and religion, and the core concept was the soul. All of this changed, however, during the twentieth century.

As this statement indicates, every area of the curriculum, according to Tyler, should be rooted in the contextual needs of individual communities.

Finally, Tyler, like other pragmatic curriculists, places confidence in empirical science as the best—indeed the only—foundation for good curriculum making. He took his degree in education and completed his dissertation on curriculum, but the basis for Tyler's views was the new empirical psychology that grew exponentially during the first half of the twentieth century. Psychology left its humanistic roots behind when it sought to become a social science. Tyler helped to make this transition a reality. He became dean of social sciences at the University of Chicago in 1948, a position that required him to serve as a leading advocate for an empirical view of scholarship. Tyler's preference for empiricism is evident throughout *Basic Principles.*

Curriculum is only effective, in Tyler's mind, if it alters the behavior of students. Learning must be measured by the observable actions of students; nothing else matters. As Tyler writes, "Since educational objectives are essentially changes in human beings, that is, the objectives aimed at are to produce certain desirable changes in the behavior patterns of the student, then evaluation is the process for determining the degree to which these changes in behavior are actually taking place."[41] Purely mental learning is nonexistent to Tyler, which is in keeping with the behavioral psychology that gave birth to his views. Tyler also builds his approach to curriculum around the concept of "selecting" and "arranging" experiences for learners, an idea that carries with it powerful assumptions about whether one person has the power to "arrange" experiences for another. All of these reasons make Tyler a good fit for pragmatic curriculum making. With regard to the major issues surrounding what a good curriculum is and ought to be, Tyler's work corresponds closely with the views of Sizer, Dewey, and Wong.

Tyler and the Roots of Curriculum Deliberation

There is, however, one way in which Tyler differs significantly from the others included in this chapter. In *Basic Principles,* he does not discuss deliberation nor does he use the language of curriculum commonplaces. He does, however, identify four "sources" of curriculum that emerge twenty years later as part of Schwab's five curriculum commonplaces. Some attention to Tyler's four sources of curriculum helps to show how a pragmatic approach is both similar and different from a deliberative one.

The four sources of curriculum that Tyler identifies are as follows: subject matter, children, societal problems, and educational values. Like deliberative thinkers, Tyler places these four curricular sources in relation to one another. Referring to the graduate-level curriculum course for which he wrote *Basic Principles*, Tyler asserts:

> The point of view taken in this course is that no single source of information is adequate to provide a basis for wise and comprehensive decisions about the objectives of the school. Each of these sources has certain values to commend it. Each source should be given some consideration in planning any comprehensive curriculum program.[42]

With his use of the four sources of curriculum, Tyler is doing something that none of the other pragmatists had done. He is trying to stop the endless battles between these four sources by placing them in relation to one another. He also makes the point that all of these sources have value. He discusses each at length, showing how curriculists should consult them when planning, creating, and evaluating a curriculum.

Discussion of the commonplaces within a pragmatic tradition is somewhat difficult because pragmatists emphasize different commonplaces depending upon the context in which problems arise. We find this emphasis on context in the work of Sizer, Wong, Dewey, and Tyler. They have their differences, but they are held together by their reverence for empirical results, their search for nonideological solutions to context-specific problems, and their respect for what works above all else. The commonplaces are not so much equal in this tradition as they are different parts of an ongoing process.

■ Pragmatic Curriculum and the Commonplaces

Teachers

As in the other traditions, teachers play a significant role in pragmatic curriculum, but teachers are best if they are effective at solving problems as they arise in experience. Teachers do not teach a subject matter so much as problem-solving

Pragmatic teachers have students design their own board games, operate a school bank, or take turns caring for a class pet. Any activity that places responsibility on students to figure out their own solutions is attractive to pragmatists.

skills, adaptability, and effective action. Within a pragmatic view of curriculum, every teacher becomes a teacher of a certain kind of science. Pragmatic curriculists conceive of teachers as directors of learning experiences. This means that effective teachers have learned to manage—indeed control—their classrooms to the point that they "give" learners highly individualized experiences. The primary role of teachers is not to serve as a moral role model or to impart knowledge but to develop skills so that learners can pursue whatever ends they choose in life. Effective teachers give rise to effective learners.

Learners

From a pragmatic perspective, learners play an important role in the curriculum-making process but not nearly the essential role they play in an existentialist view. Learners, to pragmatists, are a bundle of possibilities, a powerful source of action in the world. Like the systematic tradition, the pragmatic view contends that learners are shaped entirely by experience. Human nature is neither good nor bad, but rather neutral. Curriculists should see learners as "live creatures" (to use Dewey's phrase) who bring unique interests to schools and classrooms due to the specific history and culture they have experienced. If the curriculum they develop is to be effective, pragmatic curriculists insist that a curriculum will work only if it is connected with the experiences students have had. Developmental psychology becomes elevated, but only if it is useful within a given context. Creating an effective curriculum means studying learners to ascertain what unique experiences will release their innate power to solve problems and take action in the world.

Subject Matter

Subject matter is not on par with the other commonplaces within a pragmatic tradition. Subject matter is only useful to the extent that it informs the solution of social, political, and economic problems. To pragmatic curriculists, each discipline does not represent a timeless body of knowledge or traditions but rather a cluster of information, skills, and experiences that has the potential for use in the solution of problems. Subject matter specialists can and should be consulted during the curriculum-making process, but they are only useful if they are willing to turn their disciplinary knowledge into tool-like information that informs action.

Context

As mentioned previously, context is everything to pragmatic curriculists. Context becomes emphasized to such an extent that it takes on a meaning similar to "culture." All of the other commonplaces can be (and in fact are) dismissed if context demands it. For example, if a school context is such that annual teacher turnover is 90 percent, then the teacher commonplace should be placed at the top of the priority list, even to the detriment of the others. On the other hand, if a school prizes its academic rigor to such an extent that 75 percent of the students are failing, then the problem only can be solved if the learner commonplace takes precedence. Unlike in deliberative curriculum, the task for pragmatic curriculists is not so much to establish curricular balance among the commonplaces but to find out what works to solve immediate problems. There is no ultimate goal to pursue within the school context other than an environment in which problems are solved effectively, decisions are based on "what works," and survival is achieved.

Curriculum Making

If curriculum making assumes the issue of ultimate goals, then pragmatic curriculists want nothing to do with it. On the other hand, if curriculum making is the process of finding out what works to make instruction effective, then pragmatists engage this commonplace each and every day. Curriculum making, given this second view, requires that curriculists study the context of an individual school in order to discover what subjects, skills, and experiences will transform that school into an effective tool for social change. Because contexts change, the subjects, skills, and experiences must change as well. As a result, curriculum making becomes a scrappy, uneven affair, the results of which can only be determined after the fact by looking at the effect a curriculum has had on learners.

■ Conclusion: Strengths and Weaknesses of Pragmatic Curriculum

Like the other traditions, pragmatic curriculum has strengths and weaknesses. The tradition's greatest strength is its adaptability. At their best, pragmatists reject dogmatism and any form of ideology, so they are often successful at working with diverse groups of people. They tend to find common ground when ideological views hamper progress. Pragmatic curriculists also deserve credit for their emphasis on empirical results. They remind us that curriculum making is not only an idealistic activity but also an action-oriented task that must and should result in changes to the way students think and behave. Another strength is that this tradition can be beneficial to teachers at the beginning of their careers. The first few years of teaching are difficult for most teachers, making a pragmatic approach not only desirable but often necessary. Tips from pragmatic curriculists can be immediately useful and inspiring. The focus on context also bodes well for pragmatic curriculists. No curriculum can ever be successful if it ignores context, and pragmatists recognize this important point. A further strength of pragmatic curriculum is found in its emphasis on method. The methods of producing results inherent in this tradition can be merged with the other traditions, often without altering pragmatism's underlying assumptions. Pragmatic methods, for instance, can help radicals and existentialists alike to achieve the distinct goals they have in mind.

Pragmatic curriculum, however, also has weaknesses that must be taken into account when evaluating curriculum. This tradition's weaknesses grow from an overemphasis on its strengths. For example, adaptability is a noteworthy trait, but, taken too far, it drains pragmatic curriculists of any ideal that can serve as a source of inspiration. When applied to curriculum, the methods-driven approach supplied by pragmatists creates problems. Curriculum clings stubbornly to the idea of subject matter. Curriculum assumes content, which is why the public accepts the view that curriculum is the plan (or system) that describes what will be taught. Since pragmatism makes a sharp distinction between the "what" and the "how" of curriculum in order to establish itself as a means-only philosophy, the popular view of curriculum as the plan for what will be taught is tossed aside. When operating within the pragmatic tradition, the idea of curriculum must somehow conform to the dictates of pragmatism's methods-based philosophy. This conflict often causes pragmatic curriculists to abandon subject matter altogether. Pragmatists are willing to compromise principles, ideals, or pieces of subject matter in their effort to adapt, evolve, and produce what works. The best curricular content to select becomes that which works to produce change in a given context at a given time. In the end, nothing about curriculum can or should transcend school, district, state, or national boundaries. Once this step is made, the prospect of teaching a common body of knowledge through a core curriculum becomes impossible.

This tradition also falls short when curriculum for moral education is concerned. Curriculum for shaping students' character must take into account the internal aspect of human existence. Given their complete acceptance of empiricism, however, pragmatists reject any internal dimension of human nature—whether it is referred to as the soul, the mind, character, or consciousness. The view of human nature that undergirds pragmatic curriculum is therefore incomplete, leaving this tradition without the ability to offer a compelling case for moral education. If moral education is a crucial aspect of a truly liberating curriculum—as many teachers, curriculum makers, and other educators believe—then a pragmatic view must be left behind in favor of another tradition: deliberative. It shares a number of similarities with a pragmatic view but also includes other dimensions that make it slightly more complex and substantive, at least in the eyes of some who study and make curriculum. The next chapter explores these and other aspects of deliberative curriculum in detail.

■ Discussion Questions

1. Why is it difficult to identify a coherent tradition within pragmatic curriculum?

2. What about the work of Ted Sizer makes him a pragmatic curriculist?

3. What are some unique aspects of pragmatic curriculum?

4. Why is empirical science so closely related to a pragmatic view?

5. How did John Dewey's views change over time and how do these changes relate to his pragmatic views on curriculum?

6. What are some positive and negative aspects of Harry Wong's views on curriculum and teaching?

7. What are some strengths and weaknesses of pragmatic curriculum?

8. By the way they create and implement curriculum, what commonplaces do pragmatic curriculists consider to be the most important and why?

9. What is the "Tyler Rationale" and how is it both similar to and different from Schwab's commonplaces?

10. Why do you think the pragmatic tradition is so popular among K–12 teachers and school administrators?

CHAPTER 6

Deliberative Curriculum

*D*ELIBERATION is a term found most frequently in the field of law. People know that juries deliberate, that deliberation is about choice, and that deliberation is a social process. After being presented with evidence and hearing the arguments from both sides of a case, juries always return to their private quarters to deliberate about what should be done regarding the case before them. Juries cannot decide to do nothing. They must act. They begin by making a choice regarding innocence or guilt. Then, if a guilty verdict is reached, they must make a determination about the most appropriate punishment given the crime that has been committed.

Those who adhere to a deliberative view of curriculum see many parallels between the legal conception of deliberation and what good curriculum makers do each day. Curriculum cannot be avoided. Every year, teachers teach a curriculum. The issue is not whether a curriculum will be taught. The issue is what will be included (or perhaps more importantly what will be *excluded*) in a curriculum for any given year. Curriculum deliberators also see a parallel between law and curriculum in the sense that, similar to the problems that juries face, curriculum problems are always moral, practical, and social in nature. In the words of William A. Reid, a leading figure in the deliberative tradition of curriculum, "The deliberative model considers curriculum problems to be moral practical problems, and proposes as the means to their resolution the employment of the method of the practical. . . . The method of the practical begins, not from some prespecified statement of the problem to be addressed, so that deliberation is confined to means, but from the feeling that some state of affairs is unsatisfactory, and that it is constituted of conditions that we *wish* were otherwise and that we think *can be made* to be otherwise."[1] Instead of system, individual experience, radical action, or problem solving based on what works, the deliberative tradition places the practical art of deliberation at the center of good curriculum making. This tradition acknowledges the contributions made by the other four traditions but finds deficiencies in them that are best overcome by the strengths inherent in the deliberative tradition.

The following discussion of deliberative curriculum has three main goals. The first is to discuss the work of Reid and Ian Westbury, both of whom are contemporary writers who work within a deliberative perspective. Second, this chapter provides background on the deliberative tradition by describing the role that Joseph Schwab played in the rise of the deliberative tradition before connecting Schwab to the distinguished philosopher Richard McKeon. Finally, as in previous chapters, the five curriculum commonplaces and how they relate to one another within the deliberative tradition are reviewed, before concluding with strengths and weaknesses of this tradition. The best place to begin when discussing the deliberative tradition is with the contemporary work of William A. Reid.

■ William A. Reid and Deliberative Curriculum

William A. Reid is a British curriculum philosopher who began to contribute to the curriculum field in the mid-1970s. He completed his BA degree at Cambridge University in 1954. He then taught in English high schools for several years prior to being awarded his PhD degree from the University of Birmingham in 1977. Reid has since served in a variety of roles related to curriculum, including time as a curriculum faculty member at the University of Birmingham and as a curriculum researcher for the British government.

There are several aspects of Reid's work that make his views significant within the deliberative tradition. First, Reid accepts the notion of "universal liberal education" as the overall goal that curriculists should strive to attain. Second, Reid emphasizes the point that curriculum is both an institution and a practice. He compares curriculum to other institutions/practices such as medicine, politics, and chemistry.

Conceiving curriculum in this way has consequences that merit attention by all who create curriculum. Third, Reid integrates moral philosophy into his views, an approach that has particular relevance for twenty-first-century curriculists. All of these themes are evident in two of Reid's books, *Thinking About the Curriculum* and *Curriculum as Institution and Practice,* as well as in the many essays he has produced during the last forty years.[2] To explore the above themes, the following section draws upon *Thinking About the Curriculum* and then focuses on the way liberal education factors into Reid's views on curriculum.

Thinking About the Curriculum

As Reid's first major contribution to curriculum scholarship, *Thinking About the Curriculum* provides guidance not only to curriculum specialists, but also to members of the general public who want to improve schools. Reid invites readers to contribute to curriculum reform by thinking seriously about what curriculum is and ought to be. He challenges readers to reflect on the nature of curriculum problems so that we avoid basing our curriculum work on flawed assumptions that harm curriculum rather than improve it. He contends that curriculum is a public good to which all citizens can contribute, provided they are willing to think clearly about the types of problems that curriculum poses. He views curriculum problems as moral, practical problems that are best resolved when numerous constituent groups provide input.

Reid argues that "deliberation" as opposed to "debate" is the activity that should guide curriculum making. The goal of deliberation is to find a creative solution to a practical problem, whereas the goal of debate is to win an argument and silence one's adversaries. The latter destroys curriculum, whereas the former gives it life. In the deliberative tradition, curriculum making is an ongoing activity that cannot (and indeed should not) be "controlled" by any one group of people, whether they are viewed as "experts" within a subject matter field or elected officials charged with overseeing curriculum. Citizens have the potential to contribute to curriculum as long as they are willing to operate within the framework that curriculum deliberation provides. This framework means recognizing the public aspect of curriculum, acknowledging the views of others who may disagree with our most deeply held beliefs, and strengthening our ability to engage in

Deliberators recognize that some decisions require immediate action, whereas others can wait until the time is right.

the kind of practical reasoning that leads to the resolution of curriculum problems. As Reid puts this point:

> The method by which most everyday practical problems get solved has been variously called "deliberation" or "practical reasoning." It is an intricate and skilled intellectual and social process whereby, individually or collectively, we identify the questions to which we must respond, establish grounds for deciding on answers, and then choose among the available solutions.[3]

Reid explains how the rise of empirical science during the twentieth century relegated deliberation to an unfortunate position, one in which many people view it as less intellectually serious and significant than it truly is. From Reid's perspective, modern science, found prominently in both the systematic and the pragmatic traditions, attempted to turn all problems into procedural ones that presumably can be "solved" once and for all through the production of theoretic knowledge. This knowledge is presumed to provide "final answers" that simply tell practitioners what to do, as opposed to respecting them as deliberative agents who make value-laden judgments.

Reid makes a persuasive case that curriculum problems cannot be "solved" through the production of theoretic knowledge. Instead, curriculists must build upon a different method of connecting theory and practice, one that is found in the notion of deliberation. Deliberation joins theory and practice not by making them antagonists of one another or by making practice a handmaiden of empirical science; rather, deliberation brings the strengths of theoretic knowledge to bear on practical problems in a way that is appropriate to the problems at hand. When deliberation guides curriculum making, theoretic knowledge informs practical reasoning, but it does not control what practitioners do. Theory and practice inform one another toward the goal of universal liberal education.

Reid argues that thinking about curriculum in this way opens up possibilities that benefit all institutions tied to curriculum. One benefit is that practitioners come to be viewed as human beings who use persuasion to resolve practical problems, not technicians who implement someone else's expertise. In *Thinking About the Curriculum,* Reid makes this point by distinguishing between "procedural" and "practical" problems, and then argues that curriculum problems belong in the latter category. Contrasting a systematic approach with a deliberative one, Reid argues:

> Those who support planning by objectives would say that it [curriculum] is a procedural problem—a problem that we solve by applying a uniquely suitable formula or technique. Quite another view . . . denies that curriculum problems are of such a nature that they can be solved procedurally, and argues that solutions to them must be found by an interactive consideration of means and ends. The process through which this is achieved is called "deliberation" or "practical reasoning."[4]

Thinking about curriculum in this way means that we embrace the uncertainty that comes with practical, social problems like curriculum. The systematic view attempts to eliminate this uncertainty by providing teachers with formulas that structure what they do.

As any classroom teacher or curriculum developer knows, however, no formula can take into account every circumstance that arises in the world of practice. As opposed to the creation of increasingly complex formulas that attempt to take into account every possible scenario, what is needed in good curriculum making, Reid argues, is a practical philosophy that respects practitioners but also has broad, public significance. Practice and context matter, but too much emphasis on individual circumstances destroys the ideals inherent in deliberative curriculum. Too much idealism, on the other hand, forgets that curriculum can only be meaningful to students (and teachers) if it connects with them on a personal level. A major advantage of the deliberative tradition is that it balances the need for system with the personal side of curriculum making. Deliberators emphasize the notion of a common curriculum as something that holds a school together, while at the same time recognizing the importance of personalizing that curriculum so that it impacts learners in an individualized way. Due to its constant back and forth between means and ends, the deliberative tradition has a way of avoiding extremes that is not found in the other traditions.

Another significant contribution that grows out of *Thinking About the Curriculum* is the way in which Reid combines moral philosophy and curriculum making. Unlike a systematic view that makes a sharp distinction between "facts" and "values," the deliberative tradition embraces curriculum making as a value-laden activity. There is no way to make a curriculum, Reid contends, without taking into account questions of purpose, morality, and politics. Any curriculum carries with it assumptions about the purpose (or purposes) of schooling. When discussing the concept of "research" and how it applies to curriculum, Reid redefines the notion of "researcher" to include those who reflect on the moral ends of curriculum, not just those who produce empirical data. In Reid's words, "The commitment of the researcher should be to a conception of curriculum problems as posing questions of purpose and morality at a deep level, the solution of which cannot be known in advance, but can only be discovered through wide-ranging deliberation, drawing on many sources of information including those that the researcher himself provides."[5] Reid opens up a new path for curriculists to follow, one that has the potential to thrive now that politics and morality have reinserted themselves into every aspect of our culture. Systematic thinkers attempt to avoid politics and morality, but deliberative curriculists view the task of separating them as impossible. Deliberators embrace the socio-political nature of curriculum, believing that this dimension of curriculum making is inevitable in a world inhabited by people, not machines. To deliberators, embracing the moral nature of curriculum, however, does not mean that curriculists have an excuse to promote their political views either in a classroom or in curriculum documents. What this means, rather, is that curriculum makers must (and should) find ways to acknowledge competing perspectives as they deliberate about the means and ends of curriculum. This view of curriculum making, which deeply integrates the moral and intellectual aspects of knowledge, is inherent in Reid's conception of liberal education.

When planning a curriculum, deliberative teachers and curriculists bring together as many stakeholders as possible when making decisions. Those stakeholders could be parents, business leaders, politicians, and even other teachers or administrators.

Reid on Curriculum and Liberal Education

For those who agree that democracy requires the pursuit of universal liberal education, the deliberative tradition should be persuasive because it pursues this ideal more seriously than the others. It provides a vision of perfection that, if not attainable by everyone, is at least possible as a *pursuit* for everyone. In this respect, curriculum is a lot like justice. Both are pursuits, not necessarily destinations. As James March has written, "Justice is an ideal rather than a state of existence. We do not achieve it; we pursue it."[6] Reid expands on this point and argues that any community can only thrive if its members study a curriculum that educates them to pursue the goal of perfection, both internally and socially. The flourishing of a community therefore becomes tied to the kind of curriculum students study. Reid makes this case when he writes that a liberal curriculum must challenge students "to perfect themselves as social, political, moral, or intellectual agents."[7] Reid is working to reestablish a view of curriculum that once had prominence but has since been neglected. He argues that during the modern period the ideals of liberal education became disconnected from their social and moral ends. The ideal of an educated person became the vision of someone who is purely intellectual and has amassed a great deal of information, but who has lost his or her ability to translate intellectual knowledge into practical action. They have forgotten how to deliberate. Reid describes how curriculum changed once the ideal of an educated person evolved, draining all power from the ideal of a liberating curriculum. Deliberation is the activity that ceased to be taught once the new, purely intellectual ideal of an educated person took over. The most appropriate way to join thought and action—deliberation— was left behind in favor of systematic approaches that reduce practice to little more than the logical outgrowth of theoretic knowledge. The result is a curriculum that gives students a vision for becoming "experts" who seek to control the world of practice.

A liberal education, to Reid, is both an ideal and a plan of action. Liberal education is the end that motivates individuals and communities. It embodies the arts and methods we use to solve problems. Reid notes how the ideal of a liberal education arose in ancient times when societies like Greece and Rome needed a vision for education that would prepare young men for leadership in a free society. As Reid puts it, the notion of liberal education carries with it "an image of the leader as a person having a capacity for action informed by a mind attuned to wise and independent judgment."[8] Reid describes an educated person as someone who has become fully human because she has followed a curriculum that challenged her to attain perfection in several ways: socially, morally, politically, and intellectually. He argues that the concepts of "wholeness" and "autonomy" are at the heart of a liberally educated person. Wholeness matters because "the mark of a liberal education is the ability to marry thought and action."[9] Autonomy is essential because "liberal education is education for freedom: the person who experiences it must be able to transcend the particulars of which it consists to emerge with appetites and capacities which can be turned to problems as yet unknown."[10] Reid challenges curriculists to become liberally educated people who are comfortable in any circumstance, whether the situation is strictly intellectual, purely utilitarian, or a combination of both. A liberally educated person is highly adaptable but at the same time committed to the ideals that have served as the foundation for the liberal arts for centuries. These ideals include the unity of thought and action, the perfection of one's character, the practice of artful inquiry, an ability to serve the public interest, and a desire to foster happiness as an individual and citizen.

Creating a curriculum for liberal education is a difficult but not impossible task that is both moral and intellectual. A liberal curriculum requires diligence, reflection, and care on the part of everyone charged with cultivating it. A liberal curriculum requires reflection not only on the purpose of curriculum, but also on the purpose of the institution where this curriculum exists. A liberal curriculum demands day-to-day work that gives curriculum coherence, consistency, and structure.

> Deliberative curriculists believe that the best preparation for deliberative activity is a well-rounded liberal arts curriculum.

Reid contrasts a liberal curriculum with its opposite, a curriculum that trains students for technician-like jobs and nothing else. In his words, "The antithesis of liberal education is servile training: learning directed to the acquisition of practical skills and knowledge that can be broken down into easily assimilated packages."[11] Memorization is part of a liberal curriculum, but it is by no means an end itself. Likewise, the development of arts like reading and writing are of course part of a liberal curriculum, but they are means to the end of shaping students' character toward perfection. In Reid's words, "Liberal education seeks excellence and, beyond excellence, perfection."[12] The concept of perfection can be found in the other traditions—especially a systematic one—but only in the deliberative tradition is perfection tied to personal character, virtue, and service to the public good.

Another crucial aspect of liberal education to Reid is adaptability. He argues that if liberal education is to thrive, it must remain open to change as generations pass and cultural contexts change. At the same time, a liberating curriculum to Reid remains true to principles that endure regardless of historical context. For example, a liberal curriculum should prepare students to live as free citizens who possess the virtues necessary to extend the ancient tradition of liberal learning. These virtues include wisdom, practical wisdom, moderation, justice, truthfulness, honesty, humility, and courage.[13] Reid's conception of deliberative curriculum fosters these principles in students, teachers, and curriculists. It prepares them to unite thought and action as they deliberate about the problems they encounter.

Because of its acceptance of adaptability and permanence, a deliberative approach once again avoids two extremes that drain life from a liberal curriculum. The first, referred to as pragmatism in chapter 5, rejects ideals because it views them as hopeless, naive visions of a world that will never exist. Reid criticizes this pragmatic extreme for rejecting the need to reflect on the fundamental goals of curriculum. He goes further, arguing, "It is not simply that pragmatism is unable to respond to questions of fundamental purpose, it prides itself on not wanting to ask them."[14] Pragmatists avoid the moral question of "what should be taught," preferring instead to focus on "how to teach" or "what works." The other extreme, evident in both the systematic and the radical traditions, is found when curriculists spend so much time imagining an ideal world that they lose the capacity to solve practical problems. This second extreme destroys the ability of curriculists to move a school or school district toward the ideal they cherish. Deliberators strive to hit the midpoint between these two views.

Reid's criticism of a purely idealistic approach is embedded throughout his argument for deliberative curriculum. Curriculum, like politics, is anything but a strictly visionary activity to Reid. Curriculum is a practice that involves the discovery of problems, deliberation about the various means for resolving them, and the taking of appropriate action. As Reid writes:

Seeing curriculum problems as uncertain practical problems that have to be treated by the exercise of practical reasoning has a number of healthy results for curriculum theory and practice. From the point of view of theory, it saves curriculum thinking from the blind alleys of unwarranted seeking after science on the one hand, and denial that it can be anything more than common sense on the other.[15]

Calcification of the curriculum can be found in either extreme, whether it is ruthless pragmatism or disembodied idealism. Philosophical reflection and practical action are thus brought together as twin aspects of the same activity. Building upon the work of Schwab, Reid writes that liberal education "combines strains of both idealism and realism in that while it depends on a vision of what democracy fully informed by liberal education would be like, it is also shaped by a recognition that democracy in practice often falls short of its lofty ambitions."[16] Liberal education in a democracy holds up an ideal of what a community ought to be like, but it also recognizes that we have no choice but to make curriculum within an imperfect state of affairs.

Another contemporary author who writes within a deliberative tradition is Ian Westbury. Westbury's work differs in some respects from Reid's, but the two nevertheless share the underlying principles embedded within a deliberative tradition. Westbury's views provide additional insight that allows us not only to comprehend a deliberative approach more fully, but also to make better sense of how it relates to the others.

■ Ian Westbury and Deliberative Curriculum

Ian Westbury is a professor of curriculum and instruction at the University of Illinois at Urbana-Champaign. Originally from Australia, Westbury completed his dissertation at the University of Alberta in 1968 after writing a dissertation on communication within secondary classrooms.[17] Westbury began his academic career at the University of Chicago, where he spent four years as an assistant professor, prior to moving to the University of Illinois in 1973. Westbury has done as much as anyone to extend a deliberative view of curriculum not only in the United States but in countries around the globe. As the longtime editor of the *Journal of Curriculum Studies,* Westbury has been in a position of influence within the curriculum field for at least three decades.[18] To show how he fits within the deliberative tradition and to highlight Westbury's views on curriculum deliberation, this section concentrates on two aspects of his work: (1) his conception of liberal education, and (2) his use of the German Didaktik tradition and how it opens up new possibilities for deliberative curriculum.

Westbury on Liberal Education

Like Reid, the ideal of universal liberal education is at the heart of Westbury's work. He and Alan C. Purves, also of the University of Illinois at Urbana-Champaign, edited the eighty-seventh yearbook of the National Society for the Study of Education, the title of which was *Cultural Literacy and the Idea of General Education.* The book grew out of a rising tide of interest in the concept of general education following the publication of E. D. Hirsch's *Cultural Literacy.*[19] The choice of Westbury to serve as a coeditor of the yearbook shows his knowledge of and commitment to the liberal arts. In addition to his role as coeditor, Westbury published a chapter entitled "Who Can Be Taught What? General Education in the Secondary School."[20]

Westbury begins the chapter with a comparison of general education requirements at several high schools in Illinois before turning to what he sees as an appropriate "vision" for liberal education. He argues that "general education" is a somewhat more common term than liberal education, but both, he maintains, are closely tied to the notion of the liberal arts. Westbury then describes general education as "that minimum of education which people must have if they are to live effectively both within themselves and in society."[21] He then criticizes the elitist notion of a liberal arts curriculum that attempts to reserve a liberating curriculum for a select group of young people, relegating others to servile training. He argues that secondary schools need to restore a vision of liberal education that is truly liberating because it *combines* the liberal and the professional aspects of curriculum within a coherent whole. Westbury describes how, during the late twentieth century, liberal arts professors within elite universities attempted to hijack the liberal arts ideal for themselves, rejecting anything that was professional, practical, or applied. Westbury maintains that in doing so they emasculated the liberal arts, separating them from their true foundation, which is both intellectual and practical. He urges liberal arts professors to return to documents like *General Education in a Free Society*, produced by Harvard in the mid-1940s. The report contends that the main problem of a liberal arts curriculum, as Westbury writes, is

> one of finding a balance between the demands of a specialized and a general education. Such a balance must acknowledge the presence of diversity and, particularly, the difference between those who are of college caliber and "young people of average intelligence" who might not be suited to the traditional college but can profit from training in agriculture, nursing, and the like.[22]

Like most deliberators, Westbury believes that all students should be taught a curriculum that is both liberal and practical.

Westbury argues for a liberal arts curriculum that has a core but leaves room for specialized training in the professions. Like other deliberators, he agrees that a core curriculum has an essential role to play in providing citizens with "a body of common, tacitly shared background knowledge of the kind that would reflect the culture of the community to support conversations and debate within the community."[23] Westbury contends that this body of shared knowledge is especially important in a democracy, where everyone votes and has a voice in the nation's future. He rejects a sharp distinction between "liberal" and "professional" curriculum, arguing that both are necessary if a curriculum is to be truly liberating in a personal and social sense. In his words, "To ensure that the curriculum of a general education is a curriculum for all, the curriculum must be a curriculum for all up to some point in the school—and the core of that curriculum for all must continue to be a curriculum for all to the termination of mass education."[24] By taking this position, Westbury demonstrates several key aspects of the deliberative tradition. First, he acknowledges that all students are different, but he also recognizes their commonalities. Second, he indicates that curriculum contains ideals that hold communities together, but it also has a pragmatic side that takes into account specific school realities. Third, his position assumes that a democratic state is the best political regime in which to establish a universal core curriculum. Finally, he provides some guidance as far as what the elements of a core curriculum ought to be, but he also stresses that the liberal arts ideal is more of a vision than a set of specific courses. As he puts it, "The forms of liberal education are never settled and have always been directed toward notions of how people *should* relate to the societies in which they live."[25] The truth of this statement is nowhere more apparent than in another aspect of Westbury's work that stretches beyond the United States to Germany. In his second major contribution to the deliberative tradition, Westbury connects deliberation to the German ideals of Bildung and Didaktik. In doing so, he provides a way for students of American curriculum to renew and enrich their work.

Westbury on Bildung, Didaktik, and Curriculum

Perhaps due to his emigration from Australia to the United States, Westbury's work has an international dimension that makes it broad. The most notable contribution of Westbury's in this regard is a book he coedited in 2000 with Stefan Hopmann of Norway and Kurt Riquarts of Germany. Entitled *Teaching as a Reflective Practice: The German Didaktik Tradition,* the book builds connections between German ways of thinking about curriculum, teaching, and teacher education with views found in America. In Westbury's chapter, "Teaching as a Reflective Practice: What Might Didaktik Teach Curriculum?," he uncovers weaknesses in American curriculum and then shows how the Didaktik tradition has the potential to resolve them. Westbury answers the "What is Didaktik?" question by pointing out that Didaktik and American curriculum are concerned with the same issues but address them in distinct ways. Both discuss the goals of teaching and learning, the subject of teacher education, the topics and contents of the curriculum, the most appropriate methods of teaching, and the ways in which teaching and learning can be evaluated. The two countries resolve these issues, however, in different ways. The systematic tradition, emphasizing *organization* and *system,* has dominated American curriculum since the early 1900s. Westbury notes how most Americans conceive of curriculum as "the task of building systems of schools that have as an important part of their overall organizational framework a 'curriculum-as-manual,' containing the templates for coverage and methods that are seen as guiding, directing, or controlling a school's, or a school system's, day-by-day classroom work."[26] Westbury goes on to argue that, in America, "what is essential is the idea that public control of the schools means that . . . teachers as employees of the school system have been, and are, expected to 'implement'

their system's curricula . . . just as a system's business officials are expected to implement a system's accounting procedures."[27] Westbury describes this quintessentially American
view of curriculum in order to contrast it with the Didaktik
tradition, which he contends offers something richer.

Westbury explains how the Didaktik tradition does not
view teachers as technicians whose job is to implement the
plans of curriculum experts. Rather, in Germany, teachers
are "guaranteed professional autonomy" that provides them
with freedom to teach "without control by a curriculum in
the American sense."[28] Of course, the German state curriculum, called the *Lehrplan,* does describe specific content that
teachers should teach. The nature of subject matter found in
Lehrplan, however, differs sharply from the way "content" is
understood at least within one tradition, the systematic. Subject matter within the *Lehrplan* curriculum is "an authoritative selection from cultural traditions that can only become
educative as it is interpreted and given life by teachers."[29]
Didaktik is the art of translating subject matter into a cultural and educative force in classrooms. Teachers are viewed
as "normatively directed by the elusive concept of *Bildung,*
or formation, and by the ways of thinking found in the 'art'
of Didaktik."[30] The concept of teaching as an art has not
influenced curriculum or pedagogy in the United States for
many decades. The attempt to turn curriculum making into
a science took over pedagogical philosophy in the United
States more than a century ago.[31] As the idea of curriculum
as a systems problem gained power, art as a guiding factor
in curriculum and teaching was banished as vague, soft, and
immeasurable.

To correct this problem and to reintroduce a more
humanistic approach to curriculum, Westbury argues that
the time is right to look to Didaktik and the way it combines
system and art in a thoughtful way. As in Reid's work, we
once again find a view of curriculum that combines the moral
and intellectual aspects of knowledge. Teachers and curriculum makers, to Westbury, are normative agents who shape
students' character; they are not just technicians who deliver
information. Teachers are not limited to focusing on how to
teach, or even on what to teach. Teachers within the Didaktik tradition, rather, are expected to think seriously about the
what, the *how*, and the *why* of teaching as they concentrate
on "*their* teaching of *their* students in *their* classrooms."[32]
Didaktik is about human beings who take the state-endorsed

Lehrplan and translate it into classroom action in a way that students begin to understand and appreciate the traditions, culture, and literature of Germany. The concept of human interaction is essential to the art of Didaktik.

In addition to Didaktik, the ideal of Bildung is foundational to understanding Westbury's argument. Bildung comes from the word *bilden*, meaning "to form" or "to shape." Didaktik can be understood loosely as the art of teaching, whereas Bildung is the end toward which this art is practiced. Bildung provides the vision for what teachers ought to achieve, and Didaktik serves as the means used to achieve it. Teachers operating within the Bildung and Didaktik traditions have the responsibility to shape students internally so that they become self-directed moral agents who contribute to the public good. Within the Bildung tradition, teaching without spiritual formation is not teaching at all. Without the formation of character, training might take place, but not teaching. Bildung is the ideal that teachers should keep in mind as they translate subject matter into meaningful curriculum. Subject matter becomes a means and not an end. In Westbury's words, "Didaktik, with its starting point in a vision of the teacher transforming the bodies of content reflected in a *Lehrplan* into an educative subject matter for the classroom, has developed rich frameworks for thinking about education . . . and the reflective *transformation* of subject material into teaching."[33] Putting the point succinctly, Westbury writes, "It [Didaktik] is a teacher's rather than policymaker's or system administrator's framework."[34]

> Deliberators avoid the extremes that come with the long-standing debate between "liberal" and "professional" curriculum. To avoid the pitfalls that come with these extremes, deliberators focus on the *character* that should be the result of a high-quality curriculum.

Although Westbury does not draw direct connections between curriculum deliberation and Didaktik, the parallels are undeniable. In both traditions, teachers are seen as human beings who serve as moral and intellectual role models for their students. In addition, teaching requires the successful translation of a plan (or ideal) into classroom action. Curriculum making, moreover, requires attention to moral, intellectual, and spiritual forms of knowledge. Finally, the most appropriate method for integrating not only morality and intellect but also theory and practice is deliberation. In Westbury's words, "For Didaktik . . . it is the individual teacher who nurtures the *self-formation* that is at the heart of Bildung: Human individuality can be nurtured only by people—no abstracted and institutional 'system' can support individual, interior formation."[35] Westbury goes on to conclude that "Didaktik seeks to explicate, and then find a usable framework for thinking about, teacherly reflection and deliberation around such a task."[36] By opening up American curriculists to these forms of thinking, Westbury accomplishes at least three tasks. He critiques the excesses of systematic curriculum, he demonstrates how curriculum can be conceived more richly (in at least one other country), and he opens up new avenues for curriculum thought in the United States.

Both Westbury and Reid would acknowledge, however, that their work has not been the most influential within the deliberative tradition. That title belongs to Joseph Schwab, who inaugurated the deliberative tradition almost single-handedly about forty years ago. Careful attention to Schwab's scholarship, especially his "Practical" papers, is essential to understanding a deliberative tradition.

■ Background on Deliberative Curriculum

Joseph Schwab's Challenge to Curriculum

Joseph Schwab was a longtime professor of natural sciences and education at the University of Chicago. He arrived at Chicago in 1924 as a student at the age of fifteen and remained there for the rest of his life, retiring in 1973 at the age of sixty-four. He was deeply influenced by the sense of community that held the relatively small University of Chicago together. His BA degree combined English literature and physics, and his PhD degree, which he completed in 1939, was in genetics. Schwab became famous for his impact as a classroom teacher and also for his role as the principal designer of Chicago's core curriculum in the sciences. Schwab was a scientist but also a humanist who integrated all forms of knowledge toward the goal of shaping students morally. He was the antithesis of a scientist who attempts to separate "facts" from "values" in order to produce objective information and nothing else. Like other deliberative curriculists, Schwab thought separating the two was impossible.

Schwab valued discussion and literature as much as he did laboratory science. Westbury and Neil Wilkof make this case in their introduction to Schwab's collected works, "He [Schwab] believed in discussion teaching, in the potential importance of the Great Books, and in the tractability of science for general education; he was passionately concerned with the relationships between science, values, and education."[37] Unlike many scientists who see their lab as the

The University of Chicago and the Field of Education

Since its founding in 1892, the University of Chicago has been a powerful source of scholarship in the field of education in general and curriculum in particular. Founded by the American Baptist Education Association with funding from John D. Rockefeller, the University of Chicago was established with the goal of combining high-quality undergraduate education with an emphasis on research similar to what was found in the burgeoning German research universities of the time. The university's interest in education as a field of study took a major step forward in 1896 when John Dewey joined the faculty as a professor of philosophy, psychology, and pedagogy. The search for a "science of education" was immensely popular during this time, and the University of Chicago was one of the first universities to dedicate major resources to this effort. Dewey helped to launch Chicago's Laboratory School, which provided the university with a way to study children scientifically. Dewey left Chicago in 1906, but the university's emphasis on contributing to the field of education continues to this day. As evidenced from many of the names included in this book—for example, Dewey, Ralph Tyler, Joseph Schwab, and Richard McKeon—some of the best thinking and writing on curriculum has been produced at the University of Chicago.

only route to success, Schwab turned his back on a career as a research scientist in order to focus on curriculum, liberal education, and the role of science in undergraduate education. Schwab became friends with an author discussed in the pragmatic chapter, Ralph Tyler, who convinced Schwab to teach in Chicago's Department of Education. Following his involvement with reforms in K–12 science curriculum after the launch of *Sputnik* in the late 1950s, Schwab began to write increasingly on curriculum. He studied the existing literature within the field and was not impressed; this realization led him to deliver a far-reaching critique.

In 1969, Schwab gave the deliberative tradition in the United States a major thrust with his article "The Practical: A Language for Curriculum."[38] He challenged the field to find new ways of thinking and acting, or face certain death. His famous "the field of curriculum is moribund" statement served as a wake-up call to curriculists who had been following lines of thinking that Schwab argued had damaged the field and American schooling as a whole.[39]

The dominant mind-set against which Schwab argued is the one referred to as systematic in chapter 2. He sought to move the curriculum field away from a preoccupation

Curriculum Reform following *Sputnik*

Joseph Schwab was heavily involved in the curriculum reform movements that began following the launch of *Sputnik* by the Russians in 1957. *Sputnik*, a small satellite, orbited the earth for only a short time, but Russia's success with its launch was enough to cause something close to educational panic in the United States. The federal government suddenly became involved in initiatives that would produce more scientists, with the overall goal of competing more effectively with the Russians. Congress had created the National Science Foundation (NSF) in 1950, but following *Sputnik* curriculum reform rose to the top of the foundation's priority list. Many political leaders saw the launch of *Sputnik* as clear evidence that America had fallen behind educationally. Something had to be done.

With NSF funding, committees were formed to rewrite high school curriculum in the fields of physics, biology, and chemistry. Schwab was chosen to play a leadership role in the rewriting of the biology curriculum because of his background as a biologist, his reputation as an excellent teacher, and his interest in curriculum. Called the Biological Sciences Curriculum Study (BSCS), the group consisted almost entirely of university-based biologists, a situation that created a significant gap between the expectations of university professors and the world of high school biology teachers. Much of Schwab's writing on curriculum in the late 1960s and 1970s grows out of his experiences rewriting biology curriculum with the BSCS.

with system to one that emphasizes deliberation. The most important distinction Schwab makes to further his case is between what he calls the "theoretic" and the "practical." Schwab argues that curriculists had focused exclusively on curriculum making as a theoretic activity, when, in reality, it is a practical one. By "theoretic," Schwab means an activity that has understanding or explanation as its goal, not action. The world of the "practical," as opposed to the world of the theoretic, seeks not just to understand, but to *act* in the social world toward a desired end. Curriculists had improperly assumed that curriculum—and by extension curriculum making—were theoretic activities in which *understanding* is sufficient as an end, as opposed to practical ones in which *action* is the goal. In their attempt to model themselves after positivistic scientists, curriculists had failed to create a body of identifiable knowledge, forgotten the humanistic roots that are the basis of good curriculum making, and lost their ability to link understanding with action through deliberation.

Another way to understand Schwab's point is to look at the distinction he draws between "states of mind" and "states of affairs." These two states are linked to two modes of inquiry: theoretic and practical. Theoretic inquiry deals with states of mind, whereas practical inquiry deals with states of affairs. The end of theoretic inquiry is to influence the way people think about an object of study, for example, the structure of an atom. A recently produced study in the field of atomic theory may yield results that change the way physicists *think* about the atom, but this information does not necessarily change the way they (or we) act. Our minds may change but not much else. Practical inquiry, on the other hand, deals with states of affairs that, by definition, exist within the social and political world. Schwab shows that there is an art to determining action within a state of affairs, and this art is of the utmost significance to teachers and curriculum makers.

The goal of Schwab's first Practical paper is to make the case that curriculum is a form of practical inquiry that exists to do something within a state of affairs. Furthermore, he argues that deliberation is the central method curriculists should use as they do their work. As Schwab writes, "Curriculum is brought to bear not on ideal or abstract representatives but on the real thing, on the concrete case in all its completeness and with all its differences from all other concrete cases on which the theoretic abstraction is silent."[40] Theoretic inquiry attempts to abstract itself from specific circumstances, but Schwab's experience as a teacher and student of curriculum convinced him that particulars are always foundational to good curriculum making. Teachers do not teach a generalized version of "the sixth-grade student" or "the gifted learner," but rather Michael during third period science class in Waxahachie, Texas. The point that curriculum is a practical art does not mean that generalized knowledge is irrelevant. It means, rather, that theoretic information is only one factor that should inform teachers and curriculum makers as they practice their craft.

Instead of devoting their attention to the creation of a systematic science that is illusory at best, Schwab argues that curriculists should renew what he refers to as the "arts of the practical." These arts include writing, listening, speaking, persuading, and leading. They build upon the ancient tradition of the *artes liberales*, or the seven liberal arts, that gave meaning and purpose to curriculum prior to the modern period. Schwab wants curriculists to embody the arts of the practical so that they can become an influential force in the effort to achieve universal liberal education. Following the path of deliberative curriculum does not mean that curriculists cease to be "scientists," but it does mean that they subordinate their desire for a systematic science to their role as civic-minded leaders who serve the public interest. Schwab transforms curriculists from statistics-minded behavioral psychologists into well-schooled, philosophically informed public servants who shape communities toward civic virtue. This was not a minor challenge, and the curriculum field continues to wrestle with Schwab's critique.

Schwab and Deliberation

Beyond his distinction between theoretic and practical inquiry, the second most significant aspect of Schwab's first Practical paper is his discussion of deliberation. He wants curriculists to be educators, not just experts who understand, for example, how children learn. In Schwab's words:

> Deliberation is complex and arduous. It treats both ends and means and must treat them as mutually determining one another. It must try to identify, with respect to both, what facts may be relevant. It must try to ascertain the relevant facts in the concrete case. It must try to identify the desiderata in the case. It must generate alternative solutions. . . . It must then weigh alternatives and their costs and consequences against one another and choose, not the right alternative, for there *is* no such thing, but the best one.[41]

Deliberation means using our reasoning abilities to imagine alternatives that will move a state of affairs in the direction we want it to go. In Schwab's hands, deliberation is a deeply human activity that accepts the fact that curriculum making takes place within an imperfect world. There will never be a perfect curriculum or a perfect teacher. That does not mean, however, that teachers and curriculum makers cease to strive toward perfection. The ideal of a perfected character who knows how and why to practice the *artes liberales* is essential to Schwab's vision. He couples this vision with the art of deliberation as the means to achieving it. He recognizes that the shift for which he is calling is not minor, but he also acknowledges that the consequences for not doing so are substantial. As he puts it:

The education of educators to participate in this deliberative process will be neither easy nor quickly achieved. The education of the present generation of specialist researchers to speak to the schools and to one another will doubtless be hardest of all, and on this hardest problem I have no suggestion to make. But we could begin within two years to initiate the preparation of teachers, supervisors, curriculum makers, and graduate students of education in the uses and arts of deliberation—and we should.[42]

Schwab connects the curriculum field to a tradition that stretches back through the Middle Ages to ancient Rome and eventually to Aristotle. As a geneticist, he recognized the significant contributions that modern science has made to contemporary life, but he also knows its boundaries. In order for the field of curriculum to thrive, Schwab argues that the time has come to downplay positivistic science and instead look to ancient traditions of human inquiry for guidance. One of the main reasons Schwab was able to make this argument was because of the university context in which he was working. The University of Chicago has always been an institution that has great respect for the teaching of ancient and classical texts. As a scientist and advocate of teaching Great Books, Schwab was right at home at Chicago. One figure at the university in particular, Richard McKeon, had an especially strong influence on Schwab's work. To provide additional insight into the roots of the deliberative tradition, it is to McKeon that we now turn.

Richard McKeon: Rhetoric and Humanity in the Curriculum

At the University of Chicago, Richard McKeon was to the humanities core curriculum what Joseph Schwab was to the science core. McKeon and Schwab worked closely together during the heyday of Chicago's core curriculum, when Robert Maynard Hutchins was the university's president. Prior to arriving as a visiting professor of history at Chicago in 1934, McKeon had earned all three of his degrees at Columbia University. He studied literature and philosophy, completing his PhD with a dissertation on Spinoza in 1922. McKeon also spent time during the 1920s studying medieval philosophy in Paris, an experience that helped him to connect his views to premodern thinkers like Cicero, Quintilian, Plato, and Aristotle. McKeon is sometimes referred to as an American Aristotle, a title that perhaps narrows him somewhat, but is nonetheless accurate. He published one of the most well-known introductions to Aristotle's works, a text that did a great deal to popularize Aristotle in the United States.[43] McKeon was serving as a professor of philosophy at Columbia in the early 1930s when Hutchins recruited him to Chicago to reconstruct Chicago's core curriculum. In 1935, only one year after he arrived at Chicago, McKeon became dean of the university's Humanities Division. He also held appointments in the departments of Greek and philosophy.[44] Since Chicago was such a community-oriented institution and because both of them were instrumental in the restructuring of Chicago's core curriculum, McKeon and Schwab influenced one another significantly. Schwab's efforts to move the curriculum field toward premodern conceptions of curriculum owe much to the rhetorical and philosophical force of McKeon. To provide a sense of the source from which the deliberative tradition arises, the next section addresses McKeon's views on rhetoric and the various ways he conceived of the relationship between knowledge and action.

McKeon on Rhetoric and Premodern Curriculum

Rhetoric does not have the best reputation in our modern world. The subject is often put down as nothing other than fancy language that has no purpose beyond pleasing an audience or telling someone what they want to hear. People use the phrase "it's all just rhetoric" to make a distinction between what someone says and what they do, with the latter assumed to be sinister and the former all for show.

To McKeon, however, rhetoric is at the heart of a liberating curriculum. It is unavoidable and interwoven into every subject in the curriculum. McKeon reminds us that rhetoric is about persuasion, choice, and action. Practitioners of the art of rhetoric persuade people to make right judgments, challenge individuals and communities to move in a just direction, and solve problems using the gifts of communication, invention, and judgment. Scholars of rhetoric recognize the ambiguity surrounding their art, but this uncertainty does not mean that the art does not exist or that somehow it is less important than the other arts or sciences.

To deliberators, moral philosophy and rhetoric are foundational to good curriculum making.

McKeon refers to rhetoric as an "architectonic productive art."[45] By architectonic, he means that rhetoric, like politics, is an art of *doing*. Architectonic arts are also universal in the sense that they are concerned about ends, whereas other arts are subordinate because they only address means. Architectonic arts provide direction to the subordinate arts that contribute to them. As McKeon puts it, "Architectonic arts treat ends which order the ends of subordinate arts. The architectonic art is the most authoritative art."[46] Rhetoric is therefore elevated to one of the highest arts in McKeon's mind. In addition to being architectonic, rhetoric is also "productive" in the sense that it produces language that furthers the end that the speaker (or writer) seeks to achieve. Building upon Aristotle, McKeon contrasts the art of rhetoric as a *productive* art with the *practical* art of politics. The end of a practical art like politics is action, not production. A political leader might do something that has a significant impact without using language at all. The art of politics does not necessarily produce language, whereas rhetoric must produce language if it is to be rhetoric at all.

A person well schooled in the art of rhetoric has the ability to do several things at once. First, she has a clear end in mind that she wants to achieve with her language. Second, she understands the nature of the problems she is trying to solve as well as the people with whom she is working to solve them. Third, she surveys the rhetorical and political landscape to gain a sense of the possibilities that perhaps can solve the problem at hand. Then, she uses the right language at the right time in the right way, language that persuades people to move in the appropriate direction. To succeed in this art of persuasion, McKeon argues that "invention" and "judgment" are indispensable.[47] Invention matters because good rhetoricians are creative in their ability to imagine possibilities that can address the problems they face. They have the ability to generate lots of options, some of which may be successful and others not. In the face of numerous options for solving a problem, judgment becomes imperative because those who practice this art must be able to judge which course of action, or which language, is best among the alternatives. In discussing this process, McKeon writes, "A productive architectonic art produces subject-matters and organizes them in relation to each other and to the problems to be solved."[48] McKeon recognizes that not all problems are the same, not all people are the same, and not all contexts are the same. His vision of a well-schooled practitioner of rhetoric is someone who possesses all of the virtues necessary for political leadership but who also can take a step further and produce the language necessary to achieve the goals he has in mind. Good character without rhetorical skill is useless. Good practical skill at taking right action has limited impact if it is not combined with rhetorical capacity. Rhetorical skill *and* practical wisdom is the winning combination that animated McKeon's work.

These are some of the ideas that Schwab and McKeon discussed for decades prior to the publication of Schwab's Practical papers. McKeon, through his friendship with Schwab, was opening the curriculum field to premodern traditions that had been neglected due to the rise of purely empirical methods of curriculum making. Prior to the modern era, those who made curriculum were expected to be well-schooled civic leaders who practiced the arts of politics, rhetoric, and deliberation in the way McKeon conceived of them. McKeon and Schwab were doing something revolutionary when they began to return curriculum to its premodern roots. They hoped to give new life to curriculum through the revival of the practical and productive arts. Their argument is that curriculists should build upon humanistic sources of knowledge like rhetoric, ethics, literature, and ancient philosophy, not model themselves after physical and social scientists. McKeon never wrote specifically on curriculum like Schwab did, but the goals they worked to accomplish are similar. McKeon sought to achieve for the fields of philosophy and rhetoric what Schwab hoped to do for curriculum. Their similar goals become even more apparent when we look at McKeon's views on the theory-practice relationship and how it affects deliberation.

McKeon on the Theory-Practice Relationship and Deliberation

No issue is more central to good curriculum making than the relationship between theory and practice. The deliberative tradition contends that deliberation is the most appropriate way to bridge this gap. Perhaps the best way to show why deliberators agree on this point is by looking at an essay McKeon published in the journal *Ethics*. In the article entitled "Philosophy and Action," McKeon discusses four ways to link theory and practice, each of which can be viewed as a different kind of "practical."[49] He refers to these four modes as the following: (1) dialectic, (2) logistic, (3) inquiry, and (4) operational. They can be linked, somewhat loosely, to the four traditions discussed so far. Dialectic can be tied to radical curriculum, logistic to systematic, inquiry to deliberative, and operational to pragmatic. McKeon does not discuss a view of the practical that can be linked to an existential tradition.

In describing these four views of the theory-practice relationship, McKeon ultimately makes the case that an inquiry-based approach is the healthiest. A dialectic view sees no distinction between theory and practice. Referring to philosophers like Karl Marx and G. W. F. Hegel, who hold this view, McKeon points out that dialectic thinkers require a specific view of the world, or a set of a priori assumptions, that must be accepted by those who work within this tradition. From a dialectic perspective, only one interpretation of history is acceptable, a fact that hinders the options available to this view of practicality. It also limits the people who can participate in problem-solving activities. In his discussion of these four views, Reid points out that the dialectic view is "politically restrictive."[50] He goes on to argue that "a dialectical view of practice has to be guided by some specific account of social evolution. It will therefore cater to one possible conception of history and destiny to the exclusion of others that participants in judgment might hold."[51] In other words, those who do not accept the assumptions held by dialectic thinkers are automatically isolated from the decision-making body.

In contrast to the dialectic, a logistic view of the theory-practice relationship conceives of practical problems as the logical application of scientific knowledge to specific circumstances. As McKeon puts it, "The *logistic method* constructs formal systems of sciences on the model of mathematics, and the practical is an application of knowledge which stands in need of a science of human action to guide the uses of the sciences."[52] The logistic method makes a sharp distinction between "theory" and "practice," contending that only the production of theoretic knowledge is truly scientific. After theoretic knowledge has been produced, this knowledge must be applied deductively to solve specific problems. Rejecting practical activity as either an art or a science, the logistic view turns practice, in McKeon's words, into "the application of general scientific laws to modify processes and operations in particular practical situations."[53] Experts produce theoretic knowledge that is used to control practitioners. Solving practical problems turns into the task of managing practitioners whose role is to implement theoretic knowledge in the same way in all circumstances.

The inquiry-based method of connecting theory and practice is the one that McKeon argues is most desirable. It opens up opportunities and provides the richest basis for connecting knowledge and action. McKeon contends that the inquiry method, which he also refers to as the problematic method, "is a method of resolving problems."[54] It recognizes that not all problems are the same, indeed that some are theoretic and some are practical (a distinction, of course, that is found notably in Schwab). In the realm of practical inquiry, McKeon points out that solving problems depends on "communication and agreement."[55] He recognizes further that problems are solved within a social world, that language is key to building consensus, and that people must be persuaded in order for solutions to be invented and enacted. McKeon contends moreover that the inquiry method is just as scientific as the dialectical and logistic methods, but scientific in a different way. Science is conceived as a human activity within the inquiry method. Reason and logic are essential, but they are brought to bear within the realm of human activity. Science is therefore combined with social, political, and ethical matters. In McKeon's words:

> The problems of the practical are problems of influencing and determining moral, political, and social actions. . . . As treated according to the methods of inquiry, the problems of the practical turn on the processes by which men come to agree on a conclusion or to acquiesce in a course of action. They are problems defined by what men think, fear, desire, and believe, including what they think to be good, inevitable, or scientific.[56]

As we find in all deliberators like Schwab, Reid, and Westbury, the modern attempt to separate "facts" from "values" is rejected by the inquiry-based deliberative tradition. Science, reason, ethics, philosophy, and rhetoric all come together as practical and productive arts that contribute in their own way to the deliberative process.

The fourth and final approach to combining theory and practice that McKeon discusses is the operational. Like the pragmatic tradition discussed in chapter 5, the operational view looks to discernible results to verify that theory and practice are working together effectively. The test of productive action is what matters. The operational view differs from the dialectic because the dialectic depends on a universal theory of history, whereas the operational view relies only on results through action. As McKeon writes, "The practical as dialectic is universal and fundamental to all activities and to all knowledge. The practical as operational is universal in the application of the test of action to delimit the scope of meaningful and relevant theory."[57] All that matters in an operational view is whether an action produces discernible results, not whether it is ethically sound or in keeping with tradition or true in a philosophic sense. As McKeon puts it plainly, "The operational method tends to be antiphilosophic."[58] It also can be viewed as relativistic in the sense that all problems—as well as the solutions to them—depend entirely on context, with nothing universal holding them together. In this respect, as Reid has written critically, the operational is "simply expedient and lacking in any moral character."[59]

> Deliberators are similar to pragmatists in the sense that they want students to learn to solve problems. The difference between the two in practice, however, is that deliberators insist that students reflect on the moral framework that guides their decisions. In this respect, deliberative curriculists are as much moral philosophers as they are curriculum specialists.

Deliberation fits within McKeon's conception of the liberal arts because it is the arena in which the inquiry method is practiced and in which the art of rhetoric is possible. Deliberation is where the practical and productive arts come to bear on specific cases. Deliberation and rhetoric are separate arts, but a sharp line cannot be drawn between them. The two work together to resolve problems, strengthen virtue, and cultivate happiness.

> The concept of "practicality" is deeply rich and complex to deliberators.

Implied in McKeon's discussion of both rhetoric and the theory-practice relationship is the notion of the commonplaces. As the sources of knowledge that liberal artists should consult when trying to persuade, the commonplaces are familiar terrain for deliberative curriculists.[60] They are comfortable not only using the language of curriculum deliberation, but also with the role of language in culture generally. The deliberative tradition thrives when it comes to the commonplaces because, unlike other traditions, it has the means to balance them in theory and in practice. Through the deliberative tradition, the ancient art of rhetoric comes to bear on the field of curriculum.

■ Deliberative Curriculum and the Commonplaces

Teachers

The point of identifying curriculum commonplaces is so that the members of a deliberative team can work to balance them in practice. A curriculum is most successful when those who make it consider all five commonplaces in a thorough way. Teachers must be consulted because they know the realities inside their classrooms, they know the way their fellow teachers think, and they recognize that no curriculum can succeed if they do not support it. Teachers are expected to embody the arts of inquiry like all members of the deliberative team. They should be liberally educated and professionally trained. They should balance the five commonplaces not only as they create curriculum as part of the deliberative team, but also as they practice their art in their classrooms. They are expected to model the liberal arts ideal of a well-rounded citizen, but they also should be educated in the professional—indeed scientific—aspects of curriculum and teaching. Teaching is viewed as both an art and a science within a deliberative perspective, and teachers are expected to appreciate—indeed practice—both.

Learners

A deliberative tradition views learners as another essential component of the curriculum-making team. It does not place learners ahead of teachers or any other commonplace, but it does recognize that not all learners are the same and that the learner commonplace can serve as an important counterweight to the other commonplaces, especially the commonplace of subject matter. Deliberators acknowledge that learners pass through developmental stages that strongly influence the subject matter they are prepared to learn, the methods used to teach them, and the expectations teachers and curriculists should have for different groups of learners. At the same time, however, deliberators are not prepared to emphasize learners to such an extent that developmental stages completely overwhelm other aspects of curriculum. Learning, moreover, is not viewed as an appropriate end for curriculum, but rather as a means to a broader, deeper, and richer end like character, virtue, and happiness. A good curriculum shapes learners toward these deeper ends and is therefore not satisfied with making learning more efficient. Learners desire moral and intellectual knowledge regardless of their age. Due to the complexity of human nature, curriculum should impact learners in every aspect of their character—including its moral, intellectual, physical, civic, and spiritual dimensions. Any curriculum that fails to tap into each of these aspects of human existence will ultimately fail to turn learners into free citizens who can build and sustain community.

Subject Matter

Subject matter is an equal partner with the other common-places within a deliberative perspective. As Schwab contends in "The Practical 3: Translation into Curriculum," a common tendency is for members of the deliberative team to bestow too much influence on the subject matter specialist.[61] Other members of the team are often "overawed," as Schwab writes, by the subject matter specialist. This problem often arises due to the amount of schooling that scholars bring to deliberations or perhaps because subject matter specialists live in a university culture, which is radically different from the culture of K–12 schools. In addition, subject matter specialists have the tendency to assume that their specialized knowledge is more significant than the other sources of knowledge embodied by the other commonplaces. If the team is not careful, the views of the subject specialist can overwhelm the group's deliberations. Schwab makes a case that scholars are wrong to assume that their knowledge is more important than the other four. It is equal, not superior. In Schwab's words, "Scholars, as such, are incompetent to translate scholarly material into curriculum. They possess one body of disciplines indispensable to the task. They lack four others, equally indispensable. As scholars, they not only lack these other four, but also, as individuals, they are prone at best to ignore and at worst to sneer at them."[62] Subject specialists should never be neglected or dismissed as part of a deliberative team. At the same time, however, they must learn to listen to those who represent the other sources of knowledge and adjust their views accordingly. Scholars have valuable contributions to make when it comes to the nature of their discipline, the methods used to produce knowledge within it, and the latest avenues of research within their field.

Subject matter specialists also, however, must recognize that their knowledge is almost always theoretic, meaning that it must be translated into a usable form before it becomes a curriculum. American history, for example, is a universal field of academic study, but that does not mean that an eleventh grade American history curriculum in Massachusetts will be (or should be) the same as an eleventh grade American history curriculum in Mississippi. Of course, there will always be numerous similarities between the two curricula, but since students in Massachusetts are not the same as students in Mississippi, there will also be differences that make any particular curriculum more appropriate for one group of students compared to another. The process of translating subject matter into a usable curriculum is not something that subject matter specialists are trained to do, but it is an art they can learn to practice as they participate as equal members of a deliberative team.

Context

The context commonplace also plays a crucial role within a deliberative tradition. Problems arise out of a unique context and can only be solved if the particulars of that state of affairs are understood. The more deliberators know about the specifics of a unique problem, the better they will be able to invent solutions and take appropriate action. Experience within the environment where curriculum problems exist is essential for all members of the deliberative team. The member of the deliberative team who represents the context commonplace has the responsibility to bring knowledge about the community to bear on the group's discussions. She may be someone who knows the history of an individual school or community, or someone who is well connected to the political and economic leadership within a town. This person should be able to imagine how changes in a school or school district's curriculum will be viewed by members of the general public, as well as by business and political leaders who are directly influenced by a school's offerings.

Curriculum Making

A deliberative tradition perhaps distinguishes itself most strongly in the way it emphasizes the curriculum making commonplace. None of the other four traditions places this commonplace on par with the others. In fact, most of the other traditions ignore the curriculum making commonplace altogether. The deliberative tradition, however, recognizes that curriculum making is about action, and somebody on the deliberative team must represent and do something about this requirement of action. The curriculum making commonplace puts all of the others into motion, ensuring that curriculum is a practical activity instead of a theoretic one. If we only consider the previous four commonplaces when we deal with curriculum, we remain theoretic commentators who merely seek to understand curriculum, not educators who intend to do something with it. This desire for action is the reason that the curriculum making specialist has an essential role to play.

As the leader of the deliberative team, the curriculum maker must ensure sure that all five commonplaces are represented, consulted, and considered as the team searches for and invents solutions to curriculum problems.[63] In doing so, this leading deliberator must embody the moral, intellectual, and practical virtues that the team wants to cultivate in students. He or she must have the capacity to move swiftly back and forth between means and ends, constantly imagining creative ways to solve problems while at the same time moving the team toward the ideal of universal liberal education. Problem solving is a significant aspect of good curriculum making, but solving problems is only a means, not an end. Deliberators appreciate the emphasis on problem solving found in pragmatists, but they take their emphasis on problem solving one step further by connecting it to a liberal arts ideal. Deliberative curriculum makers retain their faith in a *telos*, whereas pragmatists reject it. In this respect, the primary difference between pragmatic curriculists and deliberative curriculists is that deliberators have not had the idealism sucked out of them.

■ Conclusion: Strengths and Weaknesses of Deliberative Curriculum

Several strengths of the deliberative tradition have become apparent throughout this chapter. Deliberative curriculum opens up new avenues of knowledge without dismissing empiricism and system. It builds upon the reality that curriculum is a value-laden subject, offering a more holistic perspective than the other traditions. Deliberative curriculum also is driven by an ideal that can serve as a source of unity, inspiration, and vision for those who make curriculum. Since it builds upon a liberal arts ideal, this tradition also has extraordinarily deep roots. It has the potential to serve the curriculum field for many years beyond the modern period that is now fading.

There are also drawbacks, however, associated with a deliberative tradition. First, it can be somewhat ambiguous. Just as terms like *practical wisdom, virtue,* and *character* can be vague, deliberators use methods and pursue ends that remain elusive no matter how much they are discussed. Another potential shortcoming is found in the discontinuity between how most members of the general public view curriculum and the views offered by deliberators. The humanistic tradition that serves as the foundation for deliberative curriculum has been marginalized to such an extent that even beginning a conversation with the language of deliberation can be difficult. Moreover, the current obsession with testing and measurement at all levels of schooling hinders the extent to which deliberators can make an impact. Deliberators by no means reject evaluation and measurement, but they place it in perspective as one aspect of a much broader process of curriculum making. Finally, the deliberative tradition perhaps pursues an ideal that is unattainable: universal liberal education. Like John Amos Comenius, deliberators assume that the overwhelming majority of the population can benefit from a liberal arts curriculum. Depending upon one's view of human nature, the pursuit of this ideal can be a strength or a weakness. It is a weakness from the perspective of those who focus on the differences in people and thereby want to differentiate curriculum to meet individual needs. On the other hand, the liberal arts ideal is a strength to those who look for commonalities among people instead of differences. Either way, the pursuit of universal liberal education as an ideal remains an unresolved issue for deliberators to address.

Part I has now surveyed the five curriculum traditions that encapsulate the various ways that curriculum is conceived not only by scholars but also by the general public. The next step is to move to part II: "From Theory to Practice." Before considering specific cases in which curriculum problems are resolved, however, the curriculum map in figure 6.1 places all of the authors covered in part I on the map introduced in chapter 1. Since this depiction of the map includes all of the authors discussed, it should help to clarify not only how the traditions relate to one another, but also how the authors can be compared. Of course, no one person ever remains static throughout his or her life, so a map like this one will

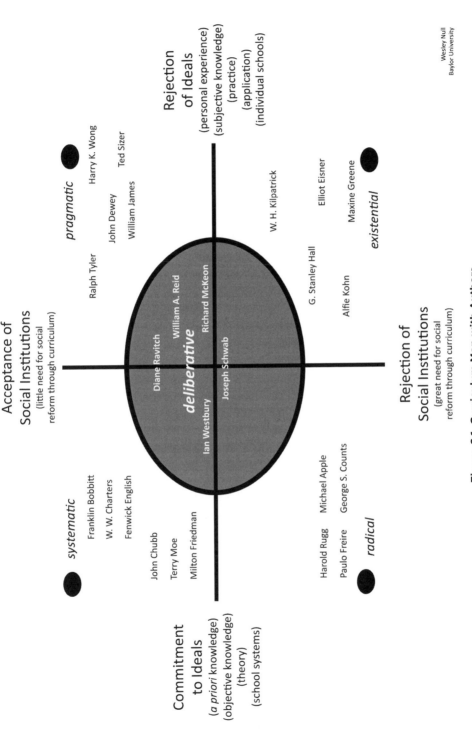

Acceptance of
Social Institutions
(little need for social
reform through curriculum)

systematic

Franklin Bobbitt
W. W. Charters
Fenwick English

John Chubb
Terry Moe
Milton Friedman

Ralph Tyler

pragmatic

Harry K. Wong

Ted Sizer

John Dewey
William James

W. H. Kilpatrick

Rejection
of Ideals
(personal experience)
(subjective knowledge)
(practice)
(application)
(individual schools)

Elliot Eisner

Maxine Greene

existential

G. Stanley Hall

Alfie Kohn

Diane Ravitch

William A. Reid

Richard McKeon

Ian Westbury

deliberative

Joseph Schwab

Harold Rugg   Michael Apple

Paulo Freire   George S. Counts

radical

Rejection of
Social Institutions
(great need for social
reform through curriculum)

Commitment
to Ideals
(*a priori* knowledge)
(objective knowledge)
(theory)
(school systems)

Wesley Null
Baylor University

Figure 6.1. Curriculum Map with Authors

always be a moving target. Nevertheless, the characterization of curriculum presented in part I leads to a map in which these authors can be located, in a relatively stable manner, in figure 6.1.

Part II discusses three ubiquitous curriculum problems by sketching the scene in which they exist. It then draws upon the five traditions to provide answers to how these problems might be resolved. The first problem is one that is on the minds of just about every teacher not only in the United States, but in countries around the globe. What should we do with state curriculum standards? As deliberative curriculists recognize, any potential answer to this question can only be generated if we study the scene in which it arises.

■ Discussion Questions

1. From a deliberative perspective, what kind of problems are curriculum problems?

2. What is deliberation and where do we see it most frequently?

3. What are the differences between theoretic and practical problems?

4. What sources of knowledge does the deliberative tradition draw upon that no other tradition does?

5. What is the relationship between liberal education and the deliberative tradition?

6. Briefly summarize Joseph Schwab's challenge to curriculum.

7. How did Richard McKeon influence the development of the deliberative tradition?

8. How does the deliberative tradition integrate theory and practice?

9. What role does rhetoric play within a deliberative tradition?

10. From the perspective of the deliberative tradition, what role should deliberation play in curriculum making?

11. What are three strengths and three weaknesses of the deliberative tradition?

FROM THEORY
TO PRACTICE

CHAPTER 7

What Should We Do with State Curriculum Standards?

THE CURRICULUM traditions presented in the previous five chapters provide a philosophical background for the way curriculum is conceived within our culture. By themselves, however, these five paradigms do not allow us to develop ourselves completely as successful teachers and curriculum makers. Part II of this text, therefore, is quite different from part I. The next three chapters present specific cases in which K–12 teachers, school administrators, and university leaders are attempting to reform curriculum. These cases are useful because they allow us to place ourselves within a specific circumstance and imagine how we might deliberate to resolve the problems that arise. This approach is useful for those who subscribe to a deliberative tradition since deliberation thrives on knowledge of specific circumstances, imaginative engagement with creative solutions, and the pursuit of a liberal curriculum for all.

With the use of the following cases, this chapter has three goals. The first is to demonstrate what happens when a reform initiative like state standards comes into contact with a specific school situation. A second goal is to raise for consideration the questions that must be addressed when any reform effort meets practical realities. Third, this chapter explains how a deliberative approach to curriculum practice would likely resolve the issues that emerge.

In order to make the cases read in a story-like manner, the tone of this chapter is different from that of part I. Each case should be useful to students of curriculum as they generate discussion about curriculum problems and devise ways

Many beginning teachers rely much more heavily on state standards than do experienced teachers.

to resolve them. A primary assumption behind the use of the following cases is that deliberative curriculum making is based on knowledge of specific circumstances. Unlike a systematic view that attempts to separate itself from practical conditions, a deliberative approach embraces contextual matters to increase the likelihood that curriculum makers will make wise judgments. A good place to begin is with the curriculum problems that have arisen in recent years due to the popularity of state curriculum standards.

■ The Idea of Curriculum Standards

A common debate when it comes to curriculum standards has to deal with how specific they should be. Some people argue that standards should be highly specific and even script what teachers say. Others support the idea of curriculum standards but think they should be general and leave individual teachers room for flexibility.

Every state in the nation has created state standards. The idea is to provide a common body of knowledge to all students within a particular state. Once these documents have been created, however, the question that teachers and school administrators face is what to do with them. Creators of state standards almost invariably approach the subject from a systematic perspective that is tied to test score results. They assume that teachers will follow the standards as if they are a script. This assumption, however, ignores the reality that any reform initiative must come into contact with a specific state of affairs.

The answer to what should be done with state standards depends upon many factors that teachers and school administrators face at any given time. The cases below are designed to help readers imagine how practitioners who take a deliberative approach can resolve the issues presented. Each person is a composite sketch, not an actual person at work within the states discussed. The schools are composites as well, but any reader will recognize the types of schools discussed. They are common in every state. These cases are based on my experience as a teacher, university faculty member, curriculum researcher, curriculum writer, university administrator, and member of numerous curriculum committees at the K–12 and university levels. Think of the following characters as representative examples of the teachers and school administrators who face similar problems each day. The first case concerns Mr. Jesse Parker, a high school U.S. history teacher at Woodvale High School in Massachusetts.

Curriculum Standards and Controversy

The creation of standards, whether at the state or federal level, is always a source of controversy. Social studies standards tend to be the most controversial. One such heated debate took place in 1994 when President Bill Clinton signed into law Goals 2000. One of the major purposes of Goals 2000 was to establish national standards, as well as assessments to measure those standards, in all core subjects. One of the first fields to attempt to create national standards was history. Dr. Gary B. Nash, a professor of history at the University of California, Los Angeles, served as chair of the National History Standards Project and, as a result, spearheaded the development of these standards. In the fall of 1994 when the new history standards were about to be released, Lynne V. Cheney attacked them in a column in the *Wall Street Journal.* She argued that the proposed standards all but ignored George Washington, presented the founding of the Sierra Club as a major event, failed to mention the Constitution even once, and in general provided legitimacy to a view of history that Cheney considered dangerous. From Cheney's perspective, on top of being historically inaccurate, the standards were written from a political perspective she thought was inappropriate. Since Cheney had served as chairman of the National Endowment for the Humanities under the George H. W. Bush administration, her opinion carried weight. A firestorm of controversy erupted following Cheney's article. Both sides claimed they were correct and that the positions of the other had been misrepresented. The debate finally calmed down, however, and the standards were used by many states to develop their own standards in history and/or social studies.

■ Jesse Parker: High School U.S. History Teacher

Jesse Parker has been teaching since 1976. He began his career immediately following the completion of his BA degree in history at a prominent university in the northeast. His first teaching job found him teaching world history, U.S. history, and a yearbook class at a junior high school in a suburban Massachusetts school district. His passion has always been U.S. history, so, after five years of teaching primarily world history and serving as yearbook sponsor, Mr. Parker jumped at the chance to switch to Woodvale High where he could focus only on U.S. history. At Woodvale, he teaches five classes of U.S. history, including one honors section, and nothing else.

Woodvale is a large school with approximately eighteen hundred students, most of whom are high achieving. The population is 85 percent white, 10 percent Hispanic, and 5 percent African American. For the most part, Mr. Parker's students are well behaved. They perform well on state tests, pay attention in class, and generally complete their homework assignments. More than 75 percent of Woodvale's graduates enroll in either a two- or four-year college, which is a good percentage but one that has been dropping in recent years. Mr. Parker's students don't come to class with much interest in history, but he enjoys trying to inspire a passion for the subject even if they arrive expecting a boring class of facts, dates, and nonstop information. Mr. Parker's five U.S. history classes typically enroll no more than twenty-five students each, with his honors section rarely reaching more than twenty. His fall course covers the first half of U.S. history, beginning with the roots of colonization and concluding with Reconstruction. In the spring, his course begins with the Industrial Revolution and ends with the events of September 11.

Jesse is well respected by his fellow teachers. He has a reputation as an inspiring, committed teacher who, due to his dedication, will likely teach another five or even ten years. He also has a reputation for wanting to do things his own way. When school administrators or outside "experts" attempt to tell Mr. Parker how to do his job, he can become quite animated, pointing out that his classroom belongs to him and that he should be free to teach the way he chooses. After all, he has been teaching for more than thirty years. He is confident in his teaching abilities and has proven that he can succeed at stimulating students' interests. Many of Mr. Parker's students have gone on to study history in college, and several have become history teachers due to his inspiration.

Mr. Parker has continued to develop himself professionally. He completed a master's degree in social studies education in 1981 at a well-known Massachusetts university. He has since turned down numerous opportunities to move into an administrative role either at Woodvale or in other nearby districts. His only experience with administration came in the mid-1980s when he served as social studies department chair for two years. He moved out of the role as quickly as possible, however, because he would rather spend time with students. He didn't enjoy the minutiae that came with administrative work. He found himself discussing test scores, book orders, and budgets with the Woodvale principal, not the kind of work he finds stimulating. Mr. Parker reads widely, both within the field of history and outside of it. He has taken his family on trips to museums up and down the East Coast, most of which revolved around his love of history, which is shared by his wife and son.

In addition to completing his master's degree, Mr. Parker has searched for ways to develop himself professionally by attending conferences and summer workshops, despite having to pay for almost all of these opportunities himself. He and his wife have one grown son, now a software developer, so the couple has plenty of time during the summers to pursue their love of travel. They typically make one trip each summer, the most recent one taking them to Spain, Portugal, and Germany. Jesse has always been interested in how Americans are viewed overseas. This interest has led him to teach U.S. history, when possible, from a global perspective that stresses international affairs. He wants students to see the various ways that America has interacted with the rest of the world beginning with the colonial period and continuing through September 11. Mr. Parker believes this international perspective will help in some small way to restore America's standing in the world, which Mr. Parker believes is in need of a great deal of work.

Since all students in Massachusetts must complete two years of U.S. history between grades eight and eleven, Mr. Parker teaches two tenth-grade and three eleventh-grade classes. All students are required to take an end-of-course exam following the year in which they complete each U.S. history course. Mr. Parker understands the importance of these tests, but he is concerned that they narrow the focus of the U.S. history curriculum, causing many teachers to teach only those facts that are found on the test. Mr. Parker works to avoid this tendency by choosing to teach his courses in much the same way he has for thirty years. He doesn't completely ignore the test, but he stresses it far less than the newer teachers. He operates on the assumption that if he teaches his course well, students' test scores will take care of themselves.

The major problem that Mr. Parker faces at this point in his career is that the state of Massachusetts recently adopted a new set of history standards. If he follows these new standards strictly, he would be required to make several radical changes to his U.S. history curriculum. His favorite part of U.S. history comes when he covers the twentieth century. Over the years he has developed two units that make a strong impact on students. The first is a unit on the space race and its relation to the Cold War. He enjoys teaching the unit because it allows for numerous interdisciplinary connections, he can show students captivating videos and photographs, and the story had a deep impact on his life when he was a young boy. He followed the efforts of astronauts as they traveled to outer space, he constructed model rockets in his family's kitchen, and he hung pictures of the planets in his bedroom. He remembers being glued to the TV set as a fifteen-year-old boy when the famous moon landing took place. He will never forget America's one giant leap for mankind. He has found that students are naturally interested in the story of space exploration, unlike other potentially mundane topics like Reconstruction or the Spanish-American War. Students enjoy hearing his stories about how the moon landing impacted him personally, something he cannot do with other periods in U.S. history.

Mr. Parker faces a problem, however, in that his curriculum from previous years emphasizes space exploration far more than the new standards. The space race is mentioned once in the standards, but it plays a minor role compared to other topics. Space exploration is only one line among a long list of topics. There is no way that Mr. Parker would have time to cover everything in the standards if he maintains his practice of teaching a two-week unit on the space race.

A second unit of Mr. Parker's, however, is one he cares about even more than the unit on space. For more than twenty years, he has taught a Holocaust unit that lasts between two and three weeks. He has found that students connect strongly with this story not just because of its emotional impact, but because of the interdisciplinary way that Mr. Parker teaches it. To connect the story to literature, he has students read Elie Wiesel's *Night*. He has them complete oral history interviews with Holocaust survivors, a process that culminates in at least two or three survivors visiting his class at the end of the unit. Mr. Parker brings in newer technology by requiring students to use digital video recorders to record their interviews, making them not only oral history interviews but videotaped documentaries as well. He has partnered with a nearby Holocaust museum to ensure that the recordings will be deposited in a permanent location. Mr. Parker's classes also watch portions of *Schindler's List* and read selections from Viktor Frankl's *Man's Search for Meaning* to help them see heroism in the face of tragedy.

The problem Mr. Parker faces when it comes to his Holocaust unit is that the new U.S. history standards make no mention whatsoever of the Holocaust. The subject is included in the world history standards, but Mr. Parker believes it should be part of U.S. history as well. He recognizes that the crimes of the Holocaust did not take place on American soil, but the influence of this event on America has been profound. For instance, Mr. Parker always discusses the many Jewish immigrants who came to the United States just before and during World War II. He teaches students specifically about Hannah Arendt, Henry Kissinger, and Albert Einstein. The impact of Jewish immigrants like these on American culture demonstrates, Mr. Parker believes, that the story of the Holocaust cannot (and should not) be contained solely within the world history curriculum.

Mr. Parker faces a series of questions that are not new given his long career. They have, however, become more urgent now that district administrators have begun to place great emphasis on test scores. Should he ignore the new standards altogether and keep doing what he has been doing? Or should he toss aside his two favorite units to make room for "covering" all of the items found in the new standards? Following the second path may result in higher test scores, but does that mean he is doing a better job of teaching? Just because students have scored well on tests does not mean they have developed a passion for history.

On the other hand, Mr. Parker agrees with the idea of state standards and subscribes to the notion that all students should learn essential aspects of U.S. history. He thinks these common pieces of knowledge (and the principles that come with them) bind Americans together. Mr. Parker also wants his high school to fare well against others in the district, just like he wants his students' test scores to be equal to or better than those of the other history teachers at Woodvale High. He wishes he had time to cover everything—including both units and all items contained in the new standards—but he recognizes that teaching everything is impossible.

What should Mr. Parker do to resolve these problems? How can he continue to teach what he enjoys while at the same time adapting to the new standards? How might he balance all of the factors that make him a good teacher while at the same time manage the new pressures that have been placed upon him? How can curriculum deliberation help Mr. Parker decide how to proceed?

Strong teachers like Mr. Parker sometimes leave the profession because of the many and sometimes contradictory demands that are placed upon them. Nationally speaking, approximately half of U.S. teachers leave the profession within five years.

Resolving Mr. Parker's Problems

Mr. Parker's problems can be resolved in a variety of ways. A systematic view would strictly enforce the system of standards adopted by the state of Massachusetts. Systematizers would remind Mr. Parker that the standards were developed for a reason, that he is an official agent of the state, and that the only way the standards can achieve their goal of delivering the same content to all students is if teachers implement them in the way they were designed. Mr. Parker should feel free to find creative *methods* to teach the state standards, but he is not at liberty to avoid material that has been adopted officially by the state. Systematizers also would insist that Mr. Parker stick with the standards for U.S. history because, if he doesn't, students will be taught a history curriculum that covers the Holocaust twice. Redundancy is something that systematic curriculists work diligently to avoid, in the name of efficiency.

An existentialist mind-set takes the opposite view and questions the value of curriculum standards altogether. If Mr. Parker feels passionate about teaching his units on space exploration and the Holocaust, he should continue to do so—especially if his students connect with these stories in a personal way. Another option from an existentialist perspective would be for Mr. Parker to consider asking his students which topics from the new standards they find most interesting and then build his curriculum around their choices. Nothing in the new standards should be retained if students do not find it intrinsically interesting.

A radical perspective also takes issue with the state standards, but for different reasons. Any set of standards created by the dominant class in society has almost invariably been designed to oppress minority students. Mr. Parker's role should be to subvert the dominant view, not reinforce it by accepting blindly what the state says he must do. A radical perspective encourages Mr. Parker to reject the hegemonic view embedded in the standards and instead introduce students to hidden groups and perspectives. Rather than learning about the virtues of Ben Franklin or the heroic efforts of George Washington, radical curriculists want Mr. Parker to teach about Thomas Jefferson as a slave owner, Malcolm X as a revolutionary leader, and Cesar Chavez as a visionary activist.

A pragmatic view would have Mr. Parker graft onto his old curriculum anything from the new standards that he thinks will turn his students into more effective problem solvers. The best approach would be for him to keep those aspects of his old curriculum that worked to get students active while trying out some new lessons based on the new standards to see how they work. If lessons based on the new standards prove effective at getting students to produce interesting products, then they should be retained. If not, they should be abandoned.

When faced with the problems before him, a deliberative approach tells Mr. Parker that he should begin to search for creative ways to address these issues while keeping all of the curriculum commonplaces in mind. He knows the teacher commonplace best. This source of knowledge tells him not to toss out everything that has been successful in previous years. He knows that he must enjoy teaching if he is to have a long-term impact on students. Mr. Parker is also well informed when it comes to the learner commonplace. He has a good sense of what interests Woodvale students, an insight that leads him to think that he should continue to teach his favorite units but perhaps adjust them slightly as he does each year anyway. When it comes to subject matter, Mr. Parker realizes that in the past he may have overemphasized space exploration. Dedicating two weeks to it is far more time than he spends on other equally significant events in U.S. history like the Great Depression and the 1960s, both of which are stressed in the new standards. Mr. Parker also considers the context commonplace when studying the new standards. He is pleased to discover that the standards stress events in Boston during the Revolutionary era. This realization leads him to imagine many creative lessons he could develop that would require students to visit historic sites in the Boston area like Lexington and Concord and Boston Harbor. All of these sites are mentioned specifically in the Massachusetts standards. He begins to consider a unit on the role of Boston during the Revolutionary period.

The commonplace that eventually helps Mr. Parker decide what he should do is curriculum making. He wants his students to receive an education that liberates them as free citizens who will shape the future of Massachusetts and the nation as a whole. He knows that his curriculum should teach students about space exploration and the Holocaust, but it must do more as well. He imagines a variety of solutions that keep common standards and test scores in mind; at the same time, he thinks of options that avoid the problem of standards and tests controlling his curriculum. One possibility he considers is to use questions from previous versions of the end-of-course exam, which have been released, as review questions that students complete as they prepare for his unit exams. By using previous exams in this way, Mr. Parker is preparing students for the types of questions they will see at the end of the year without building his entire curriculum around them.

Mr. Parker also comes to the conclusion that his Holocaust unit is important enough that he does not want to alter it significantly, but he has found a way to condense his space unit to three days instead of two weeks. This change will allow him to develop a new unit that draws upon historic sites in the area. Mr. Parker's hope is that this new unit will create the same kind of personal interest in history that his space exploration unit has done previously. By making these changes, Mr. Parker retains his ideal of teaching students a curriculum that connects with them in personal and civic ways.

The hybridized curriculum that Mr. Parker develops during the next academic year is not the same as it was before. It does, however, build upon the strengths of his experience. He finds a way to satisfy the state's expectations for what should be taught in a U.S. history curriculum, but he also figures out a path that allows him to teach subjects that interest him personally. He avoids redundancy to some extent by revising his Holocaust unit, yet he realizes that this remains an issue to address. He plans to discuss the matter with Woodvale's world history teacher to see if they can work out a plan that allows both of them to address different parts of the Holocaust standards. In doing so, Mr. Parker finds a way to teach what he enjoys teaching, but within the framework of the new U.S. history standards. Discussing the matter with the world history teacher doesn't clear up the issue of students transferring in and out of Woodvale, but it is a step toward resolving the problem for students who remain at Woodvale for four years.

A second case concerning curriculum standards, however, is not so easily resolved. This example brings the position of department chair into consideration. Introducing an administrative dimension into the state of affairs changes the situation in considerable ways, especially given that the next state, Indiana, places an even greater emphasis on test score production than Massachusetts does.

■ Kathy Waterman: Social Studies Department Chair

Ms. Kathy Waterman has been teaching social studies for five years. Recently married, she has accepted a position to teach social studies and serve as social studies department chair at Ashton High School in Ashton, Indiana. Ashton is a rural community with a population of about two thousand. The racial breakdown of Ashton High is 65 percent white, 30 percent Hispanic, and 5 percent African American. The school's graduating class is quite small, typically between thirty and forty students.

Ms. Waterman spent the past five years at a large urban high school but moved to Ashton to live with her new husband who runs a dairy farm. She completed her bachelor's degree in social studies education at a small liberal arts college in Indiana, earning teacher certification in secondary social studies and English. At her previous school, she taught a combination of freshman English, world history, and U.S. government courses. Even though her first two or three years were difficult, Ms. Waterman loves teaching. She likes the challenge of trying to convince students that subjects they think are boring—history and government—can turn out to be quite exciting. Her favorite subject is U.S. government, but she also enjoys U.S. history. Her parents were active in politics when she was young, an interest that influences the way she teaches government. She especially enjoys engaging students in current events when topics arise that interest them. Her favorite time to teach U.S. government is during a presidential election.

The move to Ashton High is a major cultural shift for Ms. Waterman. She has gone from teaching city students to a completely rural setting. She grew up in a town of about twelve thousand, so she's accustomed to a smaller city, but not as small as two thousand. In her previous school, students consistently scored above average compared to others in the state, but the same is not true for Ashton High. Ashton's test scores are always well below the state average. The school has been struggling with a student dropout problem for many years. The graduation rate is less than 50 percent, and only about 20 percent of each graduating class enrolls in a two-year college or four-year university. The overwhelming majority of students plan to remain in the Ashton area to work on their family farms, take over the family ranch, or begin a job at one of the local dairies.

> Curriculum problems change in considerable ways when viewed from the perspective of a department chair compared to a classroom teacher. Consequently, it is important for students of curriculum to look at the subject from a variety of perspectives.

Ashton students, however, love competitive athletics, especially football and basketball. They begin playing both sports at an early age, especially the boys. One of the main tools Ashton High uses to keep students in school is the prospect of playing on the varsity football or basketball teams. In addition to using athletics to retain students, the school offers numerous extracurricular activities, for example, Future Farmers of America (FFA) and even a Rodeo Club, to entice students to remain in school. Ms. Waterman played sports and was involved in multiple activities while in high school, so she understands how much fun students have with these opportunities. At the same time, however, she is first and foremost a teacher, and she intends to emphasize academics every chance she gets.

A major change came to the Ashton school district just prior to Ms. Waterman's arrival. Ashton has a new superintendent and a new high school principal, both of whom began their positions within the last three years. They are insistent upon improving academic performance for all students, but they are especially interested in the high school. Their vision of academic quality is measured entirely on how well students perform on state tests, but the good news is that they are interested in improving academic quality. This is a change from the previous administration that preferred athletics and extracurricular activities to academics. The new leadership's emphasis on test scores concerns Ms. Waterman, but she also sees it as a way to raise the profile of academics not only at Ashton High but throughout the community.

When Ms. Waterman interviewed for her position during the spring, the school's principal, Mr. Browning, asked her if she would be interested in serving as social studies department chair. She agreed to accept this extra responsibility primarily because it came with an additional conference period as well as a small stipend. "Department chair" is her official title, but the term is a bit exaggerated given what she oversees. There is only one other member of her department, Coach Wilson, who has served as the head football coach in Ashton for fifteen years. Coach Wilson, unfortunately, dedicates very little time to his teaching. He is under a great deal of pressure to win games, and the team has only won four games in the last two years. Unless the team performs better this year, Coach Wilson is not likely to return. His teaching assignment consists of two classes of U.S. history and one of U.S. government. He has the rest of the day to work on football. Ms. Waterman teaches two world history, one world geography, and two U.S. history courses. She would prefer to teach the government class instead of world geography, but Coach Wilson has been teaching government for fifteen years and doesn't want to trade it for another course. That would require too much preparation. A third teacher, Ms. Fitzgerald, also helps with the social studies classes. Her primary teaching assignment is mathematics, but she teaches an economics course every other year.

When she arrived in late July to begin preparing for her new position, Ms. Waterman discovered many problems. First, the only social studies textbooks the school had were almost ten years old. The district should have purchased new books three years ago according to the textbook adoption cycle, but the books were nowhere to be found. She realized that new textbooks would have to be at the top of her agenda. A second problem she discovered once the school year had begun was that Coach Wilson pays no attention whatsoever to the Indiana social studies standards. Every day, he simply has students read from their old textbooks and answer questions from the back of each chapter. In addition, the textbooks were so old that they were based on a previous version of the Indiana standards. Ms. Waterman quickly realized that one of the reasons Coach Wilson's students perform so poorly on end-of-course exams is because he does not introduce them to the material found on the test. Ms. Waterman has attempted to discuss these matters with Coach Wilson on several occasions, but whenever she does, he says he is busy coaching football and doesn't have the time. When it comes to Ms. Fitzgerald's economics course, she also pays little attention to state standards. Her main focus has always been mathematics. Ms. Waterman discovered that she only picked up the economics course two years ago when another teacher refused to teach it. Ms. Waterman is concerned that Ms. Fitzgerald, like Coach Wilson, spends little time addressing the economics standards, a situation that undoubtedly has a negative impact on how well students perform on the end-of-course exam.

Another problem Ms. Waterman faces is that there are so few students at Ashton High that she is often forced to teach more than one course at a time. For example, she frequently has students who are completing courses in U.S. history, world history, and world geography all in the same classroom at the same time. Many times seniors have only one credit left to complete before they graduate, but there aren't enough of them to justify another section of each course that each student needs. As a result, Ms. Waterman, as department chair, is left with the responsibility of helping these students earn their final credits. She operates these classes much like an independent study, but since students tend to work at different paces, she has a hard time keeping them on track. Ms. Waterman's role as department chair means she has no choice but to oversee the completion of this work along with her other courses. She is concerned that she is doing a poor job at the impossible task of teaching three or four courses at one time in the same classroom. She sometimes feels like a circus performer trying to juggle four or five balls at once.

Several questions are at the heart of Ms. Waterman's problems. How can she enrich the social studies curriculum at Ashton High? How can she balance the demand for high test scores from her superintendent and principal while at the same time administering a curriculum that is broad, well rounded, and opens up new opportunities for students? How can she encourage her fellow teachers to dedicate more time to the state standards without dictating to them what they must teach and how? What options are available to her to address these problems? Will the state standards be helpful or harmful given the problems she faces?

Resolving Ms. Waterman's Problems

Those who adopt a systematic framework would analyze Ms. Waterman's situation and prescribe structure, organization, and efficiency. Just about every aspect of Ashton High cries out for teachers and school administrators who will use the tools the state has developed to make the school's social studies curriculum more consistent. Books desperately need to be ordered, teachers need to be educated on how to use the state standards, and Ms. Waterman needs to find ways to use test score data to shape the school's curriculum. Systematizers would applaud the use of test scores by the superintendent and the principal. They would encourage them to spread this perspective throughout the district since school districts must have a way to measure how well students are performing. A systematic view would more than likely audit Ashton High's social studies curriculum and conclude that the state chose to adopt standards for precisely this kind of situation.

Existentialists of course emphasize the personal interests of students, so this tradition would look first to the backgrounds of students who enroll at Ashton High. If Ms. Waterman wants to improve her students' performance, she should encourage Coach Wilson and Ms. Fitzgerald to find ways to differentiate their curriculum in a way that connects history and government to the needs of their students. Perhaps they could introduce more material on the history of agriculture in U.S. history courses, additional information on political issues facing ranchers in U.S. government courses, or lessons on the economic side of running a farm in economics classes. Existentialists would applaud the move to establish extracurricular activities that draw upon the needs and interests of students. Perhaps the school should consider creating more activities to keep students interested. Another potential move would be to have all students who drop out of Ashton High complete a survey that asks them questions about why they have chosen to leave. Existentialists would contend that if she truly wants to alleviate her problems, Ms. Waterman should focus on the students and their interests, not a lifeless standards document produced by state bureaucrats. All students have natural interests, and Ashton High is obviously failing to capitalize on what students want to study.

Radical curriculists would more than likely not be attracted to a teaching opportunity at Ashton High. Since the town is overwhelmingly conservative politically, radicals would have a lot of persuading to do if they expect to convince students and parents of their curricular vision. Radicals would not look to state standards for solutions to Ms. Waterman's problems. They would encourage her to reflect on the issues behind why the new principal and superintendent were placing so much emphasis on test scores. Is there a hidden agenda behind this idea, perhaps one that has the effect of sorting minority students into low paying jobs? When given test results, radicals would want Ms. Waterman to use them for analyzing how students from the various racial groups are performing. Is their parity between white and Hispanic students? Do test scores reveal that some teachers are better (or worse) than others at working with minority learners? A radical view would be insistent on raising additional questions pertaining to equity and minority student success.

Pragmatists acknowledge that Ms. Waterman has some challenging problems that need to be addressed. Since results matter most, pragmatists would encourage Ms. Waterman to talk with other teachers and department chairs to determine what has worked to improve test scores in other subjects.

Textbooks seem like an obvious necessity, but pragmatists would want Ms. Waterman to ask more questions about recent years at the school to find out why new textbooks cannot be found. There may be good reasons behind why these books are missing, and she should avoid jumping to conclusions until she understands the context completely. As for the dropout problem, whether the current extracurricular activities (or additional ones) should be supported depends upon how effective they are at keeping students in school. If survey results and personal experience reveal that students in specific activities—for example, basketball or the Rodeo Club—remain in school longer, then these activities should be retained, perhaps even expanded. If evidence and experience indicate the opposite, then the activities should be abandoned as ineffective. As an administrator and a teacher, Ms. Waterman should always start by looking at the experiential results she wants to achieve and work backward from there.

Given her situation, a deliberative view finds many opportunities for Ms. Waterman to use her deliberative abilities to address the problems she's facing. The commonplaces provide her with a framework that she can use to organize the factors she should keep in mind as she decides what to do. To begin with, she needs to imagine numerous ways in which she can gain access to textbooks for the school year that will begin in just four weeks. Given the small number of students at Ashton High, she could more than likely call area school districts to see if anyone would allow her to borrow books until she's had a chance to find money to buy them. Perhaps even some districts could donate books, which would mean that she could keep them. Another option would be to contact publishers to see if online or electronic versions of current textbooks are available. Electronic books would give her students something to work with immediately while they wait for the hard copy texts to arrive.

Ms. Waterman also would recognize that, given the state of affairs she has found, attention to system—within reason—is paramount. The Indiana social studies standards should help to alleviate several problems that her department faces. She knows that all of Indiana's standards can be found online. She also knows that each standard comes with links to high-quality lessons developed by the National Endowment for the Humanities (NEH). One possible course of action would be for her to sit down with Coach Wilson, once the football season is complete, and show him how using the new standards would not only help his students to remain academically eligible, but also would improve their performance on state tests. State standards might even reduce the amount of time Coach Wilson spends preparing for class. In dealing with him, she also recognizes that many students look up to him as the head football coach. She knows that she could use their respect for him as a tool to improve the influence of social studies at Ashton High. If she can turn Coach Wilson into an ally, he can help her to achieve what she wants to do with social studies. She and Coach Wilson both know that athletes cannot play unless they make the appropriate grades, so a deliberative approach would find ways to build a relationship with Coach Wilson that is beneficial to everyone involved. She should avoid setting up an opposition between athletics and academics that would end up hurting both.

Just like with Coach Wilson, Ms. Waterman could show Ms. Fitzgerald how the economics standards would provide her with many new ideas for lessons, connect her curriculum to state tests, and perhaps even reduce the time she spends preparing for class. The standards also would help Ms. Waterman to address the problem of multiple students completing different courses at the same time. She already has no choice but to teach these courses as independent studies, but the standards would allow her students to know exactly what they should be studying. The standards have the potential to provide a much-needed backbone to the coursework Ms. Waterman already requires her students to complete. In addition, pointing students to the online lessons developed by the NEH would enable Ms. Waterman to continue teaching her larger class while supervising students simultaneously as they move through the social studies standards and the NEH lessons tied to them. As a supplement, the NEH lessons might be quite beneficial to students completing independent study type courses.

To create a truly liberating social studies curriculum for Ashton students, a deliberative view would find Ms. Waterman searching for ways to open up opportunities for students to see what they can accomplish beyond their immediate surroundings. She could explore many opportunities. She could arrange a trip to the state capital of Indianapolis for the highest achieving students at the end of each semester. Her principal and the superintendent want higher test scores, so Ms. Waterman could show them the benefit of rewarding high-achieving students with a trip to Indianapolis. Perhaps one of them will agree to approve funding for the trip. Other options would be to invite guest speakers from the state level to her U.S. government class, preferably leaders who are dealing with policy issues that affect farmers and ranchers. An opportunity like this may inspire Ashton High students to become leaders in the field of farming and ranching. High-profile guest speakers could gain the interest of parents, making such an opportunity a community-wide event. In all cases, a deliberative approach would find Ms. Waterman continually searching for creative solutions that will open up new opportunities for students to perform well on tests, imagine themselves in leadership positions, and raise expectations for what can be achieved by Ashton graduates.

A final case on the subject of curriculum standards shifts our focus away from high school concerns to the interdisciplinary world of elementary curriculum. We also shift from the Midwest to the state of Texas, where the emphasis on standards and tests is perhaps more powerful than anywhere else.

■ Michelle Ochoa: Fifth-Grade Teacher

Ms. Michelle Ochoa recently accepted a position to teach fifth grade at Branchwood Elementary in a suburban district outside of a large city in Texas. She completed her bachelor's degree in history at a midsized private university also in Texas. She never thought about teaching until her last semester in college, when she finally began to think seriously about what job she would find after graduation. After some soul searching, the idea of teaching elementary school is what came most powerfully to mind. As a result, she completed a six-week summer teacher certification program that certified her to teach grades four through eight. Her choice would have been to teach in a middle school, preferably eighth-grade American history, but the job she found was fifth grade at Branchwood. She knows the district well, since she graduated from one of the two high schools in the Branchwood District only four years before. Branchwood is a school with students from an upper-middle-class background. Houses surrounding Branchwood cost anywhere from $500,000 to $1 million. The district is well funded by the state, has lots of parental support (too much at times, in fact), and the students generally behave quite well.

Ms. Ochoa was extremely nervous as the school year began. She did not feel adequately prepared for the demands that come with teaching fifth grade. She learned some useful tips when completing her alternative certification program, but she now regrets not majoring in education as an undergraduate. Although the first few months have been stressful, she has managed to survive without any major problems. Fortunately, Ms. Ochoa was assigned to a magnificent mentor teacher, Ms. Gosar, who has been kind enough to share all of her materials from fifteen years of teaching. Without Ms. Gosar's help, there's no way Michelle could have survived the first few weeks of school. She expected to have more problems with classroom management, but discipline turned out not to be much of an issue since Branchwood students are generally well behaved.

Ms. Ochoa's biggest problems have come with the teaching of mathematics and in dealing with difficult parents. Mathematics is emphasized strongly at the fifth-grade level in Texas since all students must complete the state-mandated mathematics test at the end of fifth grade. Ms. Ochoa has found some of the concepts required by the fifth-grade mathematics standards—for example, fractions and volume—to be quite difficult to teach. After many weeks of trying to get these concepts across to students but having little success, she is hoping this material will simply not appear on the test in April. If her students are tested on these concepts, their scores will almost certainly reflect the difficulties she has had.

Ms. Ochoa also has run into several sets of parents who have questioned every move she has made. One mother complained to the Branchwood principal, Mr. Avant, about the amount of homework Ms. Ochoa was requiring. Ms. Ochoa has high standards for her students, and she refused, quite emphatically, to lower her standards when this mother called to complain. Mr. Avant supported Ms. Ochoa but also warned her not to get carried away with homework assignments.

Even though Branchwood's students score quite well on exams each year, the pressure from Mr. Avant to keep scores high is intense. The Branchwood district superintendent has told Mr. Avant that his potential for promotion depends on his ability to raise test scores at Branchwood. Even prior to the first day of school, Mr. Avant required all teachers to analyze test data from previous years and then show evidence on their lesson plans that demonstrates how they differentiate their curriculum for individual students based on test data. In addition to mathematics, reading and science are tested at the fifth-grade level in Texas, so these subjects take precedence in the curriculum along with mathematics. Ms. Ochoa enjoys reading and science, but her true passion is social studies. She is inspired by the opportunities that her family has been afforded after emigrating to the United States when she was only ten. Because of hard work and the freedom to innovate, Michelle's father has become a successful restaurant owner. Ms. Ochoa wants her students to understand how fortunate young Americans are to have the freedoms that too many people take for granted. Good citizenship is a major theme in Ms. Ochoa's class, something she emphasizes every day beginning with the process of establishing class rules on day one and continuing with the reciting of the Pledge of Allegiance.

Ms. Ochoa is deeply concerned that three months into her first year she has yet to teach even one social studies lesson. She feels like she is wasting everything she learned as a history major. In the weeks before the beginning of the school year, she bought almost a dozen books on teaching American history, but now that Christmas is only three weeks away, she has used none of them. She is frustrated because, much to her surprise, she has come to enjoy teaching fifth grade and would consider teaching it again next year, but only if she can find a way to incorporate her love of social studies into her curriculum. She wants to teach students about great figures like George Washington, Thomas Jefferson, Harriet Tubman, Stephen Douglas, Abraham Lincoln, Susan B. Anthony, and Martin Luther King, Jr. She believes the best way to teach citizenship is to spend time with the lives of these great Americans who exhibited the traits we want young people to emulate. Ms. Ochoa wants her students to learn about these figures not just to appreciate their role in history but to inspire her fifth graders to become visionary leaders.

She has had no opportunity to do this, however, because her fellow teachers—and more importantly Mr. Avant—have told her not to waste her time on social studies. Avant told her point blank during the third week of school: "Michelle, I'm glad you like social studies, but our school is rated based on how well students perform on tests in reading, science, and math. We'll worry about social studies when the state requires a fifth-grade test in the subject." These words struck Ms. Ochoa as a command, not a suggestion. As a first year teacher, she is naturally nervous about doing anything that would upset the administration, hence her complete neglect of social studies.

With the passage of No Child Left Behind, many people have become concerned that the emphasis on mathematics and reading within NCLB has marginalized other subjects within the elementary curriculum, for example, history, geography, and art.

Ms. Ochoa faces a host of problems that are common to first year teachers. What can she do to emphasize social studies in her fifth-grade curriculum? How might she use the Texas social studies standards to incorporate more lessons on American history? Is there a way that she can keep her principal satisfied by emphasizing the upcoming tests while at the same time introducing students to seminal figures in American history? What about the problems she has run into with parents? How might she address their concerns while maintaining her professionalism? Finally, what can she do to address her problems with teaching mathematics? How can she balance her interest in teaching social studies with the reality that mathematics matters more at this time? These questions are not easy to resolve, but Ms. Ochoa can address them successfully through creativity, imagination, and deliberation.

> The issue of curriculum standards also differs when different subjects are considered. Some elementary teachers, for example, may want more structure when it comes to their mathematics curriculum but want more flexibility with reading and writing. As a result, they may rely more heavily on the math standards than they do on the standards for other subjects.

Resolving Ms. Ochoa's Problems

A systematic view of Ms. Ochoa's situation makes the argument for change in the following way. Teaching to a specific test is not a problem, argue systematic curriculists, as long as the test includes information that is tied to state standards. The most important subjects for future economic productivity in Texas and nationally are reading, mathematics, and science. Emphasizing these subjects at the elementary level is perfectly fine, although social studies standards for fifth grade and beyond have been developed. Ms. Ochoa has a responsibility to include these social studies standards as part of her curriculum, even though the state has yet to develop a fifth-grade test. Nevertheless, prioritizing subjects that will be tested at the end of the year is just fine. There will be plenty of time for students to learn more about American history and government during the eighth and eleventh grades.

An existentialist viewpoint is sympathetic with Ms. Ochoa's desire to teach her preferred subject of social studies but wonders if fifth graders are prepared developmentally for the kind of historical understanding she wants them to have. Social studies education must be active, not just the memorization of historical facts. Existentialists would encourage Ms. Ochoa to focus students' attention on the immediate problems at Branchwood, perhaps by initiating a student council program if one does not exist already. The best way for her to teach social studies, existentialists contend, would be for her to encourage students to find problems at Branchwood that they want to solve, and then encourage them to find ways to solve them.

Radicals would appreciate the idea of using a student council to introduce social studies concepts but would want the efforts of this group to focus on community issues, not specific school problems. From a radical view, Ms. Ochoa should take the opportunity to introduce Branchwood students to the vast inequalities in wealth that are found within their extended community. Virtually all of the students at Branchwood have never experienced the poverty-stricken conditions that are found only a few miles from Branchwood, so the best approach from a radical perspective would be to find ways to open students' minds by showing them how other children in their relatively small town are forced to live. Field trips, guest speakers, poverty simulations, and role-play lessons are successful ways to introduce students to poverty and inequality from a radical perspective. When teaching these lessons, Ms. Ochoa should use her personal background to show how her family has overcome discrimination. Her story can be a powerful way to encourage students to fight for minority rights.

Pragmatists would commend Ms. Ochoa's ability to draw upon the experience of her fellow teachers, especially Ms. Gosar, as she has struggled to make it through her first semester. Given the multiple problems she is facing, a pragmatic view encourages Ms. Ochoa to focus on one problem at a time instead of trying to do everything at once. She should continue to talk with other teachers at Branchwood to see what social studies lessons they have found to work. If she can find a few minutes perhaps once per week, she should try out these lessons, during both mathematics and science, to see if they work in her classroom as well. If these lessons engage students actively, she should try them again next year. If not, she should keep searching to find lessons that produce excitement in her students.

From a deliberative perspective, perhaps the first step toward resolving Ms. Ochoa's problems is for her to recognize that her desire to incorporate more social studies could be resolved if she simply changed her wishes. Deliberators recognize that changing what we want can resolve problems quickly, or at least shift our efforts toward new problems. The challenge is that deliberators also must balance their commitment to ideals with the immediate problems they are facing. If Ms. Ochoa persists in her desire to teach social studies, a deliberative perspective would find her searching for other teachers who have found time to integrate this subject at the fifth-grade level. If none are to be found, she could consult the social studies coordinator for the Branchwood district, who is by definition an advocate of the social studies. She knows that social studies coordinators are almost always experienced teachers who have faced problems similar to what Ms. Ochoa is confronting. If her principal mentions to her again that she should focus only on reading, mathematics, and science, she could gently remind him that Texas has developed state social studies standards for fifth grade as well. Consequently, she has no choice but to incorporate social studies into her curriculum. The challenge, she could remind him, is to balance social studies with the other subjects in the curriculum.

Another possibility would be for Ms. Ochoa to incorporate social studies into her language arts curriculum. Students must read and write in order to prepare for state tests, and incorporating short biographies of figures like Abraham Lincoln and Susan B. Anthony would be a good way to introduce the material she wants to teach while at the same time teaching reading. In addition, she could require students to write about their family histories, perhaps even teaching them to complete oral history interviews with older members of their families. One more possibility would be for Ms. Ochoa to begin with a small idea such as introducing a "current events minute" following the pledge of allegiance each Friday. She could assign a different student with the task of bringing to class a current event in social studies that he or she finds interesting. Students would then be responsible for presenting their current event to the class in one minute or less. The class could spend a few minutes discussing the topic before moving on to their daily mathematics lesson. These options would not radically change what Ms. Ochoa is doing, but they would open up opportunities for her to discuss what she wants to teach. From a broader policy perspective, a long-term possibility would be for Ms. Ochoa to join the effort to encourage the state of Texas to require a fifth-grade social studies test. She knows that social studies advocates in Texas have argued for at least ten years that the lack of a fifth-grade social studies test diminishes the importance of American history in the curriculum. Ms. Ochoa could partner with the Texas Council for the Social Studies, which has led the charge for the state test, to raise the significance of social studies at the fifth-grade level.

To deal with her problems with parents, a deliberative view might find Ms. Ochoa consulting the Branchwood Parent Teacher Association to learn more about the expectations parents bring with them to Branchwood. She realizes that the better she understands Branchwood parents, the better she will be able to communicate with them about her expectations. She may realize that she needs to have a better understanding of how much homework other teachers in the school require. By the time Branchwood students enter her classroom for fifth grade, they have had four years of experience with Branchwood teachers, so Ms. Ochoa needs to make sure that her expectations aren't completely out of line with what parents have experienced during the past four years. Even though she plans to gather more information and perhaps adjust her homework expectations accordingly, Ms. Ochoa is insistent upon maintaining high standards for homework. After all, the students' next promotion will be to middle school, where rigor increases. The most likely result will be a slight accommodation in the amount of homework she is requiring, but perhaps not a radical change.

When she reflects on the problems she is facing, Ms. Ochoa realizes that the mathematics problem is the one that may take the longest to resolve. Her favorite subjects in school were history and English. Her strongest grades were never in mathematics and science. She realizes that if she continues to teach fifth grade she will need to spend time with people who are successful at teaching fifth-grade mathematics concepts. In addition to talking with other teachers, she could begin to look for professional development opportunities at area universities. Ms. Ochoa not only needs additional experience teaching mathematics, she also could benefit from a two- or three-week summer workshop on mathematics curriculum and teaching. Such a workshop could begin to make up for her lack of sufficient preparation as an undergraduate. With all of these problems, a deliberative perspective reminds Ms. Ochoa that she will never have a perfect classroom, but she can improve her situation considerably if she finds creative ways to provide a well-rounded, liberating curriculum to all of her fifth graders.

The next chapter continues the practice of using cases to show how specific curriculum problems can be resolved but shifts the context from K–12 schools to curriculum within colleges and universities. Curriculum problems within colleges and universities are not necessarily more complex, but they do become multifaceted in different ways. For example, few topics are more vexing for university administrators than the subject of core curriculum. Perhaps the difficulties surrounding this topic indicate its significance for the future of higher education.

■ Discussion Questions

1. Which of the five traditions is most closely related to the idea of curriculum standards?

2. How can state standards documents be both positive and negative from the perspective of teachers and curriculum directors?

3. How do teachers and department chairs view the idea of curriculum standards differently?

4. What about district-level curriculum directors? How might they view curriculum standards differently compared with teachers and department chairs?

5. What role can curriculum standards play in providing equal education to all students?

6. What should be the proper relationship between curriculum standards and end-of-year tests?

7. When dealing with the question of how to implement state standards, what does the deliberative tradition provide that the others do not?

CHAPTER 8

How Can We Reinstitutionalize a Core Curriculum at Our University?

A DELIBERATIVE tradition assumes there is a body of principles, arts, and methods that should serve as the foundation for any educational program, whether it's found in K–12 schools or in universities. When viewed from a deliberative perspective, the challenges that surround curriculum are similar regardless of the age of students. Consequently, students of curriculum, whether they plan to work in higher education or not, can learn from curriculum problems that arise within colleges and universities.

The title of this chapter assumes that a core curriculum at the higher education level was once commonplace and now should be reestablished. Given this view, deliberators look upon the demise of core curriculum as a significant step away from the ideal of a liberal curriculum for all. A deliberator's answer to the question "Should we reinstitutionalize a core curriculum?" is almost always yes, but deliberators also recognize that the state of affairs within which we must work to achieve the goal of a core curriculum is often far removed from the ideal. Deliberators also realize that the effort to create a core curriculum must compete with other cultural factors that often contradict the ideal of a common core. Forces such as hyperspecialization by faculty while in graduate school, extreme emphasis on graduate teaching to the detriment of undergraduates in research universities, and ideological barriers between faculty can prevent the teaching of a common core curriculum.

To understand better how the problems surrounding core curriculum arise and how they might be resolved, the

Core Curriculum

Core curriculum is a concept that is not well known to many people today. The idea behind a core curriculum is that it fosters cohesiveness and community within an educational institution. Those who argue for a core curriculum believe that there are stories, types of knowledge, and ways of thinking that should be taught as the basis for what constitutes an educated person in any community. These forms of knowledge, moreover, are represented in the traditional academic disciplines that also embody ways of thinking. Subjects almost always selected as part of a core curriculum include mathematics, history, language and literature, science, and foreign languages.

Another way to view curriculum is not so much by the subjects that are taught but by the core texts that are chosen by a school or university. This more interdisciplinary approach often selects classical texts like Homer's *Iliad*, Plato's *Republic*, Aristotle's *Ethics*, and Virgil's *Aeneid* as books that all students within a school or university must read as the glue, or core curriculum, that holds the school together. Regardless of what constitutes a core curriculum, however, the goal is for the core to provide students with similar experiences, ways of thinking, and forms of communication that hold them together as a community.

One practical way that colleges and universities can provide better curriculum leadership is to establish a position, for example associate dean for undergraduate curriculum, whose primary job is to oversee undergraduate core curriculum. Core curriculum deserves and needs this type of attention if it is to flourish.

following two cases describe scenarios in which higher education leaders desire to reestablish a common core. As in chapter 7, both scenarios derive from my experience as a curriculum writer, university professor, and member of numerous curriculum committees. Both are composite sketches, not real-life institutions. The first example comes from perhaps the most difficult circumstance in which to establish a core curriculum for all: a large state-supported research university.

■ Northern State University

Northern State University (NSU) began as a teachers college but has since emerged as a research university. Enrolling almost forty thousand students, NSU has nine academic units, including a College of Arts and Sciences, School of Education, School of Business, Nursing School, School of Engineering, School of Music, Pharmacy School, Honors

College, and a Graduate School. NSU is located in a city of approximately 150,000 and enrolls most of its students from the Midwestern states of Indiana, Illinois, Iowa, Michigan, and Wisconsin.

Dr. Martin Fitzgerald

Dr. Martin Fitzgerald, the university's provost, is in his first semester since coming to NSU from his role as dean of the College of Arts and Sciences at a research university of a similar size on the West Coast. Provost Fitzgerald's background is in English, and part of the reason he accepted his new position is because the Northern State president, as well as the board of trustees, is committed to reestablishing a common core curriculum. Dr. Fitzgerald is excited about this new opportunity. Even though the institution has had success at moving in the direction of producing additional research, many NSU alumni have become increasingly critical of the way the university has de-emphasized teaching, especially at the undergraduate level. Many alumni have strong emotional connections to the time they spent as undergraduates at NSU learning from excellent professors who were dedicated to teaching. They want to ensure that the kind of education they received will remain intact for many years. Powerful alumni groups view the school as primarily a teaching institution, despite the fact that NSU has recruited more than one hundred great researchers in recent years. An intense battle has been going on for at least a decade over the future of the institution. Some alumni support the move toward emphasizing research and grant funding, whereas others argue that the move costs too much money, belittles longtime NSU faculty, and abandons the mission of the university. Provost Fitzgerald was hired because in his previous position he faced many of these same challenges and achieved a considerable amount of success at balancing teaching and research. He also became well known for his leadership in building a new core curriculum. As a graduate of St. John's College, Dr. Fitzgerald is deeply committed to the goals of liberal arts education. He is driven by the prospect of creating an institution that values passing foundational knowledge from one generation to the next.

Recent appointees to the NSU Board of Trustees support these same ideals. They believe strongly that the institution needs to return to its roots, part of which means an increased focus on undergraduate curriculum and teaching. He must

St. John's College—located in Annapolis, Maryland, and Santa Fe, New Mexico—was established to provide a liberal arts curriculum rooted in the Great Books. Students read and discuss seminal works from the Western tradition such as Homer's *Iliad* and *Odyssey*, St. Augustine's *Confessions*, and Darwin's *Origin of Species*.

achieve this goal, however, without damaging the growing research that is a source of great pride to many new faculty. Building a high-quality core curriculum while balancing teaching with research is the goal he must keep in mind. He recognizes that if he succeeds, he will have built an institution that can serve as a model for others, since virtually every institution of the size of NSU faces these same challenges.

The president of NSU, Dr. Willow, is sixty-eight years old and has been president for eight years. He is widely rumored to be contemplating retirement, so everyone knows that Provost Fitzgerald's appointment is critical for the future of the institution. When he began to recruit Fitzgerald, President Willow was searching for someone who could provide long-term leadership. President Willow and the provost search committee believed that Fitzgerald had all of the characteristics necessary to lead NSU into the future. He is a nationally recognized scholar, a good teacher, and an effective communicator. He has a proven record of reform and has demonstrated his ability to inspire more and better research. He impressed the search committee as the kind of teacher-scholar who can help NSU tackle the university's problems. Because of his background and the impending retirement of Dr. Willow, Provost Fitzgerald began his tenure as provost with a considerable amount of influence. When he accepted the position, he knew he would begin with enough political capital to take on several reform initiatives, which is one of the main reasons he chose to accept the position. He also knows, however, that he will need to choose reform initiatives wisely to avoid spreading his opportunities too thin. Since the reform of undergraduate core curriculum was foremost on the minds of those who recruited him, Fitzgerald knows that he will need to move forward quickly with this part of his set of initiatives.

Another central person in Provost Fitzgerald's effort is Dr. Martha Curie, dean of NSU's College of Arts and Sciences. As a nationally known chemist, Dr. Curie's background is far removed from the liberal arts ideal that animates Provost Fitzgerald. At the same time, she appreciates the goals that Fitzgerald wants to push forward. Even while she supports this aspect of Fitzgerald's vision, she has many other initiatives that she must keep in mind as she works with the three hundred faculty and sixteen department chairs who make up the arts and sciences college. For one example, the university is building a $200 million science building that will bring all of the science departments under one roof. Working with department chairs and faculty to coordinate this move, in addition to normal dean work, takes up nearly all of Curie's time. Because of her connections as a scientist, she has been successful at recruiting a number of department chairs who have radically improved the grant writing and publication productivity of the science departments. She was brought to NSU to increase research productivity, which, in the minds of some faculty and alumni, runs counter to the goal of high-quality undergraduate curriculum and teaching. Much of the opposition to dedicating more time and resources to core curriculum emanates from department chairs and faculty within Curie's college.

Since he has only been on the job for three months, Provost Fitzgerald of course has not had time to make major changes. He has, however, had time to complete a careful study of the state of affairs when it comes to core curriculum. He has had time to begin the process of establishing a General Education Task Force that will make recommendations to the university faculty. Within the next month, he will appoint faculty members to the task force. Fitzgerald's review of core curriculum has revealed that all students at NSU, regardless of major, must complete twenty-seven hours of general education coursework. To some people within the NSU community, this twenty-seven-hour requirement may seem like a core curriculum, but not to Fitzgerald. Within these twenty-seven hours, no specific courses are required, no list of books is mandatory reading for all students, and no common set of curriculum standards has been developed. The university made the switch to a "cafeteria" model during the 1970s under the leadership of a provost who wanted to provide students with more choices that, in his words, would better "meet their needs and interests." Before the cafeteria system was implemented, all students completed required courses in each of three main areas: social sciences, humanities, and physical sciences. Today, however, students are allowed to choose nine hours from each block. Beyond that, each division now includes anywhere from ten to fifteen courses. When the switch was made to the cafeteria system, the decision to allow students to choose didn't seem all that significant because there were only four or five courses within each block. Over the years, however, the number of optional courses in each block has grown substantially. Another problem is that some of these courses are so narrow that they can never provide a broad, liberating curriculum that would achieve the ideals of liberal education. Examples include "The History of Film and Radio in the United States," "Race, Class, and Gender in America," and "Economics and Healthcare." Dr. Fitzgerald thinks these courses are fine for upper-level undergraduates and graduate students, but not for introductory courses that are designed to foster the liberal arts. He is adamant that they do not belong in a core curriculum.

In addition to narrow courses counting toward core curriculum credit, Provost Fitzgerald has been unable to find a document that outlines the goals NSU wants to accomplish with its general education program. He learned from experience at his previous institution that serious deliberation about the purpose of core curriculum is an essential first step to long-lasting change. No such conversation appears to have taken place at NSU, at least not for the last five or ten years. The general education program appears to have drifted as other priorities—for example, the development of new graduate programs, attention to grant writing, and the pursuit of publications—seized the attention of university administrators. The time appears to have arrived, however, for the university to turn its attention once again to its general education curriculum. Dr. Fitzgerald has many challenges before him if he expects to make significant headway, but by asking the right questions and using his influence wisely, he may be able to achieve lasting reform.

> Accrediting agencies have begun to pressure universities to define the goals they want to achieve with their undergraduate programs, especially the core curriculum that should provide a common experience for all students.

Resolving Provost Fitzgerald's Problems

The problems that Provost Fitzgerald faces are familiar to anyone who has attempted reform of core curriculum. He faces questions that require careful attention and a delicate touch. For instance, how can he foster additional support for core curriculum among the faculty? Where can he find pockets of support? What can he use to foster support? What are the strengths and weaknesses of each member of his administrative team, and how can he use their talents most appropriately? How can he balance the demands that have been placed upon him for curriculum reform with the developing research aspect of NSU? How can he reemphasize undergraduate curriculum while at the same time move forward with encouraging research? What might he draw upon to help the General Education Task Force craft goals and expectations for general education curriculum?

Fitzgerald will be wise to keep the commonplaces in mind as he formulates answers to these questions and makes decisions about what actions to take. Knowledge of the curriculum traditions and the commonplaces should guide his efforts, since virtually every argument he will hear is rooted in one or more of the commonplaces. Of the hurdles that Provost Fitzgerald faces, three stand out as most significant: lack of faculty support, lack of balance between teaching and research, and limited resources. The next section describes each of these problems and then discusses how they might be resolved from a deliberative perspective.

Lack of Faculty Support

As best he can discern, Provost Fitzgerald faces resistance regarding the core curriculum idea from almost half of the tenured and tenure-track faculty. This is the first and most significant challenge he faces. Most of the resistance is based on apathy or entrenched self-interest. The apathy results from the fact that many faculty have other priorities. They would prefer to conduct research and teach graduate students. They have little to no concern with undergraduates. Self-interest is a potential problem because core curriculum requires setting priorities. Some courses must be elevated over others. Not all courses can be part of the core curriculum. The current cafeteria approach avoids this issue by relinquishing control of general education curriculum to students in the name of meeting their "individual needs and interests." The effect, however, is that the system undermines the idea of a common cure. Fitzgerald knows that the argument based on meeting students' needs and interests is a powerful one that is rooted in the learner commonplace. He also, however, knows how to counter this argument by emphasizing the other commonplaces, specifically teachers and subject matter. The cafeteria model demotes the commonplace of subject matter, removing any ideal of a common body of knowledge for all students. It also erodes the authority of faculty. These are points that should resonate with many faculty who are committed to their disciplines.

The cafeteria method also avoids the issue of priorities when it comes to new course development. As new faculty have been added during the last fifteen to twenty years, they have created courses that have become part of the optional list from which students choose. The ideal of a core curriculum for all students has been diluted as each new course has been added to the list. Removing a course from any one of the blocks is certain to encounter resistance. Every course has its defender. In the face of this situation, Provost Fitzgerald must find a way to alter the current arrangement without alienating key faculty. Whatever action he takes, he knows that it must have the effect of treating the core departments as fairly as possible. He needs a vision that is inspiring enough to overcome the apathy that can destroy his effort.

Even though the problems he faces in gaining faculty support are substantial, Provost Fitzgerald has a number of tools on his side. To begin with, he comes into his position with a great deal of political capital. If he uses it wisely and builds support among the faculty, he can make headway. He will, however, need to use all of his political and rhetorical abilities to persuade as many faculty as possible to support the curricular effort. He will need to take the vision developed by the General Education Task Force and communicate it clearly and consistently to all NSU constituents.

Although communication is essential, the most important task Fitzgerald faces is the choice of which faculty will serve on the General Education Task Force. He will need to invite high profile, well-respected faculty from all units on campus. He will need to deliberate carefully with knowledgeable people about which members of the faculty will work well together on the task force. Members need the ability to communicate with their home units about the goals the task force recommends, they need to believe in the ideal of a liberal education for all, and they need to be able to garner support for the task force's efforts. The most important choice that Fitzgerald will make is the selection of a task force chair. He must choose someone who is widely respected throughout the university, has knowledge of how difficult curricular reform can be, can communicate effectively with constituents throughout the university, and will build rapport among the members of the task force. The choice of the chair is one of the most important decisions Provost Fitzgerald will make during his first year as provost. If he chooses poorly, his effort to reform core curriculum will have no chance of succeeding.

Another way Fitzgerald can gain faculty support is through hiring. The provost must approve every faculty hiring decision. He can use this tool to hire faculty who support the ideals he wants to achieve. He can indicate to department chairs that he wants to recruit faculty who view themselves as teachers *and* researchers, not one or the other. He also can work to find faculty who value teaching undergraduates in addition to graduate students. He can hire professors who have shown an interest in teaching broad, survey courses as well as specialized, upper-level courses. With the right vision for core curriculum, Provost Fitzgerald can begin to recruit faculty who support the reforms he has in mind. In six or seven years, perhaps the faculty can *lead* the vision for core curriculum at NSU instead of hindering it.

A third tool that Provost Fitzgerald has at his disposal is an upcoming accreditation visit by Midwestern Accreditation, the university's accrediting body. In recent accreditation reviews with other institutions, Midwestern has placed a great deal of emphasis on the idea of general education curriculum. As part of the review process, NSU must demonstrate to Midwestern that the university has a clear plan for improving its general education curriculum. At the present time, NSU does not have such a document, a problem that Provost Fitzgerald will communicate immediately to the General Education Task Force. Losing accreditation would be nothing short of a disaster for NSU. In addition to public embarrassment, one result would be that the university could no longer receive any federal funding for research or student scholarships. Fitzgerald knows the likelihood of losing accreditation is remote, but it remains a possibility that he has the duty to share with faculty. Knowledge of the possibility that federal research funding could disappear will get the attention of every faculty member on campus, especially those in the sciences and social sciences who rely on federal support for their research.

None of these actions will guarantee that Provost Fitzgerald will succeed. If he takes careful, well-conceived steps, however, he will have a much better chance of succeeding. He will need to search for opportunities to persuade faculty that renewing the university's core curriculum is not only in their own best interest, but also in the long-term best interest of the university.

Lack of Balance between Teaching and Research

A second hurdle that Fitzgerald must overcome has to deal with the relationship between teaching and research throughout the university, but especially in tenure and promotion decisions. Tenure committees at the department, college, and

The issue of how to balance teaching with research is something that universities will be dealing with for many years. At first glance, curriculum seems to be a separate matter, but until a university decides how to answer the question of where to place its emphasis when it comes to teaching and research, curriculum questions will remain impossible to resolve.

university levels have consistently struggled with how to balance teaching and research. Fitzgerald's review of tenure policies has convinced him that teaching and research are not emphasized equally. Research is by far the more dominant factor. This situation is perhaps to be expected given that NSU now bills itself as a "research university," but after talking with hundreds of faculty and alumni, he has come to the conclusion that the true vision of the university is one in which teaching and research are partners, not antagonists. He wants faculty to see how the two can build upon one another instead of competing. He would like to see service emphasized more than it is at the present time, but for now, service will need to remain a somewhat distant third to teaching and research.

One way for Provost Fitzgerald to address this problem would be to draw upon the influence of Dean Curie as a research scientist. He could develop her as the main person responsible for pushing forward the research aims of NSU, while he dedicates his time, at least initially, to core curriculum. Dr. Curie is known for her background as a researcher, so this role fits with her talents and background. Another advantage of this approach is that the twin goals of teaching and research would be institutionalized in two influential positions at NSU: the provost's office and the university's most powerful dean. Also, Dean Curie has the potential to influence the department chairs and faculty who could potentially undermine the core curriculum effort. As a consequence, building support with her is significant.

Another way to address the problem of balancing teaching and research would be for Fitzgerald to appoint a second task force that would review tenure guidelines with a specific eye to balancing teaching and research. If he chooses this path, however, he will need to think intently about when to initiate the effort. He wants to be careful not to try too many reforms at once and risk achieving nothing. His long-term goal is to build a vision for core curriculum that is sustainable, a goal he cannot achieve unless teaching and research are balanced in tenure and promotion decisions. Given that changes to tenure policy can be even more vexing than core curriculum reform, the best plan might be for Provost Fitzgerald to wait to initiate a task force on tenure until the General Education Task Force has completed its work. Provost Fitzgerald, nevertheless, recognizes that institutionalizing a balance between teaching and research is crucial if he hopes to establish a core curriculum that will last.

Limited Resources

A third impediment Fitzgerald faces is limited resources. No university has unlimited funding, so priorities must be set and budgets built accordingly. Fitzgerald recognizes that reform of undergraduate curriculum takes time and money. He will need to pay task force members for their efforts, either with stipends or with release time from teaching. He will need to provide the General Education Task Force with funds they will need to study core curriculum at other universities. They may need to travel to two or three universities to envision all possibilities for NSU. When the task force has established a document that has been reviewed by significant groups throughout the university, the resulting vision will need to be shared widely. Well-published, attractive documents that communicate the vision and plan for core curriculum will be essential to garnering support among the faculty, staff, and alumni. Publications of this quality take time and money. If he fails to budget for this part of the task, Fitzgerald will risk losing an opportunity to build support. If funds are not available, one option would be for Fitzgerald to contact granting agencies that have shown an interest in the reform of core curriculum. Several may be interested in supporting the university's efforts.

If financial constraints persist, still another possibility would be for Provost Fitzgerald to begin his reform efforts with a small pilot program of approximately 150 students. Such a program could potentially grow over time but could be initiated without sweeping changes that impact the entire university. This option is one that Provost Fitzgerald may want to encourage the task force to recommend.

Even beyond monetary concerns, another valuable resource that Fitzgerald should keep in mind is time. To busy faculty members who are completing book projects or conducting research or advising students, the wise use of time is critical. This issue may seem trivial to some, but it matters significantly to busy faculty. Provost Fitzgerald will need to make sure that the General Education Task Force collects and disseminates material to faculty in a wise manner so that they can review and provide feedback efficiently.

Even if he takes all of these steps, Provost Fitzgerald is not guaranteed to succeed. He can, however, increase his chances if he deliberates wisely with staff and faculty about the challenges before them. Perhaps most important of all, he

Core Curriculum within Universities

In 2010, the American Council of Trustees and Alumni (ACTA) conducted a study of American colleges and universities to determine the extent to which they required all students to complete courses in seven core subjects: composition, literature, foreign language, U.S. government or history, economics, mathematics, and natural or physical science. They rated every major college or university in the country based on how many of these seven subjects they require students to take. To report their results, ACTA graded these institutions on a scale of A to F, with those schools that require six to seven of the core subjects receiving an A, four or five core subjects receiving a B, three core subjects receiving a C, four core subjects receiving a D, and those that require one or no core subjects receiving an F. Of the more than seven hundred colleges and universities that ACTA studied, only sixteen (or 2 percent) received a grade of A. Many of the most well-known universities in the country did not score well. For example, Harvard received a grade of D, Princeton a grade of C, and Yale a grade of F. The majority of schools earned a grade of either B or C.

What this study indicates is that core curriculum is something that universities, especially the most prestigious, have not emphasized for quite some time. Other priorities, for example graduate programs and research, have taken precedence over core curriculum. During the early twenty-first century, however, this trend is reversing. Universities are now beginning to pay considerably more attention to core curriculum. The challenge they face, however, is how to move in a direction that is just the opposite of what they have been doing for a century.

needs to recognize that reforming core curriculum is a process that often takes five or more years to come to fruition.

A second example of a core curriculum effort is both similar and different to the situation at Northern State. Smithville College is a much different institution, but its problems are similar in the sense that core curriculum has been allowed to languish. President Elizabeth Rankin, however, is determined to improve the situation now that the opportunity has emerged.

■ Smithville College

Located in the picturesque New England countryside, Smithville College is a small liberal arts institution of approximately two thousand students. Founded in 1859 as a Methodist institution primarily for preparing pastors, Smithville attracts some of the brightest students from throughout the United

States. Students who attend Smithville are looking for an elite liberal arts college that will prepare them for graduate school or professional schools in fields like law, business, medicine, and teaching. Faculty are attracted to Smithville because of its small size, history, prestige, and dedication to undergraduate teaching, all of which have made the college famous. Smithville spends almost all of its resources on undergraduate teaching, having only three master's degree programs: one in counseling, another in music, and a third in teaching.

President Elizabeth Rankin

President Elizabeth Rankin has served as Smithville's president for eight years. Before that she taught in the history department, directed the master of arts in teaching program, and then served for a short time as dean of the College of Arts and Sciences. When she was chosen as Smithville's president eight years ago, another finalist for the position was the current provost, Dr. Greg Woodbury. Both Smithville graduates, Rankin and Woodbury have managed to work together successfully, but their relationship has been strained ever since the board of trustees chose Rankin over Woodbury. Despite her lack of experience as a provost, the presidential search committee and the board viewed Rankin as a visionary, energetic leader who embodied the characteristics they wanted in a president. Several influential board members were quite pleased to have a strong female as a finalist for the position. Upon acceptance of the presidency, Rankin became Smithville's first female president, following fifteen men. She was quite honored to break this barrier, but she has by no means let this fact dominate her presidency. Provost Woodbury served under Rankin's leadership for eight years but chose to announce his retirement six months ago after a long and distinguished career at Smithville. The college is currently in the midst of a search for Woodbury's replacement, who should be named within the next few months. President Rankin enjoyed working with Woodbury, but she also is excited about the possibilities that now open up since Woodbury is retiring.

Rankin viewed Woodbury as a competent administrator, but he served as a serious impediment to core curriculum reform, an effort that Rankin has been wanting to launch for at least a decade. She is convinced that a Great Books core curriculum is the best way to improve Smithville College at this point in its history. She believes such a program is uniquely suited to achieve three goals. First, it will offer the best liberal arts education possible; second, it will be the most direct way to preserve Smithville's traditions; and third, she thinks a Great Books curriculum is the most appropriate way to reintroduce faith into the undergraduate curriculum. The increasing influence of faith in American culture has convinced Rankin to pursue this third goal even though it will be controversial. She believes strongly that the next generation of professionals, especially in fields like medicine and teaching, will need to be well educated in a variety of religious traditions. Smithville College is also under severe competitive pressure to distinguish itself from other liberal arts colleges. Many years of deliberation with her faculty, staff, and other university presidents has convinced Rankin that reemphasizing the unique history and traditions of Smithville is the best way to remain competitive.

As she considers the five finalists for the provost position and draws upon her knowledge of Smithville, President Rankin identifies three main arguments against the Great Books idea, all of which she must answer. They can be summarized as the diversity concern, the relevant curriculum argument, and the "why more religion" critique. The following section examines each of these concerns before discussing steps that Rankin can take to address them.

Resolving President Rankin's Problems

President Rankin must keep several questions in mind as she deliberates with her faculty and staff. For example, what is the essence of Smithville College and how is it reflected in the institution's core curriculum? What assumptions, ideals, texts, traditions, metaphors, and questions should hold the institution together? What are the best arguments that counter the criticism that a Great Books core only includes white male authors? How can she respond to concerns that not all students can benefit from reading these texts? Should she attempt to institutionalize the proposed Great Books program for all students or just a select few? How can she make the case that reemphasizing faith is the best way for Smithville to retain its traditions and compete effectively for bright students? Given the emphasis on social justice that pervades Smithville, how can she argue that a Great Books curriculum will further the goal of social justice, not detract from it?

After deliberation on these and other questions, President Rankin can immediately take several steps that will help her to achieve success. She will of course need to appoint a provost who not only values a Great Books core curriculum but also understands the issues surrounding its implementation within a college like Smithville. If she and the board choose someone from outside of Smithville, this person will need to have the desire and the ability to learn the intricacies of how curriculum at Smithville operates and make decisions appropriately. She also will need to select a provost who not only shares the ideals of a liberal arts education, but is also well versed in the political realities of university administration.

The Diversity Concern

The first criticism that President Rankin knows will arise is a commonplace argument that has been around for at least fifty years. Critics of the Great Books curriculum maintain that it lacks diversity, only includes white male authors, and neglects a broad range of literary and philosophical works. Smithville enrolls a diverse student body, argue the critics, and an undergraduate curriculum should include a diverse collection of authors. Critics contend that students identify best with authors who share their racial and cultural background, so Smithville should adapt its core curriculum accordingly. Diversity is frequently an end in itself to those who criticize a Great Books curriculum.

President Rankin has several options at her disposal to counter the diversity concern. First, she is a woman, indeed the first woman president at Smithville. If she were a man, she might have more difficulty making the argument for a Great Books core. She knows, however, that her status as a woman is a unique quality that can serve her and the college in positive ways if it is handled properly. Second, she should point out to faculty, staff, and students that she is not attempting to institutionalize a curriculum that neglects women and minorities. She can make the case that there is nothing about a Great Books curriculum that prioritizes one gender or race or political party over another. The essential idea of a Great Books curriculum is that liberal arts students should read the most influential texts ever written. These are the books that have defined and shaped our culture. They transcend race and class and gender.

Nevertheless, for much of human history, white males wrote most of the books and made most of the discoveries in science. Women and minority groups, however, have increasingly published highly influential texts since at least the nineteenth century. Rankin can argue that when deciding upon which texts to include, a person's race, class, or gender should not be the deciding factor. The critical factors should be the extent to which a book (or essay or scientific experiment) influenced the direction of history, captured a piece of truth, and has withstood the criticism of time. President Rankin understands that faculty members disagree about which texts should be included, but she believes there is enough shared tradition at Smithville to identify core texts for at least two and perhaps three courses.

At this time, President Rankin thinks a first course that begins with ancients like Plato and Aristotle and continues through with authors like Virgil and Augustine would be a good option. A second course could begin with St. Thomas Aquinas and move through Dante, Luther, John Calvin, Shakespeare, and Milton. A third could bring students completely into the modern period. It could address the issue of how to broaden the curriculum to include authors from diverse backgrounds. Strong choices for a modern authors course include Mary Wollstonecraft's *Vindication of the Rights of Woman,* Jane Austen's *Emma,* Emily Dickinson's *Poems,* Harriet Beecher Stowe's *Uncle Tom's Cabin,* and Mary Shelley's *Frankenstein.* This third course could focus specifically on the twentieth century, teaching students seminal works like W. E. B. DuBois's *The Souls of Black Folk,* Elie Wiesel's *Night,* Betty Friedan's *The Feminine Mystique,* and Martin Luther King, Jr.'s *Letter from Birmingham Jail.* Including diverse authors like these is certainly important to Rankin, but she also can and should remind faculty that diversity is not an end in itself. She can argue that the end they must keep in mind is a liberating curriculum for all students, one that is rooted in the history, traditions, and character of Smithville. Appreciation for diversity is of course part of what faculty at Smithville want to teach, but it is not everything. In keeping with the history of the institution, Rankin should reiterate to faculty that character is what Smithville should emphasize first, not gender, class, or skin color.

The courses developed for the Great Books core will largely depend on the college curriculum committee, which oversees course and program development. Smithville currently has a core curriculum in which all students complete four common courses (for a total of twelve hours): one from the social sciences, one from the humanities, one from the physical sciences, and one from fine arts. These courses were designed as introductory offerings that demonstrate the commonalities among all of the disciplines represented within the four areas. The problem with the current arrangement, however, is that little commonality exists between the courses that count toward the common core. The content of these courses depends entirely on who is teaching them. There is no oversight to encourage uniformity in the various sections. One professor who teaches the introductory to social science course, for example, takes a political theory approach that begins with Plato and Aristotle and moves through modern social scientists like Max Weber and Emile Durkheim. Another professor only uses recently published case studies to analyze how the social science disciplines analyze a contemporary issue. On paper, a common core exists, but in reality students receive something quite different depending upon the professor who is teaching the course.

To reform this situation and bring a true common curriculum to Smithville, President Rankin will need to work carefully with the new provost when he or she appoints new members to the curriculum committee. Terms for committee members last three years, so reform of this group takes time. Timing for when to move forward with the Great Books initiative is crucial. If she attempts to move forward when the committee consists primarily of critics, she will of course stymie the effort. If, on the other hand, she can persuade the curriculum committee to support a well-designed two- or three-course sequence in Great Books, the full faculty will likely support it. She also can argue that, in addition to including a third Great Books course that stresses diverse authors, students can read authors from a variety of backgrounds during their remaining undergraduate curriculum. For a prestigious liberal arts college with the history and tradition of Smithville, asking that all students complete three common courses seems entirely reasonable to Rankin. If the curriculum committee proves to be an unshakable obstacle, Rankin could consider options that do not require the approval of the curriculum committee (for example, creating an entirely new unit on campus), but taking this route would require a great deal of deliberation with her most trusted advisors.

In making her case with the curriculum committee and elsewhere, President Rankin can draw upon the fact that she is a woman. She also should use her professional training as a historian. Because of this background, she should be able to place great texts like Aristotle's *Ethics* and Harriet Beecher Stowe's *Uncle Tom's Cabin* in context while at the same time arguing that works like these are timeless because they capture something eternal about human experience. She can argue furthermore that this timeless aspect of knowledge is what provides a liberating experience for students regardless of their background, and this is the most important gift that Smithville can give them.

The Relevant Curriculum Argument

During deliberations with her staff on next steps, President Rankin has discovered a second source of opposition. This criticism originates primarily from some of the newer faculty, but also from student groups like the Student Senate. They assert that a Great Books curriculum is not "relevant" to twenty-first-century students, at least not for the majority of those who attend Smithville. They would prefer to see the core remain as it is now with faculty choosing their own texts, many of which are contemporary instead of ancient. Many students appear not to share Rankin's concern with the deficiencies of the current core curriculum. If anything about the status quo must change, they would prefer that it move in the direction of more choices, not fewer.

Some faculty believe that even though Smithville enrolls bright students not all students can profit from reading texts of this kind. They argue that these books might be useful for students who plan to become college professors, perhaps those in honors programs, but requiring these texts of everyone would be forcing students to read material in which they have no interest and cannot possibly comprehend. A similar source of opposition from faculty relates to the close connection that Smithville has always had with graduate schools throughout the country. Many faculty measure the success of Smithville by the number and quality of graduate schools that admit Smithville graduates. This emphasis has a strong impact on Smithville's curriculum. Faculty from some departments, especially in the sciences and the social sciences, argue against a Great Books core because they don't believe reading these texts is the right background either for graduate school or employment once students graduate.

One more objection that Rankin has discovered is related to the "curriculum is not relevant" point. Smithville has not taught a curriculum rooted in classic texts for at least sixty years. Few of the current faculty—outside of departments like classics, philosophy, and perhaps English—have the background necessary to teach these courses. Faculty may have read some of these texts when they were undergraduates many years ago, but their doctoral education pushed them in the direction of specialization and away from a broad, liberating curriculum. Critics who use this argument claim that even if a Great Books core is established, the ideal is not practical since few faculty have the inclination, background, and time to teach Great Books courses.

To resolve the issues raised by the relevant curriculum argument, Rankin first must realize that the source of this opposition derives from at least two of the curriculum commonplaces. The first and perhaps most powerful is the learner commonplace. The rhetorical claim that Smithville's curriculum should "meet the needs and interests of all students" is a powerful one that must be checked if the integrity of Smithville's curriculum is to remain intact, regardless of whether a Great Books core is established. She can counter the claim by reminding students that their viewpoint is always an important part of curriculum development, but it also should not dominate the conversation. She can remind students that Smithville exists to give them a curriculum they ought to have and not necessarily the one they want. She can consider inviting a student representative to contribute to deliberations about curriculum reform, but she should be careful to choose someone who can be tutored on how the learner commonplace relates to all of the others.

The teacher commonplace—in this case represented by Smithville professors—is also present in the relevant curriculum argument. Rankin should recognize that behind this argument is an assumption that Smithville faculty will never change, either in the abilities of the current faculty or in the faculty who will be hired in the years ahead. This criticism may be true in some respects, but Rankin can answer the charge in several ways. First, she can dedicate resources to faculty development that will prepare interested faculty to teach the proposed new courses. There are some faculty who have shown an interest in this kind of teaching, and she should reward them for supporting the effort. She can provide stipends for faculty to participate in summer institutes,

One approach that colleges and universities can use to resolve curriculum difficulties is to return to the mission of the institution. Without a clear sense of mission, curriculum questions will be difficult, if not impossible, to answer.

she can invite consultants to campus who can help with course development, she can create a lecture series around the subject of core curriculum, and she can take an active role in hiring new faculty. Over time and through wise deliberation, she can alter the makeup of the faculty so that a core group has the background and ability to teach core texts.

If it looks as though she will not be able to recruit enough faculty to require a Great Books core for all students, then she could follow the suggestion of some faculty and establish a three-course sequence for honors students only, and then attempt to build from there. The Honors Program admits only sixty students per year, a manageable number compared to the entire freshman class.

Perhaps the most powerful step Rankin can take to achieving her goals would be to find a donor who would be willing to endow a Great Books core program. Since fundraising is a major aspect of her job, Rankin has the opportunity to visit with many donors who may be attracted to such an idea. If she can find an alumnus who shares her passion for establishing the program, an endowed gift would provide her with the economic and political capital she needs to make significant progress.

The "Why More Religion" Critique

A third complaint that Rankin must refute is the criticism against reemphasizing the Christian foundation of Smithville through a Great Books core. The arguments against this aspect of the proposal are many, but through long-term planning President Rankin believes she can respond to them.

Rankin wishes to reconnect Smithville with its Methodist heritage for three main reasons. First, her study of history and contemporary culture has convinced her that religion is becoming more prominent in our culture, not less. Second, she wants the Great Books core to introduce students to the timeless aspect of Smithville College, which she believes is best captured in the ideals that gave birth to the institution. Third, she is convinced that a truly liberating curriculum must attend to the spiritual aspect of human existence. To ignore this part of the curriculum, she maintains, is to build a core program on an incomplete view of human nature.

The first and most common objection to reintroducing Christian texts is that the Smithville faculty and students come from a variety of religious and nonreligious backgrounds. Requiring them to read Christian texts would be much too narrow, bordering even on indoctrination, some contend. Smithville chose to distance itself from Methodist control more than forty years ago, and many faculty are emphatic in their view that this development was the right direction to take.

Another objection claims that Smithville will hurt its efforts to recruit faculty and students if the institution earns a reputation for becoming more religious. This view is held mostly by faculty who have been at Smithville for twenty-five or thirty years, but not so much by the newer faculty. Younger faculty, especially those who completed their doctoral degrees since 2000, are much more open to discussing faith. Rankin believes one reason behind this development is that senior faculty completed their graduate work and began their careers during a time of increasing secularization of culture, when many social scientists believed that religion would become weaker over time. During the late twentieth and early twenty-first centuries, however, religion has become more powerful, not less. If Smithville graduates are expected to lead in the decades ahead, they will need to be well informed with regard to religion. The last thing they should do, Rankin believes, is ignore it.

President Rankin knows the volatility that can come with the religious piece of her initiative, but to her this reality only indicates the importance of the effort. She also knows she must be careful to ensure that deliberations about this matter will always be driven by reason and not emotion. She can begin by explaining to faculty why she thinks the Christian foundation of Smithville is significant. She can assure them that she is by no means interested in pushing every faculty member to discuss faith in every class, but she does want the college to demonstrate pride in its Christian heritage. She often hears faculty and alumni apologize for the Christian roots of the institution, but she thinks this tendency does more harm than good. As a historian and a Methodist, Rankin thinks Smithville should take pride in its history and use it when appropriate to distinguish itself from other liberal arts colleges. There is considerable opposition to this aspect of her plan, but there is also support that will strengthen if she has patience and shows prudence.

Rankin can counter the first objection about the diversity of the student body by reminding critics that even though students are diverse they remain deeply interested in religion and spirituality. She can argue that Smithville has a responsibility to develop students' interest in religious matters, just like they explore the intellectual, moral, and physical sides of who they are. She can also point out that the curriculum she has in mind is by no means limited to classic texts of the Christian faith. A course on religious great texts from a variety of prominent religious traditions can achieve the goals she has in mind. Such a course would include not only Christian texts like Augustine's *Confessions* and St. Thomas Aquinas's *Summa Theologica,* but also the *Bhagavad Gita* and the *Koran*. Rankin can bolster this argument by reminding faculty that Smithville graduates will be working in an increasingly global society, which means they will come into contact with numerous religious traditions. They cannot be educated enough in the history, practices, and beliefs that undergird each faith tradition. In addition, since many faculty have a deep and abiding commitment to social justice, she can make the case that much of the force behind social justice derives from the religious traditions she wants students to study.

With regard to the faculty and student recruitment objection, President Rankin will need to have her staff conduct research, if it doesn't exist already, into why students and faculty choose Smithville over other institutions. Her initial inclination is that reintroducing faith into the core curriculum may have the exact opposite effect that many critics claim. Rankin's hope is that students and faculty will begin to choose Smithville over other institutions because of the leadership the institution has shown with regard to faith matters. Rankin will, however, need to gather a considerable amount of information before she can make this determination. Critics who make the claim that reintroducing religious texts will hurt recruitment may turn out to be right, but they also may turn out to be wrong.

While taking all of the steps above, President Rankin will need to remain flexible while holding true to the ideals she wants to instill in Smithville students. She will need to listen carefully to all constituents while bearing in mind the five commonplaces that always arise when curriculum is the subject of deliberation. Rankin may not achieve every goal she wants, but with wise deliberation and the use of her rhetorical and political abilities, she can maximize her success.

A third and final major curriculum reform topic addresses the subject of teacher education. Tackling this question raises many of the same issues that come to light with core curriculum, but it also elevates additional factors that, in many ways, make it even more complex. In the next chapter, I will sketch two scenarios and then suggest ways in which teacher educators can improve their curriculum and further the goal of a liberating curriculum for all.

■ Discussion Questions

1. Why is the reform of core curriculum so difficult?
2. What are some arguments for and against the establishment of a common core curriculum?
3. What are some resources that university administrators can draw upon to achieve success in reestablishing a common core curriculum?
4. What role can accrediting agencies play in the reform of core curriculum?
5. What role can grant funding agencies play in reforming core curriculum?
6. What are some potential mistakes that would-be reformers might make when attempting to reform core curriculum?
7. How is making changes to core curriculum different at state-supported public universities compared to private religious ones?
8. Do you agree or disagree that the deliberative tradition is the best approach to use when attempting to reform core curriculum? If you think it is not, what tradition makes the most sense and why?

CHAPTER 9

What Should We Do to Create a Better Teacher Ed Curriculum?

TEACHER EDUCATION curriculum is a complex subject that too often is either neglected or assumed to be simplistic. The complexity of the subject, however, only grows as the specifics within a particular institution are considered. Curriculum for teachers is similar to core curriculum in that it impacts all subjects in a university. It is also similar to core curriculum because, when done properly, teacher ed curriculum is a university-wide responsibility. There are ways in which teacher ed curriculum,[1] however, impacts an even broader constituency than core curriculum. Every teacher ed program in the United States requires at least some practice teaching experience. Some institutions require an experience as short as a few weeks and others require a year, but practice teaching is viewed as an essential component of teacher ed curriculum. Unlike core curriculum, the practice teaching aspect of teacher ed curriculum demands a successful external relationship between universities and K–12 schools. This means that, in addition to the internal challenge of ensuring that academic departments work together constructively, teacher ed curriculum requires relationships with elementary, middle, and high schools. These schools, moreover, are almost always rooted in a culture that is much different from universities. As a result, higher education leaders who direct teacher ed programs have one of the most difficult challenges in all of university life.

This chapter consists of two cases that intend to show the difficulties that surface when leaders attempt to reform teacher ed curriculum. As in the two previous chapters, these are composite sketches that are based on my experience

Teacher education is a highly practical way that colleges and universities can serve their local communities.

with curriculum reform at the K–12 and higher education levels. The cases are designed to raise the central issues that surround teacher ed curriculum. The goal with each scenario is not to describe a real-world institution in some objective way, but rather to raise the core questions that face teacher educators, deans of education, and other higher education leaders who seek to make changes in teacher ed programs. The first case is that of Western State University (WSU), a large multipurpose university in the south that enrolls approximately thirty-five thousand students.

■ Western State University

Western State University was founded in 1892 as a normal school and has grown to include eight academic units: a College of Arts and Sciences, College of Education, College of Business, College of Computer Science and Engineering, College of Music, College of Nursing, College of Information Science, and the Graduate School. WSU is located within a large metropolitan city of more than one million people. The university attracts primarily a regional student population, with 80 percent of the students coming to WSU from within two hundred miles of the university. Just over half of the university's thirty-five thousand students are the first in their family to attend college. The student population breaks down into 40 percent Caucasian, 35 percent African American, 25 percent Hispanic, and the remaining 10 percent a combination of many other ethnic backgrounds. Each year, WSU graduates approximately three hundred students from its undergraduate teacher ed program. The College of Education offers a variety of master's and doctoral degrees, but its undergraduate teacher ed program is viewed as its most essential.

More than half of the WSU graduates who enter teaching begin their careers within an urban school setting. Teacher education has always been a central part of the mission of WSU, but, more than a century after the university's founding, preparing teachers is by no means the only purpose of the institution. As WSU changed its name from normal school to teachers college to state college and then finally to state university, the teacher education mission of the institution was gradually demoted and then isolated within the

College of Education. Not everyone views this transformation as positive.

Dean John Mason

Thirty-nine-year-old Dr. John Mason is WSU's energetic new dean. He is convinced that the isolation of teacher education has not been positive for WSU or the community that the university serves. Dean Mason came to WSU after five years as chair of the Department of Curriculum and Teaching at another large state university in the south. A former high school mathematics teacher, Dean Mason completed a master's degree in educational leadership before earning his PhD degree in mathematics education. He was attracted to WSU by the vision that the university's new president, Dr. Jenice Longfellow, has launched to reconnect WSU with its local community. Dr. Mason immediately saw President Longfellow's community-oriented mission as an opportunity to rebuild a teacher education program that could serve as a model for others. He wants to work with the faculty and staff to build a sustainable program that is in the long-term best interest not only of WSU, but more importantly of the numerous communities that it serves.

This transformation from normal school to regional state university took place with hundreds of institutions during the twentieth century. Even though many of these schools continue to graduate a significant number of teachers, the status of teacher education within the institution as a whole, in almost all cases, has been significantly diminished.

Having been on the job for only six months, Dr. Mason is in the midst of developing a plan that will guide the university's effort to reform teacher ed curriculum. The impetus for reform originates from several sources in addition to President Longfellow's community-oriented vision. First, Dean Mason recognizes that teacher ed programs have been the subject of critique in recent years, and he knows that reform is necessary. Second, he has completed a survey of superintendents and principals who employ WSU graduates, and the results indicate a severe need to provide better preparation focused on helping graduates to succeed during their first two years, especially in urban schools. Finally, Dean Mason is deeply concerned that 50 percent of teachers nationwide leave the profession within five years. The best data that Dean Mason can gather reveals that this percentage is even higher for WSU graduates. He wants to do something not only to help WSU graduates teach better during their first two years, but to increase the likelihood that they will remain in the profession long term.

With his reform efforts, Dean Mason wants to focus primarily on the school's elementary program, but he also sees the need for changes to the curriculum for secondary teachers. After six months of deliberation with faculty, staff, students, and community stakeholders, Dean Mason has decided that WSU will best serve its local community by making the following changes: (1) create additional subject-specific methods courses at the elementary and secondary levels (e.g., Teaching Elementary Mathematics, Teaching Elementary Social Studies, and Teaching High School English), (2), redesign the program's freshman-level Introduction to Teaching course to include more experience observing and working with students during their first semester in college, and (3) establish a yearlong internship for all teacher candidates during their senior year. These plans are ambitious, but Dean Mason knows that they are consistent with recent trends in teacher ed curriculum. The difficulty involved in establishing these changes becomes even more apparent once the existing program is brought into view.

WSU: The Context

The current teacher ed curriculum at WSU is a model that has been in use for at least fifteen years. Following two years of general education coursework, teacher candidates[2] begin to complete education coursework during the first semester of their junior year. Elementary candidates complete courses such as Introduction to Teaching, Foundations of Education, Multicultural Education, Learning and Development, Elementary Classroom Management, Classroom Observation, and Methods of Teaching in the Elementary School I. First-semester seniors complete Methods of Teaching in the Elementary School II and an Elementary Literacy course that focuses on the teaching of reading. All candidates then complete one semester of student teaching, typically during the spring of their senior year. Student teachers are placed in either an urban or suburban setting, without the benefit of gaining experience in more than one school.

The curriculum for middle and secondary candidates is similar to the elementary program. The primary differences are that candidates complete Middle/High School Classroom Management and then two methods courses: Teaching in Secondary Schools I and Teaching in Secondary Schools II. Of course, the Classroom Observation course and all student teaching placements are tied to middle or high schools depending upon the teaching certificate that individual

Teacher ed curriculum has always included an experiential component, whether it be only one semester during the senior year or a full-year internship. The trend in recent years has been toward more time in schools, with many programs placing candidates in K–12 schools during the first semester of their freshman year.

candidates are pursuing. This curriculum has remained relatively unchanged for the past fifteen years, but Dean Mason believes the program is ill-suited to the task of preparing teachers for twenty-first-century schools.

Before moving forward with the issues that Dean Mason faces, a more in-depth consideration of the people with whom he must work is necessary to understanding his state of affairs. The vast scope of teacher ed curriculum draws into the conversation numerous figures who have a stake in WSU's teacher ed program. Attention to the backgrounds of these figures helps to illuminate the context in which Dean Mason must work, which in turn enables readers to imagine potential solutions to his problems. No potential actions, after all, can be separated from the people who envision them, those who are responsible for taking them, and the parties impacted by them.

President Jenice Longfellow

President Jenice Longfellow became the thirteenth president of Western State three years ago. During this time she has had the opportunity to develop a comprehensive vision to integrate community service into every aspect of the university. She wants WSU to become a nationwide leader in addressing social problems through the application of research. She has been successful at raising funds through WSU alumni and several foundations to make this vision a reality. She has begun to strengthen relationships with the local chamber of commerce as well as dozens of area businesses, hospitals, museums, and governmental agencies. She also intends to deepen relationships with local schools. She recruited Dean Mason to perform just this task, since she believes he is uniquely suited to the job.

Dr. Ronnie Lopez

Another figure who is crucial to the success of Dean Mason's reform efforts is Dr. Ronnie Lopez, superintendent of the 120,000 student Valhalla school district. He has served as the Valhalla superintendent for the past seven years, rising to that position from his role as district superintendent for finance. He is extremely supportive of WSU's teacher education program, indeed recognizing that a close relationship with WSU is deeply beneficial to his district. He is pleased to have as many WSU teachers and teacher candidates involved in the Valhalla schools as possible. He views them as a valuable resource and a shot of fresh energy into the district every semester. He strongly supports all three of the reform goals that Dean Mason's team has developed, especially the yearlong internship. Dr. Lopez is anxious to develop additional relationships with Dean Mason and WSU.

Provost Barry Barnett

President Longfellow recruited Provost Barry Barnett to WSU two years ago. They worked together at their previous institution, where Barnett served as dean of the Graduate School. They both believe passionately in the community-centered vision that President Longfellow and others have developed. At his previous institution, Barnett served as dean of the College of Education before moving into the role of Graduate School dean. Because of his dean of education experience, Barnett understands the complex issues surrounding teacher ed curriculum. Although he has many constituencies to keep in mind when he makes decisions, Provost Barnett is a strong advocate for the reforms Dean Mason has in mind.

Dean Michael Leadbetter

Dr. Michael Leadbetter has served as dean of the College of Arts and Sciences at WSU for fifteen years. He has strong support from most of the faculty within his college. He is known as a competent manager who has helped the college—and by extension the university—through difficult times. He has many priorities to juggle, from recruiting department chairs to supporting faculty in their search for grants to evaluating almost three hundred faculty each year. Beyond his reputation as a competent manager, however, Dean Leadbetter is not particularly gifted as a visionary leader. Important to the state of affairs in which Dean Mason must work, Leadbetter was a finalist for the provost position when Barnett was chosen, but Leadbetter was not selected because he did not convince the search committee that he could develop a long-term vision for the university. This history has made working with Dean Leadbetter somewhat challenging, even though Dean Mason was not at WSU when Barnett was selected as provost. In addition, Dean Leadbetter has never been a strong supporter of teacher education. Leadbetter, whose background is in English, often expresses the view that teacher ed curriculum should consist of subject matter preparation and nothing else. When challenged with questions about how elementary teacher preparation should differ from secondary or how teachers can best be prepared to teach in challenging environments, Dean Leadbetter avoids these issues before ceasing to discuss teacher ed curriculum altogether. Dean Mason often wonders if Dean Leadbetter holds critical views toward teacher ed curriculum not so much because he believes these views can be defended, but because he is listening to the opinions of department chairs within his college who would benefit from a de-emphasis on teacher ed curriculum at WSU.

Given this list of colleagues, Dean Mason has several strong supporters, but also at least one influential critic. He knew of the strong support he would have at WSU before he chose to move; otherwise he would not have accepted the position. First, and perhaps most important, Provost Barnett strongly supports not only teacher education, but also the specific reform goals that Mason and others have developed. Second, Dean Mason, Provost Barnett, and President Longfellow share the community-centered vision that should shape the university for at least the next four or five years, perhaps even longer. Assuming that the upper administration remains in place, Dean Mason should have the support he needs. Third, Superintendent Ronnie Lopez recognizes the powerful impact that a newly redesigned teacher ed curriculum can have on his district. Dean Mason can draw upon Lopez's influence to build community support not only for the College of Education, but for the university as a whole. At the same time, however, Mason knows that Dean Leadbetter is a source of potential dissent. He will need to find ways either to steer clear of this likely opposition or channel it in a direction that avoids doing harm to his reform initiatives. With the above colleagues in mind, consideration of the questions Dean Mason must confront allows readers to imagine possibilities that will further the ideal of a liberating curriculum for all.

Resolving Dean Mason's Problems

The road between Dean Mason's vision for what teacher ed curriculum at WSU ought to become and the current state of affairs is littered with potential difficulties. There are many missteps that could destroy his chances at meaning-ful reform. Nevertheless, if he makes politically sound deci-sions, deliberates carefully, and persuades the various stake-holders to support the program revisions, he has a reasonable chance at institutionalizing the goals he has in mind. To do so, Dean Mason will need to generate answers to several ques-tions. First, what are his strongest sectors of support within the university and the community as a whole? How can he build support where it does not currently exist? Which of the three initiatives should be his highest priority? Should they be implemented simultaneously or piecemeal? How can he establish a new teacher ed curriculum while at the same time continue to offer the current program until all students have graduated? How can he find faculty who have the appropri-ate background and are willing to teach courses in the new program? What should Dean Mason do with the faculty who have been teaching courses that will be eliminated? How can these faculty be transitioned so that they contribute mean-ingfully to the new program?

> Political support is crucial to any curricular change, especially within colleges and uni-versities. A good guide to keep in mind is that the more extreme the change, the more essential political support will be.

As he attempts to resolve these problems, the curriculum commonplaces are helpful to Dean Mason, but they are also somewhat limiting when the subject is teacher ed curriculum. Curriculum for teacher preparation is so complex that some people involved in the effort end up belonging to two com-monplaces at the same time. For instance, teacher candidates in WSU's program are simultaneously teachers *and* learners, depending upon the context in which they are working. They are obviously teachers because of their work in the Valhalla school district, but they are also undergraduates (i.e., learn-ers) at WSU.

The subject matter commonplace takes on an added level of complexity as well. Subject matter within a teacher ed curriculum is not just about what to teach, but also about how and why to teach. Despite these complexities, the five curriculum commonplaces should remain essential to Dean Mason's thinking as he deliberates about next steps. Knowl-edge of the commonplaces will help him to recognize when someone is making an argument that emphasizes one com-monplace to the detriment of the others, whether they do so with reference to teacher candidates as teachers, K–12 stu-dents as learners, or teacher candidates as learners.

A significant step Dean Mason can take to resolve the problems he's facing is to develop a well-articulated vision that will unify the diverse constituencies who have a stake in teacher ed curriculum. An attractive title, for example, "2020 Teachers," might be useful in drawing attention to the reform initiative and generating support. Such a vision should describe how the newly redesigned program will further the community-oriented mission that President Longfellow has initiated. The vision should be written in clear language and published as an attractive document that can be used to persuade all parties that WSU's teacher ed program is central to the university's future. Mason will need to draw upon the strong support he already has from President Longfellow and Provost Barnett to garner the financial and political resources necessary to hire additional faculty, fund costly internship experiences, and recruit students who will be a good fit for the new program. The vision will need to show how a high-quality teacher ed curriculum is both liberal and professional. Breaking down barriers between "liberal" and "professional" curriculum should be at the heart of the vision. In addition, the vision should explain how and why the education of teachers is a university-wide responsibility to which all units should contribute and from which the entire university benefits. Finally, to bring together faculty from diverse departments, the vision will need to explain how it draws upon the expertise of everyone involved to further the goal of universal liberal education.

To persuade critics such as skeptical department chairs, reluctant faculty, and, perhaps most importantly, Dean Leadbetter, Dean Mason will need to draw upon several sources of influence. For starters, he can point to research, including his recently completed survey of principals and superintendents, that demonstrates how 2020 Teachers will better prepare candidates for success during their first few years of teaching and, especially, within urban schools. Likely the most beneficial source of influence is WSU's community-oriented vision. When positioning for resources and support, Dean Mason should be able to argue that no initiative better fits what the university seeks to do than teacher education. He has a strong case to make that no university program ties more directly to community service than teacher education.

Another source of support Dean Mason can use is the history of Western State. Because of his knowledge of the institution's history, Dean Mason can remind skeptical faculty and administration that the university would not exist if it were not for teacher education. One of his three main goals—the creation of subject-specific methods courses—is a direct return to the courses that once dominated teacher ed curriculum not only at WSU but at teachers colleges across the country. Dean Mason is working to reintegrate the subject matter disciplines with teaching methods after the two became separated during the second half of the twentieth century. The subject matter disciplines became isolated as purely theoretic fields within the College of Arts and Sciences, and teaching methods became the strict purview of the College of Education. Dean Mason is convinced that he must rebuild ties between these two units if teacher candidates are to receive high-quality preparation.

Still another tool for Mason is the National Council for the Accreditation of Teacher Education (NCATE). WSU has been NCATE accredited for almost fifteen years, and all three of the major reforms embedded within 2020 Teachers can be tied to the curriculum that NCATE encourages. These reforms will put WSU on track to retain its accreditation. Accreditation of WSU's teacher education program is central to the mission of the university, so reforming the school's curriculum to remain in keeping with national best practices is an influential point for Dean Mason to emphasize.

Another step that would serve Dean Mason well would be to establish an umbrella body within the university that is responsible for undergraduate teacher education. Perhaps called the Teacher Education Faculty, this body would bring together all faculty, regardless of home department, for purposes of deliberating about teacher ed curriculum. A Teacher Education Faculty that stretches across departmental boundaries would achieve several goals. First, it would raise the status of teacher education by making it a university-wide responsibility, not the purview of just the College of Education. Second, it would initiate a dialogue between disciplinary specialists and specialists in curriculum and teaching. To create more subject-specific methods courses, this type of "cross-pollination" is essential. Ideally, dialogue of this sort will result in faculty from disciplinary departments coteaching courses with education faculty. Both can benefit from the expertise of the other. Teacher candidates and K–12 students would benefit considerably from this type of collaboration. Third, the establishment of a Teacher Education Faculty would provide a long-term home for a mission-driven program that is essential to the university's future. Because of their specialized professional status, disciplinary departments will always revert to professions other than teaching.

Mathematics departments, for example, will always exist to further the profession of mathematics, not the teaching profession. Departments within the College of Education have other programs, for example graduate degrees, that siphon resources away from teacher education. Creating a Teacher Education Faculty will ensure that this body of faculty will always remain dedicated to undergraduate teacher education. As long as a unit of Teacher Education Faculty receives support from the administration, its purpose cannot be eroded.

Deliberations also may reveal to Dean Mason that the best approach will be to prioritize the three curricular changes embedded in 2020 Teachers. Initiating all three changes at once may be more than the faculty is prepared to support. If so, he will need to think through what order would be best for implementation. Given the levels at which the three changes will take place, the logical order in which to make them is to begin with the freshman-level course, then move to the subject-specific methods courses at the junior level, and then implement the yearlong senior internship. A well-formulated five-year plan will help to ensure that these changes will take place smoothly. Given his deliberative approach, however, Dean Mason knows that plans often must be revised once implementation begins. A thoughtful back and forth between the plan for what the program should look like in five years and the current state of affairs is the wisest path to balanced change.

Faculty who have taught at WSU for a significant period of time will likely have the most difficulty with the 2020 Teachers initiative. For faculty whose longtime courses will be revised or phased out, Dean Mason will need to meet with them individually to develop a plan for how each will fit into the 2020 Teachers program. Perhaps the worst occurrence Mason could allow to develop would be for senior faculty to begin to feel as though they do not have a place in the new program. To assuage this potential concern, Dean Mason will need to remind faculty that everyone's knowledge and experience is necessary for the new program to succeed. He will need to create ways to draw upon the strengths of all faculty to avoid marginalizing people who could harm the reform effort.

One of the most vexing problems Dean Mason will face is how to operate two programs at once while the university implements 2020 Teachers. He can alleviate the difficulties that come with this dilemma by requesting resources from

Provost Barnett and President Longfellow to hire additional staff while the program is in transition. During the difficult four-year process when both programs are in operation, he will need to remind faculty why 2020 Teachers is necessary and how it will benefit the university. Major curricular changes require time, patience, and deliberation to ensure that problems are resolved as they arise.

In addition to the above internal matters, Dean Mason will need to confront significant changes external to WSU. The size of the university's teacher education program—approximately three hundred graduates per year—requires a substantial number of mentor teachers throughout the Valhalla school district as well as within surrounding districts. The 2020 Teachers vision, however, calls for a yearlong internship that will double the amount of time that teacher candidates spend in the field. This expansion is excellent news for the school districts that will benefit from having interns, but it also means more work finding placements for seniors in the program. Dean Mason will need to work closely with Superintendent Lopez to expand the university's network of professional development schools. These schools generate an entirely new set of practical problems that require as much deliberation as the internal issues related to new course development. The relationships these deliberations establish with area districts, however, provide a powerful way for WSU to fulfill its community-oriented mission.

Taking the above steps will of course not produce a Utopian world in which the 2020 Teachers vision becomes implemented perfectly and without controversy. Curriculum reform is a messy practice. Any state of affairs shifts and evolves, requiring curriculum leaders to invent resolutions to current problems, search for new ones as they arise, and keep the ideal of a liberating curriculum for all in mind. If Dean Mason can master this ability, he will likely find success at improving his university's teacher ed curriculum while at the same time strengthening the community it exists to serve.

A second example of teacher ed curriculum reform shares many of the same challenges found at WSU, but also differs due to the nature of the institution. Freedom Hill College is a small, relatively new Christian institution on the West Coast that is looking to expand its influence as an institution for teacher education. This final example allows readers to recognize how curriculum deliberation at a private religious

---

Professional Development Schools and Teacher Ed Curriculum

Since the early 1980s, the concept of "professional development schools" has grown increasingly popular across the United States. Sometimes compared to teaching hospitals, professional development schools (also known as PDSs) are K–12 schools that have partnered with universities to educate K–12 students while at the same time preparing teacher candidates for their careers as teachers. PDSs first appeared on the higher education landscape during a time when teacher education programs were under heavy criticism for allegedly not preparing teachers for the "real world" of classroom practice. Many teacher education programs had grown away from classroom practice because the education schools in which they existed had begun to emphasize research, and also because teacher education was not viewed as a "prestigious" endeavor within many of the most influential universities in the country. Approximately thirty years ago, however, many education schools decided to reemphasize teacher education and practical classroom experience at the same time. PDSs address both of these needs. They are mechanisms by which universities can reconnect with K–12 schools, they are sites in which research can be conducted, and they are K–12 schools that benefit from a significant number of highly energetic teacher candidates every year.

From a historical perspective, the concept of a professional development school is quite similar to the "laboratory schools" that were foundational to every teachers college in the country before teachers colleges transformed into regional state universities. The main difference between PDSs and lab schools, however, is that lab schools were located on the campus of teachers colleges, whereas PDSs are found throughout the community where a university exists. In other words, faculty who teach in PDSs travel to the school sites in the community where their university exists, whereas K–12 students attended lab schools on the campus of the teachers colleges.

---

institution takes on a character quite different from what is found in state universities.

■ Freedom Hill College

Freedom Hill College was founded in 1968 as a Baptist institution dedicated to furthering the ideals of the Christian faith. Freedom Hill's mission "to go forth and spread Christ's light to the world" succinctly captures what the college aspires to do. Every new proposal or reform initiative is measured by the extent to which it furthers this mission. Situated within a large metropolitan city on the West Coast, Freedom Hill has grown steadily during the past forty years. With a humble beginning of only seventy-five students, the college now enrolls thirty-five hundred undergraduates who are pursuing almost eighty degree programs. Freedom Hill includes a College of Science, College of Arts and Letters, School of Business, School of Education, School of Music, School of Christian Ministries, and Seminary. Enrolling a diverse student body of 40 percent Hispanic, 40 percent Caucasian, and approximately 20 percent African American students, Freedom Hill has withstood several periods of economic difficulty during the past forty years but is currently in relatively good financial shape.

President Martin Westland

President Martin Westland is Freedom Hill College's second president. The founding president retired fifteen years ago after leading the college for more than twenty-five years. President Westland has had a remarkably successful fifteen years as president. He is well liked, has an outgoing personality, and has found success managing the political matters that come with leading a Baptist college. Westland is also a good manager. He has recruited additional high-quality faculty, managed a student recruitment effort that has reached its enrollment goals for five straight years, and established several new successful undergraduate degree programs. In addition, the endowment for the college has grown steadily, albeit not to the levels that some within the "Freedom Hill family," as they call it, would like. Freedom Hill is undoubtedly a teaching college, with all faculty teaching at least four courses per semester. The institution has not placed an emphasis on research, although some faculty do manage to write articles, publish books, and conduct research. In tenure and promotion cases, research is said to be appreciated but not required.

President Westland has been relatively pleased with Freedom Hill's undergraduate teacher education program, but he has always wished that the college could graduate more teachers. He often hears from private Christian school leaders that their schools desperately need more high-quality teachers. Freedom Hill graduates approximately forty students per year through its undergraduate teacher education program, but this number is not nearly enough to supply Christian schools in the area with the teachers they need. President

Westland believes strongly that Freedom Hill should work to rectify this situation.

In addition to the problem of finding teachers, President Westland often hears from Christian school leaders that they especially need teachers who can integrate the Christian faith into K–12 curriculum. School principals tell him that very few, if any, teacher education programs prepare teachers to do this work. President Westland knows that integrating faith into K–12 curriculum is not a simple task, which is one reason why he believes special preparation is necessary. Given the fact that few institutions even attempt this work, Westland insists that Freedom Hill College should lead the conversation.

To respond to concerns and help Freedom Hill to provide leadership to K–12 Christian schools, President Westland believes the college must make at least two changes. First, the School of Education needs to enlarge its teacher education program by recruiting additional students. These students, moreover, need to be the kind who have an interest in teaching in private Christian schools. Second, President Westland believes that the university needs to establish a master's degree program in education that not only prepares candidates to teach in private schools, but also teaches them how to integrate the Christian faith into K–12 curriculum. Despite these desires, President Westland has not been able to move forward because he has not had the right kind of leadership at the dean level within the School of Education.

Dean Eugene Barker

The dean of the School of Education is Dr. Eugene Barker. He is the only dean the School of Education has had in its twenty years of existence. As one of the earliest members of the Freedom Hill Department of Education, Barker was instrumental in establishing Freedom Hill's School of Education as it grew from a small department in the late 1960s to a large department in the early 1980s and finally into a School of Education in 1989. Dean Barker is seventy-two years old and has had a long and distinguished career as an educator. He began as an elementary school teacher and has taught every level from elementary to college. Some faculty believe the time has arrived for Dean Barker to retire, but others are satisfied with his leadership. He is well respected and admired throughout the college, especially on the Freedom

Hill Board of Trustees. Unlike President Westland, Barker is not interested in making changes to Freedom Hill's teacher ed curriculum. He is happy with the current curriculum and does not see any need to change it.

Beyond curriculum, Dean Barker is not altogether opposed to President Westland's interest in expanding Freedom Hill's program, but he sees no need to introduce coursework that teaches candidates to integrate faith into curriculum. Barker believes Freedom Hill teacher candidates should follow a curriculum that is no different from what they would encounter at a high-quality state university. The difference between Freedom Hill and state schools, to Barker, should be found in the environment that permeates the Freedom Hill campus, not its curriculum. For decades, Barker and other faculty who agree with him have prided themselves on the personal attention that faculty devote to their students. All students at Freedom Hill are required to complete two religion courses, but that's not the unique aspect of Freedom Hill that Barker emphasizes. When recruiting students and faculty, he stresses the Christian atmosphere of the college, not anything unique about its curriculum. In addition, Dean Barker is partial to the idea that Freedom Hill should continue to serve public schools, even to the detriment of private schools. He is concerned that recruiting teacher candidates who want to teach in private schools would hurt Freedom Hill's ability to support public schools, service to which he believes is foundational to the college's mission. Faculty within the School of Education are largely split on this matter, but there is at least some renewed interest, especially among newer faculty, in doing a better job serving private Christian schools.

For two main reasons, Barker is also skeptical of the idea to launch a new MEd program. First, he does not believe that Freedom Hill can recruit enough students to justify the time it will take to create or administer a new master's program. Second, Dean Barker is concerned that an MEd program will undermine the undergraduate program that Barker and his colleagues have nurtured for years. In response to President Westland's interests, Dean Barker would prefer to expand the undergraduate program slightly and perhaps place a few candidates in private schools for their student teaching semester, but not much else.

Another source of opposition to the idea of a new MEd program is Provost Richard Teller. Teller has served as provost for eight years. Prior to this time, he taught in Freedom Hill's School of Business as a finance professor for ten years, before becoming dean. He served as dean for six years before the provost position became available. Teller is quite capable at managing the fiscal side of Freedom Hill, but he is not altogether comfortable discussing a long-term vision for the college. He prefers to make decisions based on data, enrollment figures, and cost-benefit analyses. Teller is also critical of a new MEd program because several of his colleagues in the School of Business have wanted to establish an online master's in business administration program for at least five years. President Westland, however, has not been supportive. The college only has the resources to create one new program at this time. In addition, Westland is skeptical of going down the path of offering online degrees. Because of its close connection with the mission of Freedom Hill, however, President Westland is firmly behind the MEd degree. If President Westland decides to move forward with the MEd and not the MBA, there is of course not a great deal that Teller can do about it other than complain, but there is at least the likelihood of political turmoil.

> Sometimes curriculum changes simply have to wait until the institutional context is right for them to move forward.

Dr. Theresa Moore, Assistant Professor

Much to President Westland's delight, however, the prospect of creating the new MEd degree has recently improved to a considerable degree. The School of Education recently hired Dr. Theresa Moore as a new assistant professor of science education. She is a dynamic new addition to Freedom Hill. A graduate of Freedom Hill, Dr. Moore taught high school chemistry for eight years, three of which were in a private Christian school, prior to returning to earn her PhD degree at a major research university on the West Coast. The daughter of a Baptist minister, Dr. Moore is deeply committed to the mission of Freedom Hill. She was attracted to the college not just because she is an alumna, but also because she wants to impact the world as a teacher educator at an institution where she can practice her faith and teach future science teachers. Dr. Moore is only in her second year at Freedom Hill, but she has already impressed Dean Barker, Provost Teller, and President Westland as an energetic, promising teacher-scholar who will do great things for Freedom Hill, if she remains at the institution long term. She is firmly in support of both initiatives that President Westland has in

One of the major
challenges that edu-
cation faculty face
is connecting the
research-oriented world of colleges
and universities with the distinctly
different culture of K–12 schools.
One way that education faculty can
succeed at making this connection
is to spend time in K–12 schools.
They can do this by creating professional development schools
or implementing other models of
teacher ed curriculum that place
teacher candidates in schools as
early as their freshman year.

mind: to increase the size of the college's teacher education program and do a better job serving private Christian schools. As an untenured assistant professor who faces a tenure decision in just four years, however, Dr. Moore is not in a position to take a strong stand, at least not publicly, on either of these initiatives. She is willing to provide support for President Westland's interests by writing proposals, conducting studies of programs at other institutions, and encouraging support from faculty, but she also must keep in mind that several of the faculty who will vote on her tenure decision do not support the changes President Westland has in mind.

Resolving President Westland's Problems

President Westland faces problems that are not altogether difficult to resolve given his position as president, but he does need to deliberate wisely to solve them in ways that further Freedom Hill's mission and strengthen the health of the institution. Perhaps the most essential question Westland faces is not new to Freedom Hill. How do the changes under consideration further the mission of the institution? To what extent does the board of trustees support integrating faith into teacher ed curriculum? To what extent will the board support establishing a new MEd program? How can the creation of a new MEd degree help the college "to go forth and spread Christ's light to the world"? How can he address concerns from School of Business faculty who will complain because they're not able to create their program? How can President Westland expand support for both of his initiatives regarding teacher education where it doesn't exist already? Can the college afford these changes at this time? If money is not immediately available, which of these possibilities is more likely to generate donors who can endow the program, providing it with a long-term foundation? How should President Westland handle the objections of Provost Teller and Dean Barker? Can he move forward on either of these initiatives without strong support from them? If not, what are his options if he decides to replace Teller or

Barker? If the Teacher Education Faculty is not willing to introduce discussions of faith into their curriculum, are there other ways that he can help Freedom Hill to prepare teachers for Christian school service? Finally, how should President Westland develop the talents of Dr. Moore without placing her in a difficult situation?

The mission of Freedom Hill College "to go forth and spread Christ's light to the world" is the most powerful tool President Westland has available. He should have little difficulty linking the curricular changes he wants to make to the college's mission. Collecting additional comments from Christian school principals would help him to further his case for why Freedom Hill needs to expand teacher education in the way that he has proposed. Emphasizing the mission also should help him to establish additional support among the board of trustees. Westland does, however, need to think clearly about how his understanding of faith integration differs from others at Freedom Hill. As opposed to Dean Barker's "two spheres" view in which the environment of faith is separate from curriculum, President Westland believes that the Christian aspect of the college should permeate every aspect of the institution, including its curriculum.

Both of these approaches—abbreviated as the "two spheres" and "curriculum integration" models—can be viewed as equally Christian in many respects. President Westland would be making a mistake if he fails to recognize the depth of the differences that underlie these two positions. The more he reflects on his own views to clarify what he believes, the better he will be able to sympathize with those who disagree with him. Recognizing that the board of trustees includes members who hold both views, Westland will need to use all of his political and rhetorical abilities to lead careful conversations about matters that are often deeply personal. He knows that religion frequently brings out the best in people, but he also knows it can bring out the worst. Deliberations based on reason will be more important than ever when the element of faith is part of the equation. By clarifying his own views on faith integration, explaining them clearly to board members and faculty, and describing why he believes they are the best for the future of Freedom Hill, President Westland has a reasonable chance of gaining support.

Perhaps the best way for Westland to deal with Teller's interest in establishing an MBA program is to remind him that he supports the idea, but not at this time. Westland can assure Provost Teller that he realizes an MBA degree can of course further the mission of Freedom Hill in ways similar to an MEd, but, since only one program can be implemented at this time due to budget constraints, the MEd is the preferred choice. Another option would be for President Westland to show how the entire college will benefit from an MEd degree and how it ultimately will strengthen Teller's case for establishing an MBA. Given that Teller is a data-oriented administrator, figures that demonstrate how an MEd program could generate funds that would help launch an MBA degree could persuade Teller to join the effort instead of opposing it.

At least initially, Dean Barker may be the most serious obstacle to the reforms President Westland wants to enact. He could of course discuss retirement with Barker, but that might alienate him further and cause division among the university leadership. The best route to creating support with Barker is to look for common ground, of which there is a great deal. First, they both care passionately about the mission of Freedom Hill College, not a small matter, which should strengthen their ability to work together. Second, they are both strong supporters of undergraduate and graduate teacher education. Finally, both want to support Dr. Moore. She is a strong future leader for Freedom Hill, and they recognize the significance of helping her to develop a long-term home at the college.

Once this common ground is established, President Westland could begin by asking Dean Barker to move forward with those aspects of the president's plans that he supports. For example, they could immediately begin to dedicate resources to the recruitment of teacher candidates who will teach in both public and private schools. If President Westland wants to recruit candidates who will teach in Christian schools, he has options that reach beyond Dean Barker's role as dean. Westland can work with the university-wide recruitment team to develop advertisements that target students who share these interests. Until possibilities open up for the creation of new undergraduate courses that will raise questions of faith integration, Westland can encourage faculty to integrate faith into curriculum through professional development opportunities. He can invite guest speakers to campus, host summer seminars led by prominent scholars, and distribute books and other materials related to faith integration. He also can continue to hire faculty who have a desire to integrate faith into their work.

To develop Dr. Moore's talents appropriately, there are many options that Westland and Barker can pursue. They could invite her to become more involved with student recruitment. They see her as an excellent representative for Freedom Hill and believe she will find great success when recruiting future teachers to the college. They also could ask her to lead a summer workshop on faith integration. This opportunity would allow her to make new connections and it would showcase her abilities to a broader segment of the Freedom Hill community. Professor Moore also might be a good choice to lead the effort to establish the new MEd program. Given Dean Barker's objections, however, movement on that piece of the effort may not begin for another year or two. President Westland, nevertheless, could invite Professor Moore to begin working on an MEd proposal that the School of Education could present when the timing is favorable. An invitation like this from President Westland would likely have the effect of causing Professor Moore to think about her long-term role at Freedom Hill, which is exactly what would be in the best interest of the institution. Whatever the case, when working with Dean Barker, President Westland can find ways to honor Barker's many years of service while at the same time move forward in ways he thinks are in the best long-term interest of Freedom Hill.

Resolving Dr. Theresa Moore's Problems

Dr. Theresa Moore shares the curricular vision that President Westland has been promoting, but her ability to further it is of course tempered significantly compared to his. After her first year on the faculty, Dr. Moore has come to realize that she will have many opportunities at Freedom Hill if she makes wise decisions that further the mission of the institution. The questions she faces are particularly delicate given her status as an untenured professor. How can she support President Westland's proposals without alienating her colleagues? How can she maneuver an MEd program proposal through curriculum committees and other steps when she knows she will face critics? Also, after studying the state of affairs carefully, which of the leaders at Freedom Hill seem most likely to remain at the institution for the foreseeable future? Whose ideas will have the most impact on teacher ed curriculum? In addition, even though research is not a requirement for tenure, how can Dr. Moore find time to

A powerful cur-
ricular vision can
serve as a magnet
for faculty and
students. In this
respect, curriculum
changes can drive
the future of an
institution.

produce enough research to remain competitive in the job market if she decides to look elsewhere?

In many respects, Dr. Moore is in a good position since she has strong support from numerous administrative leaders, especially President Westland. To influence Freedom Hill's curriculum in the way she would like, the best path is more than likely for her to continue doing exactly what she has been doing. The best tool she has to address potential difficulties is communication. She should of course listen to President Westland and attempt to achieve the goals he has in mind, but she also must remain in close touch with Barker, her immediate supervisor. Within her classes, she can immediately begin to find ways to integrate faith into her curriculum as well as encourage teacher candidates to do the same. If she wants to expand these ideas further, she should consider establishing a book discussion group with faculty who want to learn more.

To avoid irritating faculty who may be highly critical of faith integration, however, Professor Moore will need to be prudent about how, when, and with whom she shares her views. In time, she will have more opportunities to express her beliefs publicly, but now is not the time for her to express her thoughts in an overbearing way. If Professor Moore decides to lead the effort to establish the new MEd program, she should consider a number of options to increase the likelihood that the proposal will find success. First, and perhaps most obvious, she will need a well-written proposal that ties the new program to the mission of the college, anticipates the objections that will arise, and explains how the proposed program will benefit the entire college, not just the School of Education. Even with a well-crafted proposal, however, Dr. Moore will want to discuss timing with President Westland to see if the effort is futile at this juncture if Dean Barker continues not to support it. If President Westland encourages her to move forward regardless of whether Barker supports the idea, Professor Moore could strengthen the proposal by finding a senior faculty member who will coauthor it with her. Persuading a senior member of the faculty to join the effort would establish support among a critical group of faculty. Such support would be beneficial as the proposal makes its way through the college's various curriculum committees for approval.

Second, while helping with the new program proposal as appropriate, Professor Moore would be wise to pay careful attention to which Freedom Hill leaders are likely to remain at the institution long term. If she expects to make a prolonged impact on the college's curriculum, she should avoid placing all of her eggs in one leader's basket. Dean Barker is the most likely candidate to step aside soon, but leadership within higher education changes rapidly. A wise path would be for her to keep working with President Westland as best she can, but she must always be aware of the possibility that he could leave the institution for another position at any time. Dr. Moore should ensure that she has multiple opportunities if this turn of events comes to pass.

Last but not least, Dr. Moore faces a situation that most if not all tenure track faculty face when they attempt to balance teaching and research. Finding time to conduct research will be difficult for her no matter what. She will need to decide quickly if Freedom Hill is the right type of institution for her, especially if she intends to accept leadership roles like leading the development of an MEd program. If she remains at Freedom Hill for four or five years and conducts no research, she will have few options, outside of institutions similar to Freedom Hill. At the same time, if she is satisfied with a college that focuses on teaching, then of course committing to Freedom Hill and working to influence its curriculum makes complete sense. Likely, however, she will want to continue to pursue enough research to keep doors open, at least until she has had time to learn if Freedom Hill is the right place for her long term. She will no doubt need to make sacrifices to keep her research alive. She may need to forgo summer teaching and use that time for research, even if she is not compensated for the work. She will more than likely need to take time out of her weekends, Christmas break, and spring break to carve out time for scholarship. Given that many universities only value research, however, remaining active is imperative for professional mobility. Finally, she can consider using the political capital she has built during the last year to discuss possibilities like release time from teaching or a summer sabbatical that will free up at least some time for her to dedicate to research. If President Westland, Provost Teller, and Dean Barker want to encourage Professor Moore to make a long-term home at Freedom Hill, they will search for ways to support her interest in research.

Professor Moore and all of the deliberators described in the preceding chapters share attributes that make them uniquely qualified to provide curriculum leadership. They possess a character that is shaped by specific virtues, they combine thought and practice in ways that impact students and institutions in unique ways, and they provide long-term stability that is rooted in tradition and character. In the final chapter, I want to address several key questions that, when answered, help to illuminate the deliberative tradition even further. How does character relate to curriculum deliberation? What are the virtues that make for good curriculum making? How can these virtues be cultivated? What does curriculum deliberation do for the institutions where it is practiced? What does it do for the people who practice it? Finally, why is the deliberative tradition best suited for curriculum leadership in the twenty-first century? In the final chapter, I attempt to answer these and other questions while at the same time looking toward the future.

■ Discussion Questions

1. What are some of the unique problems and circumstances surrounding teacher ed curriculum?
2. Who are the various constituencies that must be taken into account when creating and maintaining teacher ed curriculum?
3. Why is the reform of teacher ed curriculum so difficult?
4. How is teacher ed curriculum different (or how can it be different) in private institutions compared with public ones?
5. How are the curriculum commonplaces different when the subject is teacher ed curriculum compared to K–12 curriculum or university curriculum in a discipline-specific department like history or mathematics?
6. How is the history of teacher ed curriculum relevant in an institution like WSU, which was founded as a normal school/teachers college?
7. What are the two approaches to faith and curriculum found in the discussion of Freedom Hill College?
8. Why is the mission of a university or college so critical to teacher ed curriculum?

CHAPTER 10

Calling All Curriculists: Virtue and the Future of Deliberative Curriculum

A DELIBERATIVE tradition has attracted supporters during the last few decades, but it does not yet
boast the following of the other traditions described
in part I. To address this issue, this chapter has three goals.
It revisits the book's thesis from chapter 1, focuses on the
concept of virtue and how it relates to the deliberative tradition, and aims to persuade anyone interested in curriculum to
adopt a deliberative view.

In the introduction to this text, I presented a three-part
thesis. The thesis begins by stating that curriculum is in chains
and must be liberated from narrow views before true education can be established. Next, the thesis claims that the place
to begin is by liberating *the concept* of curriculum before specific problems can be addressed. Third, and finally, the thesis
argues that if we hope to create a truly liberating curriculum
for all students, curriculists need to move beyond liberating
the *idea* of curriculum to *practicing the art of deliberation*
as they resolve specific problems within unique institutions.

Readers can judge for themselves the extent to which the
previous nine chapters have furthered this thesis. The goal
has been for chapters 2 through 6 to highlight enough of the
distinctions between the five traditions that the strengths
and weaknesses of each have become apparent. Second, the
stories in chapters 7 through 9 were written to stimulate
conversation among curriculum development specialists,
curriculum faculty within universities, teachers, and school
administrators. One important step in fostering deliberation
is simply to discuss curriculum in a thoughtful and accurate
way. When discussing curriculum, the traditions presented

in part I should help readers to comprehend the assumptions various people bring to curriculum conversations. Understanding how others view curriculum is an essential first step to fostering deliberation.

■ The Premodern Turn and Curriculum Deliberation

Another essential step to improving curriculum is to recognize the uniqueness of the intellectual climate in the early twenty-first century. In the introduction, I suggested that we live in a momentous time in intellectual history. Not since the late sixteenth century and the breakdown of medieval philosophy has the world seen an intellectual milieu as dynamic as it is today. Alternatively called the postmodern turn or the death of the Enlightenment or the breakdown of positivism, something irreversible is happening in intellectual life, the full measure of which will not be understood for at least a century. Educational historian Julie Reuben recognizes the power of this shift in *The Making of the Modern University: Intellectual Transformation and the Marginalization of Morality*, which is her work on the history of twentieth-century higher education. Reuben tells the story of how twentieth-century universities, in their quest for prestige and power, attempted to separate knowledge from morality, but ultimately failed because the task is impossible. The dream of separating "facts" from "values," Reuben maintains, has run its course. Few twenty-first-century scholars attempt to uphold this outdated view. Reuben argues that instead of chasing the impossible task of separating facts from values, now is the time to return to conceptions of ethics and moral philosophy that integrate them. In Reuben's words:

> Scholars hoped that the distinction between fact and value would lead to more reliable knowledge as measured by greater agreement. The subsequent history of academic disciplines in the twentieth century indicates that this hope was illusory. . . . If universities can tolerate more conflict, we may be able to define cognitive standards by which we can address moral questions. Since it has proved impossible to completely separate fact and value, we should begin to explore ways to reintegrate them.[1]

The most successful way to explore the integration of knowledge and morality is through deliberation. The intellectual moment Reuben discerns is precisely the time when deliberative curriculists should meet the challenge to assist our culture through a time of great strife and difficulty. Put another way, now is the right moment for deliberators to gain adherents by expressing the strengths of deliberative curriculum and by showing how it resolves problems in a unique way.

In times of turmoil and change, some people race to the cutting edge to experience the new world before anyone else. Others dash to the other extreme, choosing to cloister themselves within age-old rituals, waiting for the storm to pass. Deliberators prefer a middle path that respects wisdom and tradition but also searches for new and creative ways to solve whatever problems arise in the world of practice. The method of deliberation is the route to finding this middle path. Deliberation is not strictly intellectual, nor is it purely utilitarian. It is partly idealistic, but also a touch pragmatic. It is ultimately concerned with action, but it is also deeply reflective. Joseph Schwab, William Reid, Ian Westbury, and others within a deliberative tradition embrace these aspects of deliberation while calling upon curriculists to look backward as well as forward. The term *premodern*, as opposed to *postmodern*, avoids the possibility of moving too quickly and unwisely jettisoning the many positive developments that came with the modern period. Premodern and postmodern are both difficult terms to define, but each, nevertheless, signals a break—or at least a serious separation—from the modern period.

Some scholars identify the 1960s as the time when modernism began to crumble, others emphasize the end of the Cold War, and still others point to 9/11. Regardless of the specific date, there is overwhelming evidence that the views once considered "modern" are now passing quickly into the dustbin of history. What the next stage holds is anyone's guess, but the role of those who operate within times of great change is to provide balance amid uncertainty, look beyond commonplace categories, and find ways to influence the future in ways that build healthy communities.

Philosopher Alasdair MacIntyre has done as much as anyone to shape the intellectual direction of the next century. His *After Virtue* challenges not only philosophers but also scholars from every field to return to virtue as the guidepost and map to direct our actions. Ethics may be MacIntyre's primary concern, but ethics and curriculum making are inseparable.

For those who would like to read a history of ethics, one that provides necessary background for our time of intellectual transformation, a good place to start is with Alasdair MacIntyre's *Three Rival Versions of Moral Inquiry.*

MacIntyre's work, therefore, is entirely relevant to curriculum. MacIntyre, too, recognizes the breakdown of modernism, arguing that the Enlightenment project had to fail because it rejected the concept of a *telos*, embraced a flawed conception of human nature, and built institutions on a narrow view of the moral life.

MacIntyre compares the current shift in our culture with the decline of the Roman Empire and the onset of the Middle Ages. He urges us to reconnect with the premodern tradition of virtue, specifically Aristotle's conception of it, which the modern age rejected when it abandoned a *telos*. Only by resurrecting an end to our moral lives can we revive a legitimate ethical philosophy and thereby build communities that flourish. As MacIntyre contends:

> Since the whole point of ethics—both as a theoretical and practical discipline—is to enable man to pass from his present state to his true end, the elimination of any notion of essential human nature and with it the abandonment of any notion of a *telos* leaves behind a moral scheme composed of two remaining elements whose relationship becomes quite unclear.[2]

MacIntyre identifies these "two remaining elements" as "moral content" and "untutored human nature." He argues that we no longer have a concept of either of these elements in our modern world because humanity has deprived itself of an end. Since we no longer have a goal that binds us together with a common purpose, moral deliberations have become meaningless, if not impossible to lead. Without this end, moral disagreements degenerate into screaming episodes in which one side merely attempts to overpower the other using morally bankrupt rhetoric.

Just because deliberation comes with difficulties, however, does not mean it should be avoided. We should embrace—not run from—the challenge of deliberative practice during this time of great change. Leadership during difficult times requires a deliberative leader who practices the virtues necessary to good curriculum work. As Reid urges, "Deliberation is the *practice* of the identification and resolution of curriculum problems, and, as a practice, takes on a virtuous character."[3] The virtuous character that Reid emphasizes is what the curriculum field will cultivate if a deliberative tradition finds more followers. Deliberation is the opposite of screaming matches in which one side seeks to control the other. Deliberation is the practice of using reason, language, and emotion to appreciate one another's views while at the same time persuading others to follow what we believe is right. As Robert Kunzman argues in *Grappling with the Good,* "Ethical deliberation in civic society involves a search for common ground."[4] Kunzman continues his argument, writing:

> The moral authority of difficult political deliberation depends on the inclusiveness of the discourse that precedes it. We do need the opportunity to genuinely communicate and consider our differing ethical perspectives. If we have not cultivated this ground, so to speak, then we have shown inadequate respect to others. In addition, our level of compromise and accommodation may be too shallow to sustain our life together.[5]

Nowhere in our culture is inclusiveness, respect for others, and compromise more important than curriculum.

The difficult political deliberations to which Kunzman refers, however, cannot succeed without the concepts of tradition, character, and community that MacIntyre argues have been marginalized. The modern world, especially the tradition of political liberalism upheld by political philosophers such as John Rawls, rejected these three concepts, reducing moral discussions to shrillness and not much else. Philosopher Lawrence Cahoone, when describing MacIntyre's argument in *After Virtue,* makes a similar point when he writes, "Outside of tradition, he [MacIntyre] argues, there can be no conclusive rational deliberation. . . . Man, according to MacIntyre, is a story-telling animal. By denying legitimacy to such traditional narratives, liberalism has led to nihilism and the end of rational discourse regarding conduct."[6] Whether the subject is history or science or mathematics, curriculum is about stories. MacIntyre offers curriculists a path to reenergizing curriculum through the power of narrative. A narrative, like a curriculum, is always headed toward an end. For this reason, curriculum, unlike any other subject, has the potential to bind schools and communities together, integrate knowledge and morality, and combine thought and action.

The possibilities of what can be done with the subject of curriculum are endless. Curriculum deliberation has the potential to revive liberal education in its richest sense. Curriculum deliberation offers a path to liberation not only for

> Deliberative curriculists believe that narrative and curriculum cannot be separated. In other words, a curriculum—at its very foundation—is also a story.

busy teachers who are forced to build a curriculum while being shackled with a fact-driven list of state standards, but also for state-level curriculum managers who oversee large-scale reform initiatives. State and federal leaders who direct curriculum reform efforts forget too easily that any curriculum must be implemented by practitioners and that these practitioners need wisdom to guide their practice. In the face of systematic reform strategies, now is the time for curriculum deliberators to ask questions that are central to good curriculum making but have been forgotten due to the neglect of the deliberative tradition. What virtues are essential for good curriculum making? What virtues should curriculum makers seek to uphold? How can these virtues be cultivated? The curriculum field has paid no attention to these questions. Curriculists have not attended to the internal characteristics of the people who make curriculum. This is a major oversight in the field. We find many people who

---

Three Traditions within Moral Philosophy

There are three main traditions within moral philosophy. They are referred to as utilitarian ethics, deontological ethics, and virtue ethics. Utilitarianism emphasizes the consequences of an act, meaning that whether or not an action is good is determined by the results that it produces. To utilitarian ethicists, ends are always more important than means. John Stuart Mill is often referred to as a major figure within utilitarian ethics. In contrast, deontological ethics concentrates on the rightness or wrongness of an act itself and not so much on the results that an act produces. Deontological ethics emphasizes rules. Deontologists believe that rules can be established that, at least in theory, will guide most if not all of our moral actions. Immanuel Kant is frequently referenced as a significant contributor to the deontological tradition.

Distinct from utilitarian and deontological ethics, virtue ethics concentrates on the character of the person who is doing the acting. To virtue ethicists, the circumstances in which a moral action takes place plays a significant role in the decision that ought to be made. This emphasis on situation does not mean that virtue ethicists reject rules or consequences. They consider both as necessary but not sufficient to living a moral life. What matters most of all to virtue ethicists are the habits and forms of character that moral agents have developed over time when dealing with moral decisions. Aristotle is considered to be the father of virtue ethics.

From the perspective of this book, utilitarianism can be connected to the pragmatic tradition, deontological ethics to the systematic, and virtue ethics to the deliberative tradition. The other two curricular traditions, the radical and the existentialist, share characteristics of all three ethical traditions.

connect virtue to moral education,[7] but few, if any, who combine virtue and curriculum making. Curriculum professors
have created more than enough systems, published autobi-
ographies that detail one person's curricular life, argued for
revolution against hegemonic powers, and offered pragmatic
solutions to complex issues, but the field has rejected virtue
entirely. Now is the time to correct this omission.

If the curriculum field—and indeed the practice of curriculum making—is to thrive, curriculists should follow the
lead of Schwab, Reid, and MacIntyre, which means a return
to tradition, character, and virtue. When critiquing a systematic view, Reid makes this point persuasively when he
writes, "In spite of the best efforts of the technical experts,
curriculum questions continue to be moral questions, which
is why technical measures so often result in inferior plans
and poor decisions. Where the curriculum of schooling is
concerned, to talk the language of virtue is to be realistic."[8]
From a deliberative perspective, to be practical means to be
virtuous. Practicality also means thinking far beyond "what
works" to a curriculum that will inspire students thirty, forty,
and even fifty years from now. As curriculum conversations
grow more complex, disagreements tend to become more
divisive. Communities—whether they are schools, churches,
or governmental agencies—must have leaders who can generate harmony, persuade others to find common ground, and
remain steadfast while confronting troublesome problems.

■ Virtue and Curriculum Making

But what is virtue and how can it strengthen curriculum making? Which virtues should curriculists seek to uphold first?
Perhaps the best place to turn to answer these questions is
Aristotle. His *Nicomachean Ethics* is an abundant source of
wisdom and inspiration. The breakdown of modernism has
seen a widespread, rapid increase of interest in Aristotelian
politics and ethics. Many scholars believe that virtue ethics
provides the best path out of the moral morass that has enveloped Western civilization, if not the world generally. In the
words of political philosopher Thomas W. Smith in his book
Revaluing Ethics:

> The contemporary resurgence of the study of ancient
> political philosophy can be understood as helping
> to fulfill our need for thoughtful reflection about the

past to help us manage our transition into an uncertain future. Mainly for this reason, there has been a veritable explosion in Aristotle scholarship in recent years.[9]

To recover Aristotle's work in the right way and for the right reasons, however, Smith contends that Aristotle's ethics should be viewed, first and foremost, as a pedagogy. Aristotle's goal was to *do something* to his audience, specifically to shape his audience's character toward virtue and happiness. In Smith's words, "My account rests on the view that the Aristotle behind the *Ethics* is a teacher with a profound concern for the formation of his students, rather than a philosopher who is inquiring for the sake of inquiring alone."[10] Smith's thesis supports the argument of this text for what deliberative curriculum making can, must, and should do. In addition to serving as an approach for creating curriculum, deliberative curriculum is a pedagogy that seeks to shape students' character toward permanent principles of thinking and acting. Virtue is essential because it gives life and purpose to curriculum efforts. Virtue separates humans from animals because it requires reason, a capacity that animals do not possess. Aristotle furthermore maintains that virtue is a characteristic of our souls, not an excellence of the body. It is an ability to act in an excellent way as only humans can do. This means using reason, language, and imagination to foster humaneness, happiness, and wholeness in whatever communities we influence. A virtuous human being is somewhat like a virtuous knife. An excellent knife is one that cuts quickly and powerfully. An excellent human being is someone who practices all of the virtues and attains happiness for herself and, more importantly, for the community that she serves.

To make his case for virtue and its connection to happiness, Aristotle divides virtue into two types: moral and intellectual. He maintains that both are essential if a person expects to live a happy life. He defines happiness as "activities of the soul in conformity with complete virtue," and then argues that happiness is the *telos* that binds small groups as well as communities together. The intellectual and moral virtues cannot, however, be developed only for a short time. Happiness will only result if a person embraces them for a lifetime.

Moral and intellectual virtues differ not only in how they are acquired, but also in their purpose. Moral virtues like courage and friendship are attained through practice. They admit of a mean in the sense that every moral virtue can be corrupted through excess and deficiency. The moral virtue of courage, for example, is destroyed through cowardice or recklessness. To develop courage, a person must make decisions that hit the mean between cowardice and recklessness repeatedly until doing so becomes a habit. Friendliness operates in the same manner. The two extremes are obsequiousness and peevishness. A friendly person has practiced hitting the mean between these two extremes repeatedly until doing so has become second nature. She has internalized the moral virtue of friendliness to the point that it has become habit, allowing her to concentrate on other virtues.

Intellectual virtues differ from moral virtues because they are taught, not developed through habit. Whereas Aristotle discusses numerous moral virtues, he identifies only five intellectual virtues: science, art, practical wisdom, intelligence, and theoretical wisdom. He describes science as knowledge of the necessary and eternal, art as knowledge of how to make material objects, practical wisdom as knowledge of how to make good judgments, intelligence as knowledge of the principles from which science proceeds, and theoretical wisdom as the ability to understand the relationship between science and intelligence. Intellectual virtues culminate in thought and understanding, whereas moral virtues always require action.[11]

Aristotle of course includes many more details regarding the moral and intellectual virtues, but what is useful at this point is how they relate to curriculum making. The best curriculum makers will of course be those who have cultivated all of the virtues over time. This goal, however, is not easy to attain. No school, college, or university can expect to maintain a high-quality curriculum if those who deliberate about it do not seek to uphold the virtues. The character of the people who deliberate is what gives a curriculum its vitality, infuses it with meaning, and makes it liberating for those who follow it. If for example the moral virtue of generosity is not present in the character of those who make a school's curriculum, then that school's program will lose its identity as a public good. It will become a balkanized product that special interests seek to control for their private gain, not a public trust that holds communities together. Courage is another virtue that is indispensable to good curriculum making. Anyone who has embarked on a major curriculum reform effort, regardless of the grade level, knows that courage is necessary for achieving lasting change. Without courage, a curriculum

Politically speaking, virtue is neither conservative nor liberal. People with the reputation of having a virtuous character—for example, Winston Churchill or Martin Luther King, Jr.—come from a range of points along the political spectrum.

becomes anemic and therefore fails to challenge students or change when circumstances demand it.

Practical wisdom, also referred to as prudence, is perhaps the most essential of the virtues to curriculum making. Aristotle begins his discussion of practical wisdom by arguing that the best place to begin when seeking to cultivate this virtue is by looking at the people who possess it. Those who have a reputation for making wise judgments should serve as role models. Aristotle goes on to argue that we only deliberate about things we can change, not eternal matters. Practical wisdom, therefore, is not a pure science like chemistry or physics because the goal in those fields is to produce eternal knowledge, whereas the end of practical wisdom is judgment. Aristotle concludes by defining practical wisdom as "a truthful rational characteristic of acting in matters involving what is good for man."[12] He then discusses how deliberation is the method we use to discern how to act in the interest of what is good for man. He summarizes the relationship between practical wisdom and deliberation by stating that good deliberation "brings success in relation to what is, in an unqualified sense, the end."[13] The end he has in mind, of course, is happiness, not just for individuals but also for communities and institutions.

> The relationship between practical wisdom and curriculum making is an area that deserves much further attention in the field of curriculum.

Other virtues like wisdom, justice, honesty, moderation, persistence, compassion, and honesty all breathe life not only into curriculum, but into the process of curriculum making as well. Without wisdom, deliberators cannot envision a long-term future for students, a school, or a community. If persistence is absent, a curriculum will not succeed, nor will it influence students for any appreciable period of time. Compassion is especially useful when students face difficult material or when a school is beset by trauma. Honesty builds trust among deliberators, yielding people who address problems quickly without allowing them to overwhelm a school's ability to flourish.

Given two of the examples found in chapters 7 and 8 regarding faith-based institutions, the question of how faith can infuse even more virtues into curriculum making is worth considering. Should deliberation within religious schools take on a different character from deliberation within secular ones? Most people would answer yes to this question. The

Christian tradition, for example, upholds the spiritual virtues of faith, hope, and love, which transcend and transform the virtues found in both Plato and Aristotle. Faith, hope, and love transform the cardinal virtues of wisdom, courage, moderation, and justice by adding an even longer term dimension to deliberations within religious schools. The spiritual virtues also can strengthen deliberation within public institutions, but of course within the constraints required by law. Faith extends knowledge to a higher dimension, providing deliberators with another source of wisdom that can bind schools, colleges, and communities together. Hope provides inspiration to curriculum workers as they deliberate, power to students as they struggle to make sense of a challenging course, and confidence to teachers as they work in difficult circumstances. Much like faith, love strengthens communities by transforming Aristotle's happiness into a broader end that has love for one another and eternal peace in the presence of God as its end.

> The debate over the proper relationship between the cardinal and spiritual virtues has taken place for centuries, and it will not end anytime soon.

There are no doubt other virtues that can breathe meaning, life, and purpose into curriculum making. The purpose of the above discussion has been to highlight only a few to show the benefits that will develop when curriculists pay increased attention to virtue. The relationship between virtue and curriculum making has not been explored, and the curriculum field has suffered because of it. Curriculum deliberators need a book-length study of the virtues and how they can and should impact curriculum deliberation.

The chart in figure 10.1 depicts how the virtues can serve as the moral and intellectual foundation for a team of curriculum deliberators. Ideally, all members of the team should strive to uphold the moral, intellectual, and (where appropriate) spiritual virtues. If all of them do so while making curriculum decisions, then a school, college, or university will be well on its way to establishing a liberating curriculum for all.

> Universal liberal education will never be achieved until the conversation over curriculum turns to the character of the people who make curriculum decisions.

■ John Amos Comenius and a Liberating Curriculum for All

Now that the virtues and how they relate to curriculum making have been brought into view, the time is right to return to the curriculum map introduced in chapter 1 (see figure 1.1). The map is not an absolute, unchanging portrayal of the five curricular traditions, but it is a tool for everyone who is interested in curriculum to use as they address curriculum

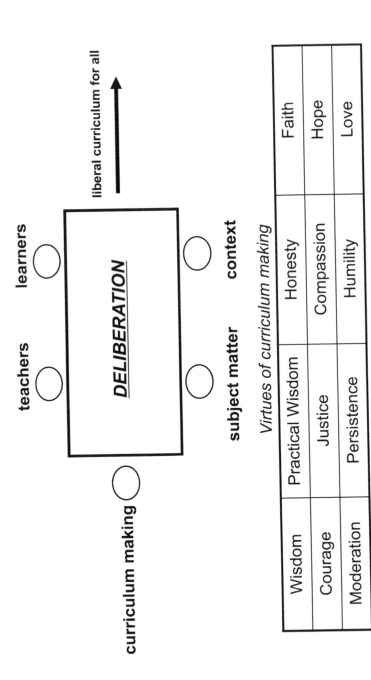

Virtues of curriculum making

Wisdom	Practical Wisdom	Honesty	Faith
Courage	Justice	Compassion	Hope
Moderation	Persistence	Humility	Love

Figure 10.1. Curriculum Deliberation Team

problems. The opportunity to use the map arises, of course, in educational institutions like schools, colleges, and universities. The occasion, however, also presents itself whenever curriculum is the subject of conversation. In this respect, every conversation about curriculum offers the opportunity to infuse deliberation into our communities and pursue the ideal of a high-quality curriculum for all.

One person who recognized the significance of pursuing a liberating curriculum for all is John Amos Comenius. Concluding with Comenius makes sense because we have yet to fulfill the vision he set forth almost four hundred years ago. In *The Great Didactic,* Comenius's masterpiece, he was the first to introduce the ideal of universal liberal education. He had a powerful, wide-ranging intellect, but he was also uniquely skilled at the practical tasks required to run a school. He was the kind of teacher-scholar who could shift from discussing the latest works of philosophy with Rene Descartes to writing a deeply practical book on what parents should do to rear their children properly and prepare them for their first day of school.[14]

Comenius's goal was not just to set forth a vision, but to accomplish the task of teaching a high-quality liberal arts curriculum to all young people. Comenius's vision also included women, a radical view at the time. Comenius provides deliberative curriculists with a role model because of his unique ability to discuss intellectual matters at the highest level while at the same time knowing how to resolve practical problems and build community.

Comenius is not well known today for a variety of reasons, but chief among them is that his work does not fit neatly into one of the modern-day categories that dominate intellectual life. He was a theologian, philosopher, historian, curriculist, and psychologist all at the same time. His books are part theology, part philosophy, part curriculum philosophy, part literature, part psychology, and even part educational administration. Modern universities have no idea what to do with someone like Comenius.

Found in *The Great Didactic,* Comenius's argument for universal liberal education can be summed up in three points: (1) all of us are made in the image of God, (2) the part of us that is God-like is our ability to reason, and (3) all people have the responsibility to make themselves more completely human by strengthening their God-given ability to reason. This line of reasoning can serve as a tremendous source of inspiration. Comenius's argument means that the job of a teacher, or curriculum maker, is to make himself more God-like by training his ability to reason and by contributing to the ideal of a liberating curriculum for all. Faith working alongside reason is what enables curriculum workers to overcome evil and serve as a source of liberation. Each of us has the tools to resist corruption, but we have to fend off the dark side of our nature with the twofold light of reason and faith. Teachers are responsible for showing how to make this happen—in their curriculum, character, and conduct.

To Comenius, all of us can reason, but our reason is clouded by the dark side of human nature. Good curriculum making—and indeed good teaching—clears away the fog of fallenness so that the twofold light of reason and faith can illuminate our lives. As Comenius puts it:

> The seeds of knowledge, of virtue, and of piety are . . . naturally implanted in us; but the *actual* knowledge, virtue, and piety themselves are not so given. These must be acquired by prayer, by education, and by action. He gave no bad definition who said that man was a "teachable animal." And indeed it is only by a proper education that he can become a man.[15]

Be sure to keep in mind that to Comenius "man" is a general term. By no means does he exclude women from deliberations about curriculum or the ideal of universal liberal education.

Comenius's views were consistently criticized by at least two groups. One group thought his vision for educating everyone was naive. Certain souls cannot reason, argued these critics, so teachers and other educators should not even try to develop reason where it never existed in the first place. A second group also thought Comenius was naive, but for a different reason. They emphasized the fallenness of man to such an extent that they outright rejected Comenius's view that mankind could be improved through curriculum and teaching.

Comenius, of course, had an answer to both of these groups. To the first, he responded with his lifelong argument that *everyone* is made in the image of God. He understood that some people may reason more strongly than others, but that does not mean that reason is nonexistent in some people.

Good teachers and curriculum makers strengthen reason wherever they find it, regardless of how strong it may be.

To the second group, Comenius responded by pointing out that in their overemphasis on fallenness these critics rejected the entire point of education. If a curriculum cannot make people better, then does it not follow that we should just stop trying to teach people anything at all? Perhaps we can just eliminate the idea of curriculum, teachers, and teaching? As Comenius made the point:

> Our inner strength, some one will remark, has been weakened by the Fall. I reply, weakened, yes, but not extinguished. Even our bodily force, if it be in bad condition, can be restored to its natural vigour by walking, running, and other forms of exercise. . . . Shall not a man be easily taught those things to which nature—I will not say admits him or leads him—but rather *urges* and *impels* him?[16]

Comenius omitted nobody from his vision—and *plan*—for universal liberal education, and neither should we. My hope is that, whenever curriculum is discussed, this book will provide deliberators with the inspiration and courage necessary to attain virtue, ask curriculum questions, and teach deliberation. Those who make curriculum—and indeed the general public—can continue to choose one of the other paths that neglects deliberation and virtue, but the result will be a curriculum that culminates in slavery, not liberation. Twenty-first-century students, their teachers, and the communities they create deserve far better.

■ Discussion Questions

1. What are the three parts to this book's thesis?

2. How is intellectual life changing during the early twenty-first century?

3. What does virtue have to do with curriculum making?

4. How is happiness related to curriculum deliberation?

5. What are Aristotle's two types of virtue and what are some examples of each?

6. What does it mean for virtue to serve as the foundation for curriculum making? What does the author argue are the benefits of this approach?

7. What virtues are most essential to curriculum making?

8. How can or should curriculum deliberation be different in religious compared to secular schools? Should deliberations within private religious schools take on a different character? If so, how?

9. Why is Comenius a good role model for deliberative curriculists?

Appendix
Curriculum Dilemmas

THE FOLLOWING curriculum dilemmas can be used to foster deliberation about curriculum. They are composite sketches of common curriculum problems that arise within K–12 schools. Students should be encouraged to justify their decisions using reason, logic, and a sound view of the moral life.

■ Curriculum Dilemma #1

"Intelligent Design versus Evolution: Teach It or Ignore It?"

You are a twenty-two-year-old, first year biology teacher at Mossy Bogs High School in the Houston, Texas, area. You recently graduated from a successful science teacher education program at a major university in Texas, and you feel quite well prepared to begin your first year as a teacher. While an undergraduate, you completed a yearlong internship during which you had a great experience with an inspiring biology teacher. Your mentor teacher was quite successful at addressing the debates surrounding evolution and intelligent design. He was particularly good at raising the issues surrounding this controversy without taking a strong stance in one direction or another. You admired what you saw your mentor teacher doing in the classroom, and you are looking forward to modeling much of what he did in your own science classroom.

About two weeks prior to beginning a new unit on evolution, however, you had a conversation with your science department chair during which he raised the issue of teaching evolution at Mossy Bogs High School. You mentioned to your department chair that you were working hard to develop lessons that present a balanced view of the evolution/intelligent design debate. Your department chair then says to you, in a quite straightforward manner, "We do not discuss intelligent design at Mossy Bogs High School. Through the years, we have learned that it is much better to ignore intelligent design altogether and focus only on the material that is found on state tests. You should know that our science department has a strong stance on this issue."

You are, of course, quite disappointed to hear your department chair's views on this matter. You feel as though your students will be cheated if your science curriculum does not include serious discussion about evolution and intelligent design, which you consider to be a major debate that is taking place within both scientific and religious communities. At the same time, however, you realize that you cannot ignore what your department chair is telling you. You are caught between creating the kind of science curriculum that you think should be taught and following the demands that are being made of you by your supervisor.

What would you do and why?

■ Curriculum Dilemma #2

"Should I Talk to the Principal or Not?"

You are a third year first-grade teacher at Whispering Pines Elementary School in a suburban district in the Seattle, Washington, area. Your school enrolls a mix of students who come from sharply different socioeconomic backgrounds. About half of the 650 students in your school come from homes that cost at least $1 million, and many of them come from homes that cost in the $10 million to $20 million range. The other half of the school's students, however, are almost all on free and reduced lunch. Many of them have little or no support at home, their families have almost no money, and most of these children have never even touched a computer before they arrive for kindergarten. You know that many of these students will be lucky to make it to their junior year, let alone complete high school.

Your problem is that two of the other first-grade teachers always get the students who come from the higher socioeconomic class of students. You don't mind teaching the students who struggle to perform, in fact you enjoy the challenge, but you wonder why you never seem to get students who come from the wealthier backgrounds. You think that all of the students in the school would benefit from being in mixed classrooms, but the principal of the school apparently disagrees with you.

You realize that you need to do something before classroom assignments are made for your fourth year at the school. You know that the two teachers who always get the more privileged students, however, are very good friends with the principal. The principal and these two teachers have been together at Whispering Pines Elementary for almost fifteen years. They attend church together, they play golf together on the weekends, and their children are star athletes together at the district's high school.

You also know that parents of some of the more privileged students have requested, in years past, that their children be in your class, but you have never gotten any of these students in your room. To make matters worse, your students' test scores are always lower than those in the other two classes. The teachers are made to look as though they are outstanding educators when you know that most of their success is due to the students they have in their classrooms.

Because of test scores, you look bad each year, even though you know that you are doing just as good a job—if not a better job—than the other first-grade teachers. You have begun to feel angry, not only at the other two teachers, but also at the principal. The fourth first-grade teacher is only in her first year, so she isn't all that aware of what is going on. You have begun to think about requesting a transfer to another school, but, despite these problems, you like this school. You have become good friends with many of the other teachers from other grade levels. You also live across the street from the school and enjoy being able to walk to work every day. You love teaching, but all of these problems have taken a serious toll on the idealism that drew you into the teaching profession in the first place.

Parents will be making requests for the following academic year during the next week, so you know that you need to act quickly if you intend for something different to happen with assignments for the next year. You realize that you have at least four questions to answer at this point: Should I talk to the principal about my concerns? Should I talk with one of the other first-grade teachers? Should I talk with someone else? Or, should I just ignore the situation, with the realization that things may get worse in the years ahead instead of better?

What would you do and why?

■ Curriculum Dilemma #3

"Must I Teach Phonics?"

You have been teaching second grade for fifteen years at Woodrow Wilson Elementary School in a rural district in upstate New York. You have enjoyed the last fifteen years very much. You have had the freedom to teach just about any way you have wanted. As a reading teacher, you see yourself as a "whole language" teacher who enjoys surrounding students with good reading material and then allowing them to explore the books and lessons that they enjoy most. You see yourself as a creative teacher who loves her students and who enjoys meeting their needs and interests. You have a strong dislike for phonics. You think it is counterproductive and makes the students dislike reading. Two of the other second-grade teachers use phonics every day, but, since there has not been a district-wide policy in years past, all of you have had the freedom to teach however you wish.

Last year, however, your small district got a new superintendent who has hired a new principal for Woodrow Wilson Elementary. The new principal is a radical supporter of phonics. He has told everyone in the school that in order to raise test scores, every teacher, beginning next year, must use phonics. You are angry about this attack on your professionalism. Your students do just fine in your class, and they also score well on all of the end-of-year tests, even though you think these tests are overemphasized. You are angry that Mr. Battle, the new principal, thinks that he can come into the school and dictate how everyone should teach.

Many other teachers in the school are angry as well. They know that you are a whole-language supporter and that you are a well-known, outspoken advocate for the teaching profession. As a result, at least half a dozen teachers have come to you to complain (albeit privately) and to ask your advice about what they should do to fight this new mandate from the principal. Several of the teachers have told you that they plan to quit if they are not allowed to teach in the way they want. Some of these teachers are the most gifted and successful in the school. You are seriously concerned that the school is being damaged by what Mr. Battle is doing. You have no interest in teaching phonics. In fact, you have no idea how to use phonics even if you wanted to. You also refuse to change everything that you have been doing for the past fifteen years just because your school has a new principal. You see these mandates as a direct attack on who you are as a professional.

You are not sure what to do, but you know you need to do something. You realize that you have several important questions to consider: Should I just stay quiet and do what the principal is telling us to do even though I know that it will do long-term damage to the students, the school, and to me as a professional? Should I join with the other teachers and begin a campaign to battle this new mandate? Should I contact one of the school board members and inform him of what is going on? Or, should I just ignore what the principal is saying, shut my classroom door, and continue to do what I have been doing for the past fifteen years?

What would you do and why?

■ Curriculum Dilemma #4

"Should I Confront the Principal or Ignore What I Saw?"

You are a first year sixth-grade mathematics teacher at Rosie Oaks Middle School in a small school district in suburban Memphis, Tennessee. Although you think your school district is obsessed with test scores, you have had a good first year. Your school recently completed its final round of state testing, and everyone in your school is quite pleased that the testing season is over. Everyone is anxious, however, about how the school will do. Your school should learn the test results in about three weeks. Rosie Oaks has been under tremendous pressure to raise test scores. Last year, your school was rated "Academically Unacceptable" by the state. The school's new principal, Mr. Shades, is under extreme pressure to raise your school's scores. In fact, you know that he was hired on a two-year contract that will not be renewed unless your school's rating improves from "Academically Unacceptable" to "Meets Expectations."

The Friday evening following the week of testing, you realize that you have forgotten a set of student papers in your classroom, papers that you promised to grade and return to your students on Monday. As a result, you make a trip back to the school late on Friday evening to get the papers. You didn't expect to see anyone at school this late on a Friday, so you are quite surprised when you see a light on in the library as you are walking to your classroom. You are curious to see who is there, so you peak through the door's window to see what is going on. When you do, you see Mr. Shades in the library with all of the scantron forms, a large eraser, and a box of #2 pencils. You see him erasing scores and marking new answers. You watch him do this to at least twenty or thirty scantron forms. You are shocked at what you see. You can't believe your eyes. You then become scared that Mr. Shades will see you. You run to your classroom, grab your papers, and then leave the school as quickly as you can. You are quite sure that Mr. Shades did not see you.

Your first instinct is to try and forget about the entire situation. You try to forget what you saw, but your conscience will not let you put the incident behind you. In addition, you recall hearing Mr. Shades, a few weeks earlier, joking to one of the assistant principals that he will do "whatever it takes" to improve the school's test scores, including "taking the test for them, if I have to." At the time, you thought nothing of what Mr. Shades said, but now you realize that he may have been serious.

You enjoy teaching at your school. With the exception of the testing pressure that he has been placing on everyone, you think Mr. Shades is a good principal. You think the emphasis on testing is completely out of control, and, in some strange way, you can even sympathize with Mr. Shades, if he in fact was changing students' answers. You know that Mr. Shades has six children at home, ages six months to nine years old. You would feel terrible if Mr. Shades lost his job because of what you have seen. At the same time, you have no direct evidence that he was changing students' scores. Moreover, he is the person responsible for boxing up all of the testing forms and returning them to the state education agency. Who knows, perhaps Mr. Shades was erasing and changing scores for a legitimate reason. Still, however, you cannot think of any reason why he would be doing what you saw. If he was changing students' scores, you know that such a practice is absolutely wrong and he should be punished. You know that the consequences are severe for school personnel who either cheat on state testing or who do not report any cheating that they see. Like all teachers, you signed an oath that states you will not compromise test score data in any way, or be an accomplice to others who do engage in falsifying test score data. You are tempted to do nothing, but your conscience will not let you forget what you witnessed. There are legal reasons for not ignoring what you witnessed as well. You want to forget the incident and get on with the last three weeks of school, but you just cannot let it go.

What would you do and why?

■ Curriculum Dilemma #5

"Should I Give the Star Running Back a Break or Uphold Standards?"

Your name is Mrs. Searight, and you are a fifteen-year veteran English teacher at Piney Woods High School, an award-winning school in suburban Charlotte, North Carolina. Your school enrolls some of the wealthiest and most academically well-prepared students in the country. Upon graduation, students from Piney Woods routinely enroll and succeed remarkably well at some of the most prestigious universities in the country.

You are currently teaching one honors section of British literature, but you would like to teach three additional sections beginning next year. Teaching four sections of British literature per year to academically gifted students is your dream job. This teaching situation is currently in your grasp because Mrs. Turner, who currently teaches the other honors British literature courses, has announced that she will be retiring at the end of the year. You realize that you are in a perfect position to take over her classes. The principal, Mr. Moses, has even mentioned to you that you would be a perfect fit "to take over Mrs. Turner's classes next year," if you want to.

Your school, however, has recently become increasingly obsessed with athletics. Your football team has never been that good, but suddenly, they find themselves undefeated after having won three games in the playoffs. They are one win away from playing in the state football championship. You are uneasy about your school's newfound fascination with athletics. You think students at Piney Woods should focus on their academic studies and leave athletics to, at best, a second-place status in their lives. The school board, your principal, and even many teachers at the school are quite enthusiastic about how the football team is doing.

In your one honors section, you happen to have Brian Axe, the star running back, as one of your students. Brian has scored an average of three touchdowns in every game this season. Without Brian, the Piney Woods Rattlers are almost certain to lose. He carries the team on his shoulders. Brian, however, has not been performing well at all in your class. He has not turned in any papers since the end of October. He comes to class, but he doesn't pay any attention to what is going on. For the past six weeks, you have drawn attention to these problems in the weekly progress reports that all athletes must complete. You have not, however, heard anything from the coaches. Brian seems to be doing worse every week. You then decide to e-mail the head coach, Coach Bubbers, to let him know that Brian will be receiving a failing grade at the end of the semester. You tell him that you realize that this failing grade will make Brian ineligible to play in the last two games, but you must uphold moral and intellectual standards. You tell Coach Bubbers that Brian has little chance of improving his situation at this point and that the team needs to make plans to play the last two games without him.

After school that day, you are grading papers in your classroom when Coach Bubbers and Mr. Moses, the principal, walk into your room and shut the door. They then proceed to tell you, in no uncertain terms, that Brian should receive a passing grade for the semester. They tell you that what the football team is doing is of great benefit not only to the school, but to the entire community. They say that the school has been making lots of money at the playoff games, money that can be used for academic purposes. They say that you should give Brian a break and that he will get back on track once the football season is over.

You tell Coach Bubbers and Mr. Moses that you simply will not lower your standards simply to win some silly football game. Brian has not been doing the work, and he should receive the grade that he deserves. You ask Coach Bubbers and Mr. Moses, "How is giving Brian a grade that he does not deserve fair to the other students in the class? What about the students who have been working hard and who will receive grades of C? Is it fair that Brian will receive the same grade as them, even though he has not been doing anything?" Coach Bubbers and Mr. Moses are not interested in hearing what you have to say. Mr. Moses then says, quite rudely, "Well, Mrs. Searight, maybe you aren't the right person to teach our honors British literature sections after all." Mr. Moses goes on to say, "We can continue this conversation when you turn in your grades on Friday. Be sure to bring your grade forms directly to me in my office." Coach Bubbers and Mr. Moses then storm out of your room.

You are crushed by what has just happened. You pride yourself on upholding high moral and intellectual standards for your students and for the teaching profession. At the same time, however, you want to please your principal, you don't like disobeying authority, and your dream teaching situation is only one year away.

What would you do to address this problem and why?

Notes

Foreword

1. William H. Schubert, "Toward Lives Worth Sharing: A Basis for Integrating Curriculum," *Educational Horizons* 73 (1994): 26.

2. John Dewey, *Art as Experience* (New York: Perigee, 1934); William F. Pinar, William M. Reynolds, Patrick Slattery, and Peter M. Taubman, *Understanding Curriculum: An Introduction to the Study of Historical and Contemporary Curriculum Discourses* (New York: Peter Lang, 1995); Paulo Freire, *Pedagogy of the Oppressed* (Boston: Beacon, 1970/1997); and Michael W. Apple, *Teachers and Texts: A Political Economy of Class and Gender Relations in Education* (New York: Routledge, 1988).

3. Freire, *Pedagogy of the Oppressed*.

4. Michael Lewis, *Moneyball* (New York: Norton, 2003).

5. Lewis, *Moneyball*, xiv.

6. William H. Schubert, "Journeys of Expansion and Synopsis: Tensions in Books That Shaped Curriculum Inquiry, 1968–Present," *Curriculum Inquiry* 40 (2010): 1.

7. Robert Dahl, *After the Revolution?* (New Haven: Yale University Press, 1970/1990).

8. William H. Schubert, *Curriculum: Perspective, Paradigm, and Possibility* (New York: MacMillan, 1986); and William F. Pinar, William M. Reynolds, Patrick Slattery, and Peter M. Taubman, *Understanding Curriculum: An Introduction to the Study of Historical and Contemporary Curriculum Discourses* (New York: Peter Lang, 1995).

9. Elliot Eisner, *The Educational Imagination: On the Design and Evaluation of School Programs* (New York: Prentice Hall, 1979).

10. Roselynn Nguyen and J. Wesley Null, "From the Unity of Truth to Technique and Back Again: The Transformation of Curriculum and Professionalism within Higher Education," *American Educational History Journal* 35 (Summer 2008): 103–16; J. Wesley Null, "Educational Foundations for Teachers: Why We Lost and What to Do About It," *Journal of Philosophy and History of Education* 56 (Fall 2006): 130–32; J. Wesley Null, *Peerless Educator: The Life and Work of Isaac Leon Kandel* (New York: Peter Lang, 2007); J. Wesley Null, "Is There a Future for Teacher Ed Curriculum? An Answer from History and Moral Philosophy," *American Educational History Journal* 35 (Summer 2008): 3–18; J. Wesley Null, "Back to the Future: How and Why to Revive the Teachers College Tradition," *Journal of Teacher Education* 60 (November/December 2009); J. Wesley Null and Chara Haeussler Bohan, "Teacher Education

Curriculum: What, How, and Why," *Curriculum and Teaching Dialogue* 7 (Fall 2005): 39–49; J. Wesley Null and Diane Ravitch, eds., *Forgotten Heroes of American Education: The Great Tradition of Teaching Teachers* (Greenwich, CT: IAP–Information Age Publishing, 2006).

11. Eric Hobsbawn, *Interesting Times* (London: Allen Lane, 2002), 417.

12. David M. Callejo-Pérez, "Curriculum and Transformation: Re-thinking Leadership and Schools All Over Again," *Journal of Curriculum and Instruction* 3 (November 2009): 6–21; David M. Callejo-Pérez and A. Swan Dagen, "Teachers as Decision Makers: Narratives of Power in an Era of Standards," *Revista Contrapontos* 10 (January/April 2010): 41–48; David M. Callejo-Pérez and S. Diaz, "The Future of Policy Development in Education: How a Rural County Can Maximize Its Resources through Collaboration." In J. Slater and R. David, eds. *Collaboration in Education* (New York: Routledge, 2010), 65–72.

13. Freire, *Pedagogy of the Oppressed*.

14. Michael Kreyling, *Inventing Southern Literature* (Jackson: University of Mississippi Press, 2001).

15. Kreyling, *Inventing Southern Literature*, 18.

Introduction

1. Lawrence A. Cremin, *Traditions of American Education* (New York: Basic Books, 1977).

2. William A. Reid, *Curriculum as Institution and Practice: Essays in the Deliberative Tradition* (Mahwah, NJ: Lawrence Erlbaum, 1999).

3. At the university level, this assertion holds whether the social science researchers I am referring to are found in colleges of arts and sciences or in schools of education. Either way, the goal of social science research (when practiced in this way) is to explain social phenomena and simultaneously disconnect from curriculum and ethics. I am arguing that this disconnect is impossible, problematic, and wrongheaded.

4. See, for example, Alasdair MacIntyre, *After Virtue: A Study in Moral Theory*, 3rd ed. (Notre Dame, IN: University of Notre Dame Press, 2007); William M. Sullivan, *Work and Integrity: The Crisis and Promise of Professionalism in America*, 2nd ed. (San Francisco: Jossey-Bass, 2005); and William F. May, *Beleaguered Rulers: The Public Obligation of the Professional* (Louisville, KY: Westminster John Knox, 2001).

5. Steven H. Miles, *The Hippocratic Oath and the Ethics of Medicine* (Oxford: Oxford University Press, 2004).

6. Pierre Hadot, *Philosophy as a Way of Life*, ed. Arnold I. Davidson (Malden, MA: Blackwell, 1995), 265.

7. William A. Reid, *The Pursuit of Curriculum: Schooling and the Public Interest*, ed. J. Wesley Null (Greenwich, CT: IAP, 2006).

8. Donald N. Levine, *Powers of the Mind: The Reinvention of Liberal Learning in America* (Chicago: University of Chicago Press, 2007), 114–45.

9. Joseph J. Schwab, "The Practical 3: Translation into Curriculum," *School Review* 81 (August 1973): 501–22.

Chapter 1: The March to Liberal Curriculum for All

1. Allan Bloom, trans., *The Republic of Plato* (New York: Basic Books, 1968), 221–49.

2. C. D. C. Reeve, trans., Aristotle, *Politics* (Indianapolis, IN: Hackett, 1998), 65–133.

3. Readers should note the parallel between these three soul types and the Olympic medals awarded every four years.

4. For more on the history of the idea of liberal education, see Bruce A. Kimball, *Orators and Philosophers: A History of the Idea of Liberal Education* (New York: College Board, 1995).

5. See, for example, R. P. H. Green, trans., *On Christian Teaching* by Augustine (Oxford: Oxford University Press, 1997); Ralph McInerny, trans., *Thomas Aquinas: Selected Writings* (London: Penguin Books, 1998); and M. W. Keatinge, trans., *The Great Didactic* by John Amos Comenius (Whitefish, MT: Kessinger Publishing, 1992).

6. M. W. Keatinge, trans., *The Great Didactic* by John Amos Comenius (Whitefish, MT: Kessinger Publishing, 1992); Ernest M. Eller, ed., *The School of Infancy* by John Amos Comenius (Chapel Hill: University of North Carolina Press, 1956); and John Amos Comenius, *Orbis Pictus* (Syracuse, NY: C. W. Bardeen, 1887).

7. J. Wesley Null and Diane Ravitch, eds., *Forgotten Heroes of American Education: The Great Tradition of Teaching Teachers* (Greenwich, CT: Information Age, 2006); see also, Christine A. Ogren, *The American State Normal School: "An Instrument of Great Good"* (New York: Palgrave Macmillan, 2005).

8. B. Edward McClellan, *Moral Education in America: Schools and the Shaping of Character from Colonial Times to the Present* (New York: Teachers College Press, 1999), 1–30.

9. See, for example, Robert Kunzman, *Grappling with the Good: Talking about Religion and Morality in Public Schools* (Albany, NJ: SUNY Press, 2006); David Carr and Jan Steutel, eds., *Virtue Ethics and Moral Education* (London: Routledge, 1999); Susan D. Collins, *Aristotle and the Rediscovery of Citizenship* (New York: Cambridge University Press, 2006); Jon Elster, ed., *Deliberative Democracy* (Cambridge: Cambridge University Press, 1998); and Gail McCutcheon, *Developing the Curriculum: Solo and Group Deliberation* (White Plains, NY: Longman Publishers, 1995).

10. For more on this point, see J. Wesley Null, "Teaching Deliberation: Curriculum Workers as Public Educators," in William A. Reid, *The Pursuit of Curriculum: Schooling and the Public Interest*, ed. J. Wesley Null (Greenwich, CT: IAP, 2006), xiii–xxi.

11. John Dewey, *Democracy and Education* (New York: Macmillan, 1916), 239.

12. Dewey, *Democracy and Education*, 194–206.

13. Donald N. Levine, *Powers of the Mind: The Reinvention of Liberal Learning in America* (Chicago: University of Chicago Press, 2007), 142–45.

14. Joseph J. Schwab, "The Practical: A Language for Curriculum," *School Review* 78 (November 1969): 1–23.

15. Joseph J. Schwab, "The Practical 3: Translation into Curriculum," *School Review* 81 (August 1973): 501–22.

16. William A. Reid, *The Pursuit of Curriculum: Schooling and the Public Interest*, ed. J. Wesley Null (Greenwich, CT: Information Age Publishing, 2006).

17. William A. Reid, *Thinking About the Curriculum: The Nature and Treatment of Curriculum Problems* (London: Routledge, 1978).

Chapter 2: Systematic Curriculum

1. *Chief Executive*, no. 207, April 2005.

2. William L. Bainbridge, "Teacher Pay Key in Fixing Public Schools," *Columbus Dispatch*, April 23, 2005, 08A.

3. "Fixing America's Future: To Stave Off a U.S. Work Force Crisis, CEOs Are Getting More Involved in Improving the Nation's Schools," *Chief Executive*, no. 207, April 2005, 23–25.

4. "Final Word: Editorials," *Chief Executive*, no. 207, April 2005, 72.

5. U.S. Department of Education, *No Child Left Behind: A Toolkit for Teachers* (Washington, DC: U.S. Department of Education, 2004), 30.

6. U.S. Department of Education, Office of the Secretary, Office of Public Affairs, *No Child Left Behind: A Parents Guide* (Washington, DC: U.S. Department of Education, 2003), 18.

7. U.S. Department of Education, *No Child Left Behind: A Parents Guide*, 15.

8. U.S. Department of Education, *A Parents Guide*, 19.

9. U.S. Department of Education, *A Parents Guide*, 19.

10. U.S. Department of Education, *A Parents Guide*, 13.

11. D. K. Cohen, S. Raudenbush, and D. L. Ball, "Resources, Instruction, and Research," in F. Mosteller and R. Boruch, eds., *Evidence Matters: Randomized Trials in Education Research* (Washington, DC: Brookings Institution Press, 2002), 196.

12. *No Child Left Behind: A Desktop Reference,* prepared by the Under Secretary of Education (Washington, DC: U.S. Department of Education, September 2002), 13.

13. Diane Ravitch, *National Standards in American Education: A Citizen's Guide* (Washington, DC: Brookings Institution Press, 1995), 23.

14. There are other curriculum standards that combine systematic curriculum expectations with local adaptation in a way similar to what Ravitch advocates. For example, the National Science Education Standards establish goals for science education but also recognize that different curricula within different school districts can achieve the goals they describe; see National Academy of Sciences, *National Science Education Standards* (Washington, DC: National Academy Press, 1996).

15. Larry E. Frase, Fenwick W. English, and William K. Poston, Jr., eds., *The Curriculum Management Audit: Improving School Quality* (Lancaster, PA: Technomic, 1995); Fenwick W. English, *Educational Administration: The Human Science* (New York: HarperCollins, 1992); Fenwick W. English, *Deep Curriculum Alignment: Creating a Level Playing Field for All Children on High-stakes Tests of Educational Accountability* (Lanham, MD: Scarecrow, 2001); and Fenwick W. English, *Curriculum Auditing* (Lancaster, PA: Technomic, 1988).

16. Fenwick W. English, *Deciding What to Teach and Test: Developing, Aligning, and Auditing the Curriculum* (Thousand Oaks, CA: Corwin Press, 2000), xiv; emphases and quotation marks in original.

17. English, *Deciding What to Teach*, 2; emphasis in original.

18. Larry E. Frase, "Introduction," in *The Curriculum Management Audit: Improving School Quality,* eds. Larry E. Frase, Fenwick W. English, and William K. Poston, Jr. (Lancaster, PA: Technomic Publishing, 1995), ix.

19. Frase, "Introduction," 5–6.

20. Fenwick W. English, "Standards and Assumptions of the Curriculum Management Audit," in *The Curriculum Management Audit: Improving School Quality,* eds., Larry E. Frase, Fenwick W. English, and William K. Poston, Jr. (Lancaster, PA: Technomic Publishing, 1995); quotation marks in original.

21. For more on this point, see Larry Cuban, *The Blackboard and the Bottom Line: Why Schools Can't Be Businesses* (Cambridge, MA: Harvard University Press, 2007); see also, David Tyack and Larry Cuban, *Tinkering toward Utopia: A Century of Public School Reform* (Cambridge, MA: Harvard University Press, 1997).

22. Raymond E. Callahan, *Education and the Cult of Efficiency: A Study of the Social Forces That Have Shaped the Administration of the Public Schools* (Chicago: University of Chicago Press, 1964).

23. John Franklin Bobbitt, *The Curriculum* (New York: Macmillan, 1918).

24. Bobbitt, *The Curriculum*, 43.

25. Franklin Bobbitt, *How to Make a Curriculum* (New York: Houghton Mifflin, 1924), 8.

26. See, for example, Herbert M. Kliebard, "The Rise of Scientific Curriculum Making and Its Aftermath," *Curriculum Theory Network* 5 (1975): 27–38.

27. Bobbitt did, however, undergo a transformation later in life. He recognized that his earlier work had been misguided; nonetheless, Bobbitt's early books were the ones that became popular, and the views contained within them are the ones that remain powerful today. For more on Bobbitt's transformation, see J. Wesley Null, "Efficiency Jettisoned: Unacknowledged Changes in the Curriculum Thought of John Franklin Bobbitt," *Journal of Curriculum and Supervision* 15 (Fall 1999): 35–42; and J. Wesley Null, "Social Efficiency Splintered: Multiple Meanings Instead of the Hegemony of One," *Journal of Curriculum and Supervision* 19 (Winter 2004): 99–124.

28. I have chosen to use the phrases "teacher training" and "teacher training curriculum" not because those are the phrases that I prefer, but because those are the phrases used by Charters. The use of teacher *training* as opposed to teacher *education* reveals Charters's underlying views on curriculum. Systematic thinkers like Charters make a sharp distinction between liberal and vocational curriculum and then focus almost exclusively on training for occupations and not liberal education for citizenship, hence Charters's use of training instead of education.

29. J. Wesley Null, "Curriculum for Teachers: Four Traditions within Pedagogical Philosophy," *Educational Studies* 42 (August 2007): 43–63.

30. W. W. Charters, *Curriculum Construction* (New York: Macmillan, 1923), 4; emphasis in original.

31. W. W. Charters and Douglas Waples, *The Commonwealth Teacher-Training Study* (Chicago: University of Chicago Press, 1929), 223–25.

32. Charters and Waples, *Commonwealth Teacher-Training Study*, 10.

33. See, for example, W. W. Charters, *Methods of Teaching: Their Basis and Statement Developed from a Functional Standpoint* (Chicago: Row, Peterson, and Company, 1912).

34. See, for example, W. W. Charters, *How to Teach Ideals* (Madras: Methodist Publishing House, 1927); W. W. Charters, *The Teaching of Ideals* (New York: Macmillan, 1928).

35. Milton Friedman, *Capitalism and Freedom* (Chicago: University of Chicago Press, 1962).

36. Friedman, *Capitalism and Freedom*, 85–107.

37. Milton Friedman and Rose Friedman, *Free to Choose: A Personal Statement* (New York: Harcourt Brace Jovanovich, 1980), 170.

38. John E. Chubb and Terry M. Moe, *Politics, Markets, and America's Schools* (Washington, DC: Brookings Institution Press, 1990).

39. Chubb and Moe, *Politics, Markets*, 25.

40. Chubb and Moe, *Politics, Markets*, 33.

41. Chubb and Moe, *Politics, Markets*, 13.

42. Chubb and Moe, *Politics, Markets*, 186.

43. Chubb and Moe, *Politics, Markets*, 189.

44. John E. Chubb and Terry M. Moe, "American Public Schools: Choice *Is* a Panacea," *Brookings Review* 8 (Summer 1990): 4–12; emphasis in original title.

45. Neal McCluskey, "Corruption in the Public Schools: The Market Is the Answer," *Policy Analysis* 542 (April 20, 2005): 12.

46. McCluskey, "Corruption in the Public Schools," 16.

47. Mortimer J. Adler, "Teaching and Learning," in *From Parnassus: Essays in Honor of Jacques Barzun*, eds., Dora B. Weiner and William R. Keylor (New York: Harper and Row, 1976), 57–65.

48. See, for example, John E. Chubb, "Saving No Child Left Behind," in *Within Our Reach: How America Can Educate Every Child*, ed. John E. Chubb (Lanham, MD: Rowman and Littlefield, 2005), 1–34.

Chapter 3: Existentialist Curriculum

1. Maxine Greene, "Literature, Existentialism, and Education," in *Existentialism and Phenomenology in Education*, ed. David E. Denton (New York: Teachers College Press, 1974), 75.

2. Alfie Kohn, *Punished by Rewards: The Trouble with Gold Stars, Incentive Plans, A's, Praise, and Other Bribes* (Boston: Houghton Mifflin, 1993), 252.

3. Alfie Kohn, *Punished by Rewards: The Trouble with Gold Stars, Incentive Plans, A's, Praise, and Other Bribes* (Boston: Houghton Mifflin, 1993); Alfie Kohn, *No Contest: The Case Against Competition*, rev. ed. (Boston: Houghton Mifflin, 1992); Alfie Kohn, *What to Look For in a Classroom . . . And Other Essays* (San Francisco: Jossey-Bass, 1998); and Alfie Kohn, *The Schools Our Children Deserve: Moving Beyond Traditional Classrooms and "Tougher Standards"* (New York: Houghton Mifflin, 2000).

4. Kitty Thuermer, "In Defense of the Progressive School: An Interview with Alfie Kohn," *Independent School* 59 (Fall 1999): 95.

5. Kohn, *Punished by Rewards*, 217.

6. Kohn, *No Contest*, 11–44.

7. Kohn, *Punished by Rewards*, 225.

8. Greene, "Literature, Existentialism, and Education," 84.

9. Greene, "Literature, Existentialism, and Education," 84.

10. Maxine Greene, *The Dialectic of Freedom* (New York: Teachers College Press, 1988), 1.

11. Maxine Greene, "'Excellence,' Meanings and Multiplicity," *Teachers College Record* 86 (Winter 1984): 293.

12. Jean-Jacques Rousseau, *Emile, or On Education*, trans. Allan Bloom (New York: Basic Books, 1979).

13. Elliot Eisner, *Cognition and Curriculum Reconsidered*, 2nd ed. (New York: Teachers College Press, 1994), 39.

14. Eisner, *Cognition and Curriculum Reconsidered*, 19.

15. Elliot Eisner, *The Educational Imagination: On the Design and Evaluation of School Programs*, 2nd ed. (New York: Macmillan, 1985), 358.

16. G. Stanley Hall, "The Contents of Children's Minds," *The Princeton Review* 11 (May 1883): 249–72.

17. G. Stanley Hall, "The Contents of Children's Minds on Entering School," in *Readings in American Educational Thought: From Puritanism to Progressivism*, eds. Andrew J. Milson, Chara Haeussler Bohan, Perry L. Glanzer, and J. Wesley Null (Greenwich, CT: Information Age, 2004), 243–53.

18. Hall, "The Contents of Children's Minds on Entering School," 252.

19. Ellen Key, *The Century of the Child* (New York: G. Putnam's Sons, 1909).

20. See, for example, William Heard Kilpatrick, *Education for a Changing Civilization* (New York: Macmillan, 1928), and William Heard Kilpatrick, *Philosophy of Education* (New York: Macmillan, 1951).

21. William Heard Kilpatrick, *Remaking the Curriculum* (New York: Newson and Company, 1936), 31–32.

22. William Heard Kilpatrick, *The Project Method: The Use of the Purposeful Act in the Educative Process* (New York: Teachers College, Columbia University, 1918), 12.

23. Kilpatrick, *Remaking the Curriculum*, 28.

24. National Research Council, *How People Learn: Brain, Mind, Experience, and School*, 2nd ed. (Washington, DC: National Academy Press, 2000).

Chapter 4: Radical Curriculum

1. George S. Counts, *Dare the School Build a New Social Order?* (Carbondale: Southern Illinois University, 1978), 51; originally published in 1932.

2. Michael W. Apple, *Ideology and Curriculum*, 2nd ed. (New York: Routledge, 1990), 156.

3. Michael W. Apple, *Official Knowledge: Democratic Education in a Conservative Age* (New York: Routledge, 1993), 179.

4. Michael W. Apple, "Relevance and Curriculum: A Study in Phenomenological Sociology of Knowledge," EdD diss., Teachers College, Columbia University, 1970, 1.

5. Apple, *Official Knowledge*, 11.

6. Apple, *Official Knowledge*, 11.

7. Apple, *Official Knowledge*, 40.

8. Michael W. Apple, *Educating the "Right" Way: Markets, Standards, God, and Inequality* (New York: Routledge, 2006), 4.

9. Apple, *Official Knowledge*, 28.

10. Apple, *Official Knowledge*, 40.

11. Apple, *Official Knowledge*, 118.

12. Eugene F. Provenzo, *Critical Literacy: What Every American Needs to Know* (Boulder, CO: Paradigm, 2006).

13. Apple, *Ideology and Curriculum*, ix–x.

14. Apple, *Ideology and Curriculum*, 1.

15. Apple, *Ideology and Curriculum*, 86.

16. Apple, *Official Knowledge*, 180.

17. Paulo Freire, *Pedagogy of the Oppressed*, 30th anniversary ed. (New York: Continuum, 2002).

18. Freire, *Pedagogy of the Oppressed*, 73.

19. Freire, *Pedagogy of the Oppressed*, 138.

20. Paulo Freire, "Education, Liberation, and the Church," *Religious Education* 79 (Fall 1984): 524–45.

21. Freire, "Education, Liberation, and the Church," 536.

22. Freire, "Education, Liberation, and the Church," 535.

23. Freire, "Education, Liberation, and the Church," 536.

24. Freire, "Education, Liberation, and the Church," 540.

25. Freire, "Education, Liberation, and the Church," 542.

26. Freire, "Education, Liberation, and the Church," 543.

27. Freire, "Education, Liberation, and the Church," 544.

28. Freire, "Education, Liberation, and the Church," 544.

29. Freire, "Education, Liberation, and the Church," 545.

30. Paulo Freire, "Know, Practice, and Teach the Gospels," *Religious Education* 79 (Fall 1984): 547.

31. George S. Counts, *A Ford Crosses Russia* (Boston: Stratford, 1930); and George S. Counts, *The Soviet Challenge to America* (New York: John Day, 1931).

32. Counts, *Dare the School Build a New Social Order?* (Carbondale: Southern Illinois University, 1978); originally published in 1932.

33. Counts does not use this term, but, for purposes of my argument, I will continue to use it.

34. Counts, *Dare the School*, 4.

35. Counts, *Dare the School*, 5

36. Counts, *Dare the School*, 26.

37. Counts, *Dare the School*, 27.

38. Counts, *Dare the School*, 33.

39. Counts, *Dare the School*, 19–20.

40. Counts, *Dare the School*, 25.

41. Ronald W. Evans, *This Happened in America: Harold Rugg and the Censure of Social Studies* (Greenwich, NC: Information Age, 2007).

42. Harold Rugg and George S. Counts, "A Critical Appraisal of Current Methods of Curriculum-Making," in *Twenty-Sixth Yearbook of the National Society for the Study of Education* (Bloomington, IL: Public School Publishing Company, 1926), 427.

43. Rugg and Counts, "Critical Appraisal of Current Methods," 447.

44. Evans, *This Happened in America*," 101.

45. Evans, *This Happened in America*," 101.

46. Evans, *This Happened in America*,"189.

47. Harold Ordway Rugg, *That Men May Understand: An American in the Long Armistice* (New York: Doubleday, 1941).

48. Charles Dorn, "'Treason in the Textbooks': Reinterpreting the Harold Rugg Textbook Controversy in the Context of Wartime Schooling," *Paedagogica Historica* 44 (August 2008): 457–79.

49. Harold O. Rugg, "How Shall We Reconstruct the Social Studies Curriculum?" *Historical Outlook* 12 (May 1921): 184–89.

50. Apple, *Official Knowledge*, 6.

51. Evans, *This Happened in America*, 103–4.

Chapter 5: Pragmatic Curriculum

1. William James, "What Pragmatism Means," in *Essays in Pragmatism by William James*, ed. Alburey Castell (New York: Hafner, 1948), 150.

2. Theodore R. Sizer, *Horace's Compromise: The Dilemma of the American High School* (Boston: Houghton Mifflin, 1984), 20.

3. Sizer, *Horace's Compromise*, 206.

4. Sizer, *Horace's Compromise*, 225–27.

5. Sizer, *Horace's Compromise*, 230.

6. Sizer, *Horace's Compromise*, 230.

7. Sizer, *Horace's Compromise*, 228.

8. Theodore R. Sizer, *Horace's Hope: What Works for the American High School* (Boston: Houghton Mifflin, 1996).

9. Harry K. Wong, "Behavioral Objectives, Teacher Help, and Academic Achievement," EdD diss., Brigham Young University, 1980.

10. "Dr. Harry K. Wong," American Entertainment International Speakers Bureau, www.aeispeakers.com/speakerbio.php?SpeakerID=1094.

11. Harry K. Wong and Rosemary T. Wong, *The First Days of School: How to Be an Effective Teacher* (Mountain View, CA: Harry K. Wong Publications, 1998), xii.

12. Wong and Wong, *The First Days of School* (1998), 169.

13. Harry K. Wong and Rosemary T. Wong, *The First Days of School: How to Be an Effective Teacher*, 4th ed. (Mountain View, CA: Harry K. Wong Publications, 2009), 68.

14. Wong and Wong, *The First Days of School* (1998), 217.

15. Wong and Wong, *The First Days of School* (1998), 65.

16. Wong and Wong, *The First Days of School* (1998), 75.

17. Jay Martin, *The Education of John Dewey: A Biography* (New York: Columbia University Press, 2002).

18. Robert B. Westbrook, *John Dewey and American Democracy* (Ithaca, NY: Cornell University Press, 1991), 15–29.

19. Westbrook, *John Dewey*, 22.

20. Daniel N. Robinson, *A History of Intellectual Psychology* (Madison: University of Wisconsin Press, 1995).

21. John Dewey, *The School and Society/The Child and the Curriculum*, ed. Philip W. Jackson (Chicago: University of Chicago Press, 1991), 34.

22. John Dewey, "The Primary-Education Fetich," *Forum* XXV (May 1898): 315–16.

23. For another work of Dewey's in which he praises Rousseau and again makes the case for a curriculum rooted in children's interests, see John Dewey and Evelyn Dewey, *Schools of Tomorrow* (New York: E. P. Dutton & Company, 1915).

24. John Dewey, *Democracy and Education* (New York: Macmillan, 1916), 309.

25. Dewey, *Democracy and Education*, 310.

26. Dewey, *Democracy and Education*, 313.

27. Dewey, *Democracy and Education*, 313.

28. Dewey, *Democracy and Education*, 313.

29. Dewey, *Democracy and Education*, 314.

30. The idea of "social efficiency" has received a good deal of attention from curriculum theorists and historians. Dewey has sometimes been wrongly portrayed as a critic of social efficiency, but the evidence belies this interpretation. Dewey argued passionately in favor of social efficiency in *Democracy and Education,* dedicating an entire chapter to the concept. See Dewey, *Democracy and Education,* 111–23; see also, J. Wesley Null, "Social Efficiency Splintered: Multiple Meanings Instead of the Hegemony of One," *Journal of Curriculum and Supervision* 19 (Winter 2004): 99–124; and Michael Knoll, "From Kidd to Dewey: The Origin and Meaning of 'Social Efficiency,'" *Journal of Curriculum Studies* 41 (June 2009): 361–91.

31. John Dewey, *The School and Society/The Child and the Curriculum,* ed. Philip W. Jackson (Chicago: University of Chicago Press, 1991), 34.

32. John Dewey, "Can Education Share in Social Reconstruction?," *Social Frontier* 1 (October 1934): 12.

33. Dewey, *Democracy and Education*, 49–50.

34. John Dewey, "The Teacher and His World," *Social Frontier* 1 (January 1935): 7.

35. Ralph W. Tyler, "Statistical Methods for Utilizing Personal Judgments to Evaluate Activities for Teacher-Training Curricula," PhD diss., University of Chicago, 1927.

36. Craig Kridel and Robert V. Bullough, *Stories of the Eight-Year Study: Reexamining Secondary Education in America* (Albany, NY: SUNY Press, 2007).

37. Ralph W. Tyler, *Basic Principles of Curriculum and Instruction* (Chicago: University of Chicago Press, 1949).

38. Tyler, *Basic Principles of Curriculum*, 36.

39. Tyler, *Basic Principles of Curriculum*, 128.

40. Tyler, *Basic Principles of Curriculum*, 23.

41. Tyler, *Basic Principles of Curriculum*, 106.

42. Tyler, *Basic Principles of Curriculum*, 4–5.

Chapter 6: Deliberative Curriculum

1. William A. Reid, *Curriculum as Institution and Practice: Essays in the Deliberative Tradition* (Mahwah, NJ: Lawrence Erlbaum, 1999), 42–43.

2. William A. Reid, *Thinking About the Curriculum: The Nature and Treatment of Curriculum Problems* (London: Routledge and Kegan Paul, 1978); and William A. Reid, *Curriculum as Institution and Practice: Essays in the Deliberative Tradition* (Mahwah, NJ: Lawrence Erlbaum, 1999).

3. Reid, *Thinking About the Curriculum*, 43.

4. Reid, *Thinking About the Curriculum*, 41–42.

5. Reid, *Thinking About the Curriculum*, 39.

6. James March, "Model Bias in Social Action," *Review of Educational Research* 42 (Autumn 1972): 414.

7. William A. Reid, "Democracy, Perfectability, and the Battle of the Books: Thoughts on the Conception of Liberal Education in the Writings of Schwab," *Curriculum Inquiry* 10 (Fall 1980): 259.

8. Reid, "Democracy, Perfectability, and the Battle of the Books," 249–250.

9. Reid, "Democracy, Perfectability, and the Battle of the Books," 250.

10. Reid, "Democracy, Perfectability, and the Battle of the Books," 250.

11. Reid, "Democracy, Perfectability, and the Battle of the Books," 250.

12. Reid, "Democracy, Perfectability, and the Battle of the Books," 250.

13. In chapter 10, I return to these virtues and discuss them in more detail.

14. William A. Reid, "Principle and Pragmatism in English Curriculum Making, 1868–1918," *Journal of Curriculum Studies* 29 (November-December 1997): 681.

15. Reid, *Curriculum as Institution and Practice*, 35.

16. Reid, "Democracy, Perfectability, and the Battle of the Books," 258.

17. Ian Westbury, "An Investigation of Some Aspects of Communication," PhD diss., University of Alberta, 1968.

18. Ian Westbury and Geoffrey Milburn, *Rethinking Schooling: Twenty-five Years of the Journal of Curriculum Studies* (New York: Routledge, 2006).

19. E. D. Hirsch, Jr., *Cultural Literacy: What Every American Needs to Know* (New York: Houghton Mifflin, 1987).

20. Ian Westbury, "Who Can Be Taught What? General Education in the Secondary School," in *Cultural Literacy and the Idea of General Education: Eighty-seventh Yearbook of the National Society for the Study of Education, Part II*, eds. Ian Westbury and Alan C. Purves (Chicago: National Society for the Study of Education, 1988), 171–97.

21. Westbury, "Who Can Be Taught What?," 183.

22. Westbury, "Who Can Be Taught What?," 186.

23. Westbury, "Who Can Be Taught What?," 191.

24. Westbury, "Who Can Be Taught What?," 193.

25. Westbury, "Who Can Be Taught What?," 195.

26. Ian Westbury, "Teaching as a Reflective Practice: What Might Didaktik Teach Curriculum?," in *Teaching as a Reflective Practice: The German Didaktik Tradition*, eds. Ian Westbury, Stefan Hopmann, and Kurt Riquarts (Mahwah, NJ: Lawrence Erlbaum Associates, 2000), 16–17.

27. Westbury, "Teaching as a Reflective Practice," 16–17.

28. Westbury, "Teaching as a Reflective Practice," 17.

29. Westbury, "Teaching as a Reflective Practice," 17.

30. Westbury, "Teaching as a Reflective Practice," 17.

31. J. Wesley Null, "Curriculum for Teachers: Four Traditions within Pedagogical Philosophy," *Educational Studies* 42 (August 2007): 43–63.

32. Westbury, "Teaching as a Reflective Practice," 17.

33. Westbury, "Teaching as a Reflective Practice," 33.

34. Westbury, "Teaching as a Reflective Practice," 33.

35. Westbury, "Teaching as a Reflective Practice," 31–32.

36. Westbury, "Teaching as a Reflective Practice," 32.

37. Ian Westbury and Neil J. Wilkof, *Joseph J. Schwab: Science, Curriculum, and Liberal Education* (Chicago: University of Chicago Press, 1978), 9.

38. Joseph J. Schwab, "The Practical: A Language for Curriculum," *School Review* 78 (November 1969): 1–23.

39. Schwab, "The Practical," 1.

40. Schwab, "The Practical," 11.

41. Schwab, "The Practical," 20–21.

42. Schwab, "The Practical," 22.

43. Aristotle, *Introduction to Aristotle,* ed. Richard McKeon (New York: Modern Library, 1947).

44. Donald N. Levine, *Powers of the Mind: The Reinvention of Liberal Learning in America* (Chicago: University of Chicago Press, 2006), 92.

45. Richard McKeon, *Rhetoric: Essays in Invention and Discovery,* ed. Mark Backman (Woodbridge, CT: Ox Bow Press, 1987), 3.

46. McKeon, *Rhetoric,* 3.

47. Richard McKeon, "The Methods of Rhetoric and Philosophy: Invention and Judgment," in *Rhetoric: Essays in Invention and Discovery,* ed. Mark Backman (Woodbridge, CT: Ox Bow Press, 1987), 56–65.

48. McKeon, "The Methods of Rhetoric," 6.

49. Richard McKeon, "Philosophy and Action," *Ethics* 62 (January 1952): 79–100.

50. Reid, *Curriculum as Institution and Practice*, 14.

51. Reid, *Curriculum as Institution and Practice*, 14.

52. Richard McKeon, "Philosophy and Action," *Ethics* 62 (January 1952): 84; italics in original.

53. McKeon, "Philosophy and Action," 85.

54. McKeon, "Philosophy and Action," 85.

55. McKeon, "Philosophy and Action," 85.

56. McKeon, "Philosophy and Action," 86.

57. McKeon, "Philosophy and Action," 86.

58. McKeon, "Philosophy and Action," 87.

59. Reid, *Curriculum as Institution and Practice*, 14.

60. For one book on the commonplaces and their relation to the liberal arts, see Joan Marie Lechner, *Renaissance Concepts of the Commonplaces* (Westport, CT: Greenwood, 1962). An entire book dedicated to the notion of the commonplaces and how they relate to curriculum could be useful.

61. Joseph J. Schwab, "The Practical 3: Translation into Curriculum," *School Review* 81 (August 1973): 501–22.

62. Schwab, "The Practical 3," 501.

63. For more on deliberation as a concept and how it plays out in practice, see J. T. Dillon, *Deliberation in Education and Society* (Westport, CT: Ablex Publishing, 1994).

Chapter 9: What Should We Do to Create a Better Teacher Ed Curriculum?

1. I realize the phrase "teacher ed curriculum" is shorthand, but "teacher education curriculum" is too long to repeat numerous times. On the other hand, "teacher education" avoids the issue of curriculum that is at the heart of this chapter. As a result, I have chosen to use "teacher ed curriculum" even if the phrase does come across as somewhat informal.

2. For those who may not be accustomed to this language, the term *candidate* is used to distinguish between undergraduate teachers-in-training and K–12 students. *Candidate* is the term of choice because these undergraduates are candidates for teacher certification. I reserve the term *students* to mean children and young adults who attend elementary, middle, or high schools.

Chapter 10: Calling All Curriculists: Virtue and the Future of Deliberative Curriculum

1. Julie A. Reuben, *The Making of the Modern University: Intellectual Transformation and the Marginalization of Morality* (Chicago: University of Chicago, 1996), 269.

2. Alasdair MacIntyre, *After Virtue: A Study in Moral Theory*, 2nd ed. (Notre Dame, IN: University of Notre Dame, 1984), 54–55.

3. William A. Reid, *Curriculum as Institution and Practice: Essays in the Deliberative Tradition* (Mahwah, NJ: Lawrence Erlbaum, 1999), 45.

4. Robert Kunzman, *Grappling with the Good: Talking about Religion and Morality in Public Schools* (Albany, NY: SUNY, 2006), 58.

5. Kunzman, *Grappling with the Good*, 84.

6. Lawrence Cahoone, ed., *From Modernism to Postmodernism: An Anthology* (Cambridge, MA: Blackwell, 1996), 534.

7. See, for example, Thomas W. Smith, *Revaluing Ethics: Aristotle's Dialectical Pedagogy* (Albany, NY: SUNY Press, 2001).

8. Reid, *Curriculum as Institution and Practice*, 49.

9. Smith, *Revaluing Ethics*, 2.

10. Smith, *Revaluing Ethics*, 6.

11. Aristotle, *Nicomachean Ethics*, ed. Martin Ostwald (Upper Saddle River, NJ: Prentice Hall, 1999); see also, J. Wesley Null and Andrew J. Milson, "Beyond Marquee Morality: Virtue in the Social Studies," *Social Studies* 94 (May/June 2003): 119–22.

12. Aristotle, *Nicomachean Ethics*, 153.

13. Aristotle, *Nicomachean Ethics*, 163.

14. John Amos Comenius, *School of Infancy: An Essay on the Education of Youth during the First Six Years* (Whitefish, MT: Kessinger Publishing, 2003); originally published in 1633.

15. John Amos Comenius, *The Great Didactic*, M. W. Keatinge, ed. (Whitefish, MT: Kessinger Publishing, 1992), 52.

16. Comenius, *The Great Didactic*, 85; emphasis in original.

Bibliography

Adler, Mortimer. 1976. "Teaching and Learning." In *From Parnassus: Essays in Honor of Jacques Barzun*, edited by Dora B. Weiner and William R. Keylor. New York: Harper and Row, 57–65.

Apple, Michael W. 1970. "Relevance and Curriculum: A Study in Phenomenological Sociology of Knowledge." EdD diss., Teachers College, Columbia University.

———. 1990. *Ideology and Curriculum.* 2nd ed. New York: Routledge.

———. 1993. *Official Knowledge: Democratic Education in a Conservative Age.* New York: Routledge.

———. 2006. *Educating the "Right" Way: Markets, Standards, God, and Inequality.* New York: Routledge.

Aristotle. 1947. "Introduction to Aristotle." In *Aristotle*, edited by Richard McKeon. New York: Modern Library.

———. 1999. *Nicomachean Ethics.* Translated by Martin Ostwald. Upper Saddle River, NJ: Prentice Hall.

Bainbridge, William L. 2005. "Teacher Pay Key in Fixing Public Schools." *Columbus Dispatch,* April 23, 08A.

Bloom, Allan, ed. and trans. 1968. *The Republic of Plato.* New York: Basic Books.

Bobbitt, Franklin. 1924. *How to Make a Curriculum.* New York: Houghton Mifflin.

Bobbitt, John Franklin. 1918. *The Curriculum.* New York: Macmillan.

Cahoone, Lawrence, ed. 1996. *From Modernism to Postmodernism: An Anthology.* Cambridge, MA: Blackwell.

Callahan, Raymond E. 1964. *Education and the Cult of Efficiency: A Study of the Social Forces That Have Shaped the Administration of the Public Schools.* Chicago: University of Chicago.

Callejo-Pérez, David M. 2009. "Curriculum and Transformation: Re-Thinking Leadership and Schools All Over Again." *Journal of Curriculum and Instruction* 3, no. 2: 6–21.

Callejo-Pérez, David M., and S. Dagen. 2010. "Teachers as Decision Makers: Narratives of Power in an Era of Standards." *Revista Contrapontos* 10, no. 1: 41–48.

Callejo-Pérez, David M., and S. Diaz. 2010. "Policy Development and Sustainability in Education: How a Rural County Can Maximize Its Resources through Collaboration." *Collaboration in Education*: 65–72.

Carr, David, and Jan Steutel, eds. 1999. *Virtue Ethics and Moral Education.* London: Routledge.

Charters, W. W. 1912. *Methods of Teaching: Their Basis and Statement Developed from a Functional Standpoint.* Chicago: Row, Peterson, and Company.

———. 1923. *Curriculum Construction.* New York: Macmillan.

———. 1927. *How to Teach Ideals.* Madras: Methodist Publishing House.

———. 1928. *The Teaching of Ideals.* New York: Macmillan.

Charters, W. W., and Douglas Waples. 1929. *The Commonwealth Teacher-Training Study.* Chicago: University of Chicago.

Chubb, John E. 2005. "Saving No Child Left Behind." In *Within Our Reach: How America Can Educate Every Child*, edited by John E. Chubb. Lanham, MD: Rowman and Littlefield, 1–34.

Chubb, John E., and Terry M. Moe. 1990a. "American Public Schools: Choice Is a Panacea." *The Brookings Review* 8: 4–12.

———. 1990b. *Politics, Markets and America's Schools.* Washington, DC: Brookings Institution Press.

Cohen, D. K., S. Raudenbush, and D. L. Ball. 2002. "Resources, Instruction and Research." In *Evidence Matters: Randomized Trials in Education Research*, edited by F. Mosteller and R. Boruch. Washington DC: Brookings Institution Press, 196.

Collins, Susan D. 2006. *Aristotle and the Rediscovery of Citizenship.* New York: Cambridge University.

Comenius, John Amos. 1887. *Orbis Pictus.* Syracuse, NY: C.W. Bardeen.

———. 1992. *The Great Didactic.* Translated and edited by M. W. Keatinge. Whitefish, MT: Kessinger.

———. 2003. *School of Infancy: An Essay on the Education of Youth during the First Six Years.* Whitefish, MT: Kessinger.

Counts, George S. 1930. *A Ford Crosses Russia.* Boston: Stratford.

———. 1931. *The Soviet Challenge to America.* New York: John Day.

———. 1978. *Dare the School Build a New Social Order?* Carbondale: Southern Illinois University.

Cremin, L. A. 1977. *Traditions of American Education.* New York: Basic Books.

Cuban, Larry. 2004. *The Blackboard and the Bottom Line: Why Schools Can't Be Businesses.* Cambridge, MA: Harvard University Press.

Dewey, John. 1898. "The Primary-Education Fetich." *Forum* XXV: 315–16.

———. 1899. *The School and Society.* Chicago: University of Chicago.

———. 1916. *Democracy and Education: An Introduction to the Philosophy of Education.* New York: Macmillan.

———. 1934. "Can Education Share in Social Reconstruction?" *Social Frontier* 1: 12.

———. 1935. "The Teacher and His World." *Social Frontier* 1: 7.

———. 1991. *The School and Society/The Child and the Curriculum.* Edited by Philip W. Jackson. Chicago: University of Chicago.

Dewey, John, and Evelyn Dewey. 1915. *Schools of Tomorrow.* New York: E. P. Dutton and Company.

Dillon, J. T. 1994. *Deliberation in Education and Society.* Westport, CT: Ablex Publishing.

Dorn, Charles. 2008. "'Treason in the Textbooks': Reinterpreting the Harold Rugg Textbook Controversy in the Context of Wartime Schooling." *Paedogogica Historica* 44: 457–79.

Eller, Ernest M., ed. 1956. *The School of Infancy by John Amos Comenius.* Chapel Hill: University of North Carolina.

Elster, Jon, ed. 1998. *Deliberative Democracy.* Cambridge: Cambridge University Press.

English, Fenwick W. 1988. *Curriculum Auditing.* Lancaster, PA: Technomic.

———. 1992. *Educational Administration: The Human Science.* New York: HarperCollins.

———. 1995. "Standards and Assumptions of the Curriculum Management Audit." In *The Curriculum Management Audit: Improving School Quality,* edited by Larry E. Frase, Fenwick W. English, and William K. Poston, Jr. Lancaster, PA: Technomic.

———. 2000. *Deciding What to Teach and Test: Developing, Aligning, and Auditing the Curriculum.* Thousand Oaks, CA: Corwin.

———. 2001. *Deep Curriculum Alignment: Creating a Level Playing Field for All Children in High-Stakes Tests of Educational Accountability.* Lanham, MD: Scarecrow.

Evans, Ronald W. 2007. *This Happened in America: Harold Rugg and the Censure of Social Studies.* Greenwich, NC: Information Age.

"Final Word: Editorials." 2005. *Chief Executive* 207, 72.

"Fixing America's Future: To Stave Off a U.S. Work Force Crisis, CEOs Are Getting More Involved in Improving the Nation's Schools." 2005. *Chief Executive* 207, 23–25.

Frase, Larry E. 1995."Introduction." In *The Curriculum Management Audit: Improving School Quality,* edited by Larry E. Frase, Fenwick W. English, and William K. Poston, Jr. Lancaster PA: Technomic, ix.

Frase, Larry F., Fenwick W. English, and William K. Poston, Jr., eds. 1995. *The Curriculum Management Audit: Improving School Quality.* Lancaster, PA: Technomic.

Freire, Paulo. 1984a. "Education, Liberation, and the Church." *Religious Education* 79: 524–45.

———. 1984b. "Know, Practice, and Teach the Gospels." *Religious Education* 79: 547.

———. 2002. *Pedagogy of the Oppressed.* 30th anniversary ed. New York: Continuum.

Friedman, Milton. 1962. *Capitalism and Freedom.* Chicago: University of Chicago.

Friedman, Milton, and Rose Friedman. 1980. *Free to Choose: A Personal Statement.* New York: Harcourt Brace Jovanovich.

Green, R. P. H., trans. 1997. *On Christian Teaching by Augustine.* Oxford: Oxford University.

Greene, Maxine. 1974. "Literature, Existentialism, and Education." In *Existentialism and Phenomenology in Education,* edited by David E. Denton. New York: Teachers College Press, 75.

———. 1984. "'Excellence,' Meanings and Multiplicity." *Teachers College Record* 86, no. 2: 283–97.

———. 1988. *The Dialectic of Freedom.* New York: Teachers College Press.

Hadot, Pierre. 1995. *Philosophy as a Way of Life.* Edited by Arnold I. Davidson. Malden, MA: Blackwell.

Hall, G. Stanley. 1883. "The Contents of Children's Minds." *The Princton Review* 11: 249–72.

———. 2004. "The Contents of Children's Minds on Entering School." In *Readings in American Educational Thought: From Puritanism to Progressivism,* edited by Andrew J. Milson, Chara Haeussler Bohan, Perry L. Glanzer and J. Wesley Null. Greenwich, CT: Information Age, 243–53.

Hirsch, E. D., Jr. 1987. *Cultural Literacy: What Every American Needs to Know.* Boston: Houghton Mifflin.

James, William. 1948. "What Pragmatism Means. "In *Essays in Pragmatism,* edited by William James. New York: Hafner, 150.

Keatinge, M. W., trans. 1992. *The Great Didactic by John Amos Comenius.* Whitefish, MT: Kessinger.

Key, Ellen. 1909. *The Century of the Child.* New York: G. P. Putnam's Sons.

Kilpatrick, William H. 1918. "The Project Method: The Use of the Purposeful Act in the Educative Process." *Teachers College Bulletin* 10, no. 3: 3–18.

———. 1928. *Education for a Changing Civilization.* New York: Macmillan.

———. 1936. *Remaking the Curriculum.* New York: Newson and Company.

———. 1951. *Philosophy of Education.* New York: Macmillan.

Kimball, Bruce A. 1995. *Orators and Philosophers: A History of the Idea of Liberal Education.* New York: College Board.

Kliebard, Herbert M. 1975. "The Rise of Scientific Curriculum Making and Its Aftermath." *Curriculum Theory Network* 5: 27–38.

Knoll, Michael. 2009. "From Kidd to Dewey: The Origin and Meaning of 'Social Efficiency.'" *Journal of Curriculum Studies* 41: 361–91.

Kohn, Alfie. 1992. *No Contest: The Case against Competition.* Revised ed. Boston: Houghton Mifflin.

———. 1993. *Punished by Rewards: The Trouble with Gold Stars, Incentive Plans, A's, Praise, and Other Bribes.* Boston: Houghton Mifflin.

———. 1998. *What to Look for in a Classroom . . . and Other Essays.* San Francisco: Jossey-Bass.

———. 2000. *The Schools Our Children Deserve: Moving Beyond Traditional Classrooms and "Tougher Standards."* New York: Houghton Mifflin.

Kridel, Craig Alan, and Robert V. Bullough. 2007. *Stories of the Eight-Year Study: Reexamining Secondary Education in America.* Albany, NY: SUNY Press.

Kunzman, Robert. 2006. *Grappling with the Good: Talking about Religion and Morality in Public Schools.* Albany, NY: SUNY Press.

Lechner, Joan Marie. 1962. *Renaissance Concepts of the Commonplaces.* Westport, CT: Greenwood.

Levine, Donald N. 2007. *Powers of the Mind: The Reinvention of Liberal Learning in America.* Chicago: University of Chicago.

MacIntyre, Alasdair. 1991. *Three Rival Versions of Moral Enquiry: Encyclopedia, Genealogy, and Tradition.* Notre Dame, IN: University of Notre Dame Press.

———. 2007. *After Virtue: A Study in Moral Theory.* 3rd ed. Notre Dame, IN: University of Notre Dame Press.

March, James G. 1972. "Model Bias in Social Action." *Review of Educational Research* 42, no. 4: 413–29.

Martin, Jay. 2002. *The Education of John Dewey: A Biography.* New York: Columbia University.

May, William F. 2001. *Beleaguered Rulers: The Public Obligation of the Professional.* Louisville, KY: Westminster John Knox.

McClellan, B. Edward. 1999. *Moral Education in America: Schools and the Shaping of Character from Colonial Times to the Present.* New York: Teachers College Press.

McCluskey, Neil Gerard. 2005. *Corruption in the Public Schools: The Market Is the Answer.* Washington DC: Cato Institute.

McCutcheon, Gail. 1995. *Developing the Curriculum: Solo and Group Deliberation.* White Plains, NY: Longman.

McInerny, Ralph, trans. 1998. *Thomas Aquinas: Selected Writings.* London: Penguin Books.

McKeon, Richard. 1952. "Philosophy and Action." *Ethics* 62, no. 2: 79–100.

———. 1987a. "The Methods of Rhetoric and Philosophy: Invention and Judgment." In *Rhetoric: Essays in Invention and Discovery,* edited by Mark Backman. Woodbridge, CT: Ox Bow, 56–65.

———. 1987b. *Rhetoric: Essays in Invention and Discovery.* Edited by Mark Backman. Woodbridge, CT: Ox Bow.

Miles, Steven H. 2004. *The Hippocratic Oath and the Ethics of Medicine.* Oxford: Oxford University.

National Academy of Sciences. 1996. *National Science Education Standards.* Washington DC: National Academy Press.

National Research Council. 2000. *How People Learn: Brain, Mind, Experience, and School.* 2nd ed. Washington, DC: National Academy Press.

No Child Left Behind: A Desktop Reference. 2002. Prepared by the Under Secretary of Education. Washington, DC: U.S. Department of Education.

Null, J. Wesley. 1999. "Efficiency Jettisoned: Unacknowledged Changes in the Curriculum Thought of John Franklin Bobbitt." *Journal of Curriculum and Supervision* 15: 35–42.

———. 2004. "Social Efficiency Splintered: Multiple Meanings Instead of the Hegemony of One." *Journal of Curriculum and Supervision* 19: 99–124.

———. 2006. "Teaching Deliberation: Curriculum Workers as Public Educators." In *The Pursuit of Curriculum: Schooling and the Public Interest*, edited by J. Wesley Null. Greenwich, CT: Information Age, xiii–xxi.

———. 2007. "Curriculum for Teachers: Four Traditions within Pedagogical Philosophy." *Educational Studies* 42: 43–63.

Null, J. Wesley, and Andrew J. Milson. 2003. "Beyond Marquee Morality: Virtue in the Social Studies." *The Social Studies* 94: 119–22.

Null, J. Wesley, and Diane Ravitch, eds. 2006. *Forgotten Heroes of American Education: The Great Tradition of Teaching Teachers.* Greenwich, CT: Information Age.

Ogren, Christine A. 2005. *The American State Normal School: "An Instrument of Great Good."* New York: Palgrave Macmillan.

Provenzo, Eugene F. 2006. *Critical Literacy: What Every American Needs to Know.* Boulder, CO: Paradigm.

Ravitch, Diane. 1995. *National Standards in American Education: A Citizen's Guide.* Washington, DC: Brookings Institution Press.

Reeve, C. D. C. trans. 1998. *Aristotle, Politics.* Indianapolis: Hackett.

Reid, William A. 1978. *Thinking About the Curriculum: The Nature and Treatment of Curriculum Problems.* London: Routledge and Kegan Paul.

———. 1980. "Democracy, Perfectability, and the Battle of the Books: Thoughts on the Conception of Liberal Education in the Writings of Schwab." *Curriculum Inquiry* 10, no. 3: 249–63.

———. 1997. "Principle and Pragmatism in English Curriculum Making 1868–1918." *Journal of Curriculum Studies* 29, no. 6: 667–82.

———. 1999. *Curriculum as Institution and Practice: Essays in the Deliberation Tradition.* Mahwah, NJ: Lawrence Erlbaum.

———. 2006. *The Pursuit of Curriculum: Schooling and the Public Interest.* Edited by J. Wesley Null. Greenwich, CT: Information Age.

Reuben, Julie A. 1996. *The Making of the Modern University: Intellectual Transformation and the Marginalization of Morality.* Chicago: University of Chicago.

Robinson, Daniel N. 1995. *A History of Intellectual Psychology.* Madison: University of Wisconsin.

Rousseau, Jean-Jacques. 1979. *Emile, or On Education.* Translated by Allan Bloom. New York: Basic Books.

Rugg, Harold Ordway. 1921. "How Shall We Reconstruct the Social Studies Curriculum?" *The Historical Outlook* 12: 184–89.

———. 1941. *That Men May Understand: An American in the Long Armistice.* New York: Doubleday.

Rugg, Harold, and George S. Counts. 1926. "A Critical Appraisal of Current Methods of Curriculum-Making." In *Twenty-sixth Yearbook of the National Society for the Study of Education.* Bloomington, IL: Public School Publishing Company, 427.

Schwab, Joseph J. 1969. "The Practical: A Language for Curriculum." *School Review* 78, no. 1: 1–23.

———. 1973. "The Practical 3: Translation into Curriculum." *School Review* 81, no. 4: 501–22.

Sizer, Theodore R. 1984. *Horace's Compromise: The Dilemma of the American High School.* Boston: Houghton Mifflin.

———. 1996. *Horace's Hope: What Works for the American High School.* Boston: Houghton Mifflin.

Smith, Thomas W. 2001. *Revaluing Ethics: Aristotle's Dialectical Pedagogy.* Albany, NY: SUNY Press.

Sullivan, William M. 2005. *Work and Integrity: The Crisis and Promise of Professionalism in America.* 2nd ed. San Francisco: Jossey-Bass.

Taylor, Frederick. 1911. *Principles of Scientific Management.* New York: Harper and Bros.

Thuermer, Kitty. 1999. "In Defense of the Progressive School." *Independent School* 59, no. 1: 90–95.

Tyack, David B., and Larry Cuban. 1997. *Tinkering toward Utopia: A Century of Public School Reform.* Cambridge, MA: Harvard University Press.

Tyler, Ralph W. 1927. *Statistical Methods for Utilizing Personal Judgments to Evaluate Activities for Teacher-Training Curricula.* PhD diss. University of Chicago.

———. 1949. *Basic Principles of Curriculum and Instruction.* Chicago: University of Chicago.

U.S. Department of Education. 2004. *No Child Left Behind: A Toolkit for Teachers.* Washington DC: U.S. Department of Education.

U.S. Department of Education, Office of the Secretary, Office of Public Affairs. 2003. *No Child Left Behind: A Parents Guide.* Washington DC: U.S. Department of Education.

Westbrook, Robert B. 1991. *John Dewey and American Democracy.* Ithaca, NY: Cornell University.

Westbury, Ian. 1968. *An Investigation of Some Aspects of Communication.* PhD diss. University of Alberta.

———. 1988. "Who Can Be Taught What? General Education in the Secondary School." In *Cultural Literacy and the Idea of General Education: Eighty-seventh Yearbook for the Study of Education, Part II,* edited by Ian Westbury and Alan C. Purves. Chicago: National Society for the Study of Education, 171–97.

———. 2000. "Teaching as a Reflective Practice: What Might Didaktik Teach Curriculum?" In *The German Didaktik Tradition,* edited by Ian Westbury, Stefan Hopmann, and Kurt Riquarts. Mahwah, NJ: Lawrence Erlbaum Associates, 16–17.

Westbury, Ian, and Geoffrey Milburn. 2006. *Rethinking Schooling: Twenty-five Years of the Journal of Curriculum Studies.* New York: Routledge.

Westbury, Ian, and Neil J. Wilkof. 1978. *Joseph J. Schwab: Science, Curriculum, and Liberal Education.* Chicago: University of Chicago.

Wong, Harry K. 1980. "Behavioral Objectives, Teacher Help, and Academic Achievement." PhD diss., Brigham Young University.

Wong, Harry K., and Rosemary T. Wong. 1998. *The First Days of School: How to Be an Effective Teacher.* Mountain View, CA: Harry K. Wong Publications.

———. 2009. *The First Days of School: How to Be an Effective Teacher.* 4th ed. Mountain View, CA: Harry K. Wong Publications.

Index

Note: Italic page numbers refer to figures. When there are multiple identical note numbers on one page, they are preceded by the chapter number, e.g., 296:9n2 refers to note 2 in chapter 9.

About the Author

WESLEY NULL is associate professor of Curriculum & Foundations of Education in the School of Education and the Honors College at Baylor University. He completed his PhD degree at the University of Texas at Austin, where he studied curriculum theory and the history of education. At Baylor, Null teaches foundations of education in the School of Education and interdisciplinary courses on social science and great texts in the Honors College. He also serves as associate dean of Baylor's Honors College.

Null is the author of *Peerless Educator: The Life and Work of Isaac Leon Kandel* (2007) and *A Disciplined Progressive Educator: The Life and Career of William Chandler Bagley* (2004). He is coeditor, with Diane Ravitch, of *Forgotten Heroes of American Education: The Great Tradition of Teaching Teachers* (2006). He has coedited several other books as well, including *Readings in American Educational Thought: From Puritanism to Progressivism* (2009) and *The Pursuit of Curriculum: Schooling and the Public Interest* (2006). Null is president of the American Association for Teaching and Curriculum and serves as editor of the *American Educational History Journal*. He lives in Hewitt, Texas, with his wife, Dana, and their two children, Corbin and Raegan.